Michelle Engeler
Youth and the State in Guinea: Meander

Culture and Social Practice

For Maëlyne and Louane

Michelle Engeler (PhD) works at the Department of Social Sciences at the University of Basel. Her research interests focus on youth, political change and mobility, particularly in West Africa.

MICHELLE ENGELER

Youth and the State in Guinea:
Meandering Lives

[transcript]

Bibliographic information published by the Deutsche Nationalbibliothek
The Deutsche Nationalbibliothek lists this publication in the Deutsche Nationalbibliografie; detailed bibliographic data are available in the Internet at http://dnb.d-nb.de

© 2019 transcript Verlag, Bielefeld

Cover layout: Maria Arndt, Bielefeld
Cover illustration: Michelle Engeler (2010)
Proofread by Alexa Barnby & Simon Pare
Printed by Majuskel Medienproduktion GmbH, Wetzlar
Print-ISBN 978-3-8376-4570-5
PDF-ISBN 978-3-8394-4570-9
https://doi.org/10.14361/9783839445709

Content

List of tables and abbreviations

Tables

Table 1: Chronology, 1895-2013 (p. 175)
Table 2: Selected informants (p. 179)

Abbreviations

AJG	Association des Jeunes de Guéckédou
BPN	Bureau Politique National
CEM	Cercles d'études Marxistes
CENI	Commission Electorale Nationale Indépendante
CMRN	Comité Militaire de Redressement National
CNDD	Conseil National pour la Démocratie et le Développement
CRD	Communautés Rurales de Développement
CTRN	Comité Transitoire de Redressement National
CU	Commune Urbaines
DPJ	Département Préfectoral de la Jeunesse
DPE	Département Préfectoral de l'Education
DPM	Département Préfectoral pour la Réalisations des Microprojets
ECOMOG	Economic Community of West African States Monitoring and Observation Group
ECOWAS	Economic Community of West African States
GTZ	Deutsche Gesellschaft für Technische Zusammenarbeit (German NGO, today known as GIZ)

GIZ	Deutsche Gesellschaft für Internationale Zusammenarbeit
GJG	Guides des Jeunes de Guéckédou
JRDA	La Jeunesse du Rassemblement Démocratique Africaine
MSF	Médecins sans Frontières
NGO	Non-government organisation
NPFL	National Patriotic Front of Liberia (rebel movement in Liberia, headed by Charles Taylor and ally of the RUF)
PDG	Parti Démocratique de Guinée
PRL	Pouvoir Révolutionnaire Local
RDA	Rassemblement Démocratique Africain
RDIG	Rassemblement pour le Développement Intégré de la Guinée (political party lead by Jean-Marc Téliano, originating from Guéckédou)
RPG	Rassemblement du Peuple de Guinée (well-known party member and leader is the current Guinean President Alpha Condé)
RUF	Revolutionary United Front of Sierra Leone (the main rebel movement in Sierra Leone, fighting from 1991 until 2002)
PUP	Parti de l'Unité et du Progrès (well-known party member/leader: Lansana Conté, Guinea's president from 1984 to 2008)
UFDG	Union des Forces Démocratiques de Guinée (well-known party member/leader: Cellou Dalein Diallo, presidential candidate in 2010)
UNDP	United Nations Development Program
UNHCR	United Nations High Commissioner for Refugees
UNICEF	United Nations International Children's Emergency Fund
USTG-CNTG	Union syndicale des travailleurs de Guinée – Confédération nationale des travailleurs de Guinée
WFP	World Food Programme

Acknowledgments

Writing this book has been a most challenging yet rewarding process, not least because doing anthropology is not an isolated endeavour but builds on encounters and conversations. Accordingly, there have been many people along the way who have contributed to my work, and I would like to thank everyone who helped me in a variety of ways during the research process that led to this monograph.

First and foremost, this study was only possible because of the many Guineans who generously allowed me to gain insights into their lives by sharing their time, describing their experiences and discussing their views with me. I owe them a great deal! In addition, I am indebted to my Guinean hosts and to my research assistant, all of whom contributed to my well-being and progress over the years, particularly Jackie Kadiatou Condé, the extended Diallo family including Mr Diallo and Alpha Diallo, and Tamba Augustin Koundouno. Thank you for being with me come rain or shine, for giving me your food, your trust and your worldviews; thank you for the shared memories and endless conversations. Your friendship was the best support I could have wished for. Likewise, on-site I was able to count on assistance and logistical help from the GIZ (*Gesellschaft für Internationale Zusammenarbeit*) and the Belgian MSF (*Médecins sans Frontières*). I am most grateful to these institutions for their support, in particular Leen Diels, Franco Fava, Stefan Grünbaum, Faya Moïce Ouéndéno, Lucile Peter and Marc Yombouno. These people not only provided technical, logistical and medical assistance but also shared their insights and regional knowledge with me.

This book derives from my doctoral dissertation 'At the Crossroads: Being Young and the State in the Making in Guéckédou, Guinea' (Engeler, 2015), carried out under the auspices of the Institute of Social Anthropology at the University of Basel. I am thus grateful to my supervisors, Till Förster and Gregor Dobler, for their support and to all my other colleagues at the Institute of Social Anthropology and the Centre for African Studies Basel who read or commented on the proposal and the various draft chapters, articles and presentations related to this book. Carole Ammann, Jana Gerold, Kathrin Heitz, Andrea Kaufmann, Lucy Koechlin and Noemi Steuer in particular supported me through fruitful discussions and the constructive comments they made during my research and the write-up. Likewise, I would like to thank the researchers from the Department of Geography at the University of Zurich, in particular the Political Geography Unit, including Tobias Hagmann, Pia Hollenbach, Benedikt Korf and Mark Starmanns, who assisted me especially when I was developing the research idea for this monograph. Equally I would like to thank Anita Schroven for providing me with key insights and valuable information on Guinea and helpful survival strategies for Conakry in particular. I would also like to thank Elisabeth Idris, may she rest in peace, for having been a supportive librarian and Alexa Barnby and Simon Pare for careful and attentive language editing at different stages of this book project.

I also wish to thank my family and friends for their patience during my absence on research trips and the hours I spent in front of the computer. Writing this book would have been a very lonely process without them. In particular, I would like to thank Sonja Egger, Urs and Gabrielle Engeler-Fontaine, Jeannine Engeler, Sven Falk, Itta Lohrer and Martina Schmidt for their interest in my work and for remaining in touch when abroad.

My deepest gratitude goes to the greatest loves in my life: my daughters Maëlyne Yaëlle Mougnou-sin and Louane Imany Hancyouo. Although both of you were born after most arduous part of this research and book project was completed, your presence was and is the most precious support and source of inspiration! Thank you!

The extended fieldwork on which this book is based was made possible by a grant from the KFPE (*Kommission für Forschungspartnerschaften mit Entwicklungsländern*) and the FAG (*Freiwillige Akademische Gesellschaft*). The publication of this study was enabled thanks to grants from the Werenfels-Fonds of the FAG and the Dissertationsfonds of the University of Basel.

Prologue
Who is young, is courageous!

One of my Guinean friends, Albert, once said that we can distinguish the young from the elderly through courage. "The young person is the one who always has courage", he said.[1] He gave war as an example and talked about the courageous young warriors who had fought on the battlefields during the recent conflicts in the Guéckédou borderland. On another occasion, he described himself as having been young and courageous early on in his life. He said that back then, when he started studying in a town far away from home, he had faced challenging times, "however, with courage, I made it through the first year."[2]

In fact, I heard people equating courage with the youth on several occasions. Once, for instance my neighbours talked about the apprentices working on big trucks. They explained that these men were courageous young people because they were on the road day and night and sat on the load bed without any protection from the rain or dust. From up there, they could keep an eye on the oncoming traffic and could jump down to guide the truck around the potholes. During their few breaks, they protected the cargo, taking turns to sleep under the truck, sometimes on mats, sometimes in hammocks. This is not a job for an old man! Another time, they mentioned a brave young woman who sold rice on a street corner to contribute to her family's income. She arrived to sell food for breakfast around seven thirty each morning. To do this, they explained, she had to get up very early to prepare the rice and the garnishes. She would also have had to manage other household obligations. However, every morning she there was, selling rice without ever complaining. A courageous young woman!

People expressed themselves differently when talking about old men and women. Sometimes I got the impression that the elders needed no further adjectives to describe them. Youngsters, on the other hand, were not just associated with

---

1 *"Le jeune, c'est celui qui a toujours le courage"*, 10.10.2010, communication with Albert, one of my key informants. His life trajectory is further explained in Chapter V.

2 *"[...] mais quand-même, avec du courage, [...] j'ai fait la première année"*, 18.11.2009, communication with Albert.

courage but could also be rude or angry, beautiful or clumsy. The attribute of courage and being courageous, however, was expressed in respectful terms and sometimes regarded with a hint of incomprehension, but never contempt. Thus, unlike in the West, where youth (also in the context of Africa) is often portrayed as "bad" or as a potential threat to social stability, young people in Guinea are often described in terms of positive values such as courage and bravery.

When meeting young people in Guinea and talking to them about their life stories, their activities in different youth groups, their strategies for earning a living, or their relationships with other members of the community, I was indeed amazed at how many of them courageously and actively set out to shape their everyday lives amid political changes and economic hardship. I dedicate this book to all the young people I met in Guinea. May you continue to have the courage to constantly shape your society's future while creating the meandering courses of your lives.

I.   Introduction

"Que la grève commence",

graffiti on a building in Conakry, seen in 2008.[1]

My desire to study youth and the state in the Guéckédou borderland originated in my first preparatory field trip to Guinea in 2008.

At the time, I spent the first couple of weeks in Conakry, Guinea's capital. Besides visiting the administrative centre and making contact with different people from universities, ministries and non-governmental organisations (NGOs), I went for a walk every day around the neighbourhood I was staying in. Through these walks I became familiar with some of my neighbours, got to know the owners and employees of a couple of small restaurants, shops and Internet cafés, and regularly visited the beach where many youngsters were playing football or revising for their exams. Here and there we started to chat on an almost daily basis. We would usually discuss the political situation, which was quite turbulent at the time. Besides current affairs, almost every conversation confronted me sooner or later with tales of the general strikes that had taken place a year previously and had paralysed almost every Guinean town. Back then, in 2007, the trade union confederation, the USTG-CNTG (*Union syndicale des travailleurs de Guinée – Confédération nationale des travailleurs de Guinée*) had called for nationwide strikes and masses of people, among them many youths, were mobilised. They had demonstrated for political change and a better future, and for almost the first time in Guinea's recent history proved their strength in changing the direction of the president's politics. Then head of state, Lansana Conté, had to acknowledge some of the accusations and finally appointed a new prime minister of national consent. However, in 2008, many of my interlocutors were dissatisfied with the current state of affairs and told me that Conté had resumed his political machinations of constantly dismissing ministers and favouring his entourage of party members and business people. According to them, their calls for change had vanished into thin air. They

---

1   The phrasing can be translated as "may the strike begin", the respective photography is published in 'Bilder von Staat', Engeler (2009).

explained in disappointment that Guinean politics was only for the old and that youths were supposed to keep quiet and simply play football.

During this first stay in Guinea I kept asking myself what it meant to be young and to grow older in Guinea and in what kind of spaces young people could negotiate their own and their society's and country's future. Would it be first and foremost by means of demonstrations and therefore by occupying the streets to demonstrate against the current government? And what role was ascribed to trade unions, political parties or state institutions?

During a short trip to Guéckédou, the town which I later decided should become my main research site, I had another formative encounter. In front of a small video shop I met a man of about thirty who was part of a youth association that tried to make a living through animal breeding. Previously, however, he had been a member of the *Jeunes Volontaires*. He described the *Jeunes Volontaires* as a young vigilante group that had emerged in the Guéckédou borderland in 2000 after rebels from Sierra Leone and Liberia had attacked the region. During our conversation the young man explained how he had become involved in taking up arms to defend his country. Apparently, the Guinean state did not provide enough security for its citizens in this remote borderland. How did it come about that young people instead protected the nation's borders? What happened to those young armed fighters after the fighting was over? And what do local identities, national feelings and youth associations in that particular context mean?

Besides talking about the war, the young man also pointed out the ethnic relations in the cross-border space of the *pays Kissi*. He described the Kissi as the autochthons of Guéckédou. But the Kissi also inhabit the nearby towns and villages in Sierra Leone and Liberia. Fascinated by this territorial complexity, I became very interested in how it related to the making of ethnic and national identities. Back home, while researching the topic, I soon learnt that these relations and identities are also strongly linked to the management of generational relations and young lives more generally. Moreover, Guinea's First Republic, which took the shape of a socialist one-party state, seriously unsettled and shaped the local social fabric of intergenerational relations and power configurations in Guéckédou, not least through the Demystification Campaign, the Cultural Revolution, and various socialist youth groups and associations.

My preliminary field trip not only stirred my interest in studying young people growing up in complex political terrains but also revealed to me some of the topic's complexities and peculiarities, particularly in Guinea. As a result, I decided to focus on young people's meandering lives and associative activities to shed light on the broader topic of the relationship between youth and the state in Guinea.

1. Meandering lives and the state in the making

The goal of this book is to examine the relationship between youth and the state in the Guéckédou borderland, thus the edge of the Guinean nation-state. The years between 2000 and 2010 take centre stage here while the main body of data was collected between 2008 and 2010. Thus, more recent events such as the Ebola outbreak in late 2013 and the subsequently declared epidemic from 2014 to 2016, or the presidential elections in 2015 and related political turmoils are not discussed. However, the insights provided by this study may give valuable background information for these complex contexts and related future developments. Moreover the book demonstrates that being young and growing up in the Guéckédou borderland is and has always been shaped by major events, (geo-)political circumstances, population movements and different, often overlapping political organisations and ideologies. However, the lives of both individuals and (state) institutions interact not only with more general socio-political transformation processes but also with each other to finally follow their very own, often unpredictable, meandering.

By combining a detailed ethnographic study of youth with an analysis of the local state, this monograph can be seen as contributing to the growing body of literature on the youth and the state in contemporary Africa and beyond.

Researching young people

Research on youth has become a major subject for social scientists working in Africa and elsewhere (Maira and Soep, 2005, Furlong, 2012). For Diouf, for instance, young people represent a key concern for African studies and Straker even identified a "boom" in youth studies arising in Africa over the last decade (Diouf, 2003, Straker, 2007b). Goerg and co-authors argue that this scientific interest in African youth (Goerg et al., 1992: 6) is prompted by demographic characteristics in particular – the so-called youth bulge – and African conceptions of age, knowledge and power. However, as Bucholtz notes, until recently surprisingly little of this research was informed by anthropology but was instead dominated by sociology of youth (Bucholtz, 2002: 525).

With Kirschner (2010), I argue that one can distinguish three key discourses in youth studies focusing on Africa. One trend is based on the conception of a "youth crisis". This perspective may be seen as interlinked with the perception of Africa as a triple crisis, involving the nation, the state and the family (Diouf, 2003). Diouf explains this as follows: after independence, African states conceptualised young people as both the bearers of the project of modernity and the source of a return to African culture (Diouf, 2003: 4). This nationalist project on the twofold role of young people sought to do two things: firstly, sustain a clear differentiation between the elders and the youngsters and, secondly, place youth at the centre of economic development and national liberation. However, in the 1970s, in a context of economic hardship and political turbulence, this project was embroiled in crisis: "In this new situation, the construction of youth as 'the hope of the world' has been replaced by representations of youth as dangerous, criminal, decadent, and given to a sexuality that is unrestrained and threatening the whole society" (Diouf, 2003: 4). The youth crisis debate received prominent support, branding African youth a "lost generation" (Cruise O'Brien, 1996: 56) or "loose molecules in a very unstable social fluid" (Kaplan, 1994: 46; 1997). Very often, the discourse about a youth crisis is related to demographics, thus to the youth bulge on the African continent and the notion that huge masses of unemployed youths, mainly young men, result in a security risk in both rural and urban spaces. However, various publications have also critically questioned this perspective.

A second trend in youth studies perceives young people in Africa to be merely victims, thus as marginalised young people or as subaltern in the context of war, HIV/AIDS pandemics, rapid urbanisation and economic decline. Hence, this perspective may be seen as the other side of the "youth crisis" coin; young people are not regarded as the mere perpetrators of the crisis but as its victims (Galperin, 2002, Bøås, 2007). This conceptualisation of youth as a subaltern identity also implies that young people constantly oppose those in power: "Youth, as political position, has long played the role of critiquing those in power (the elders) for not doing what they should" (Shepler, 2010b: 631). As a consequence, young people tend to be discontented, to resist or revolt (Mbembe, 1985: 77, 228, Jeffrey, 2012).

The third trend within youth studies tries to overcome the perpetrator/victim dichotomy by emphasising that young people should instead be seen as actors of social change. Thus, they are simultaneously related to crisis and constantly creating new meanings. Various authors address this dual situation of powerless youth lost in crisis on the one hand and powerful and creative youth on the other, mirrored in publications entitled *Makers and Breakers* (Honwana and De Boeck, 2005) and *Vanguard and Vandals* (Abbink and Van Kessel, 2005). Most of these contributions address youth as ambivalent actors of social change in the context of urban spaces, violent conflict, health and/or economic challenges. Another common characteristic of the most recent scholarly debates about young people in Africa is to conceptualise and define "youth" in a very broad sense. They examine young people as plural and heterogeneous categories related neither to biological age nor to a fixed group of people (Christiansen et al., 2006: 11). However, one can nevertheless distinguish three slightly different conceptions. The first perceives youth as a transition period between child and adult status, thus as life stage; the second emphasises youth as a subculture; and the third tackles youth merely as a social construction. Many of the early anthropological investigations of the 1930s form part of the first approach, conceptualising youth merely as a clearly bounded life stage. Thus, research centred on initiation into age groups or the transitions or rites of passage from youth to adulthood (Mead, 1929, Evans-Pritchard, 1960 [reprint]). The second definition, then, perceives youth merely as a subculture. Hence, this perspective highlights youth as a separated or isolated segment of society. Accordingly, young people form subcultures, which, for instance, become observable in specific dress, musical styles or forms of expressions (Boesen, 2008, Tait, 2000).

Both of the youth definitions mentioned above give crucial insights into youths' everyday life in different regional and thematic contexts. Both perspectives also risk underemphasising youths' agency and sociality. Christiansen and co-authors appropriately state: "The consequence of the life-stage perspective is that we gain a picture of youth as having very little agentive capacity to change or move within or between generational categories. The focus on youth culture, on the contrary, can easily paint a picture of youth as an entity, which is socially and culturally detached from the surrounding world" (Christiansen et al., 2006: 16). The third conception may serve as an alternative as it approaches youth as a socially constructed category rather than as a time-delimited state with a universal definition (Shepler, 2010b: 630). Thus, age boundaries are dependent on time, place and social context: "Within the same day a person can be positioned as child, youth and adult, depending on the situation and the stakes involved in the relationship" (Christiansen et al., 2006: 12). Hence, life *stages* are rather perceived as a fluid part of life *courses*, which often follow uneven trajectories. As Burgess writes: "Youth status can be lost or gained through the aging process and a variety of personal decisions and life events. Often invisible to censuses and maps, youth consists of a constantly shifting population moving in and out of locally determined notions of youthfulness" (Burgess, 2005: viii).

Following up on these perspectives, the most important analytical premise guiding this study is the idea that "youth" represents a socially constructed category; thus, age boundaries are conceptualised as loose. This book therefore aligns itself with studies that understand youth as relational and focus on youthful agency rather than grasping youth as a clear-cut transition period between child and adult status (thus a clearly defined life stage) or as a mere subculture (often highlighting youth as a separate or isolated segment of society).

Finally, this research monograph combines the analytic category of agency, which Emirbayer and Mische (1998) understand as a temporally embedded process of social engagement, with the theory of vital conjunctures proposed by Johnson-Hanks (2002) and introduces the perspective of "meandering lives" to grasp youth as a state of being *and* becoming, of actively shaping *and* of simply following the course of life. Inevitably, these meandering lives are interwoven with the socio-political context of the Guinean state in the making. Hence, unlike other youth studies, this monograph aims at a historically sensitive analysis of the youth–state nexus, which represents a fruitful lens for not only depicting youthful lives and associative activities in present-day Guéckédou but also drawing a nuanced picture of state–society relations and of political changes and continuities more broadly in postcolonial Guinea.

Approaching state–society relations

Importantly, this book avoids a broad-brush analysis of the state versus socie-ty in line with studies that examine specific places, events and groups – which Hagmann and Péclard (2010) understand as arenas – in which the boundaries of state and society are blurred, become discussed or are negotiated by a variety of actors (Kerkvliet, 2001, 2003). Significantly, "a state is not only built as a delibe-rate means to contain and direct power for the benefit of the few, a state is also formed, out of the anonymous actions of many" (Lonsdale, 1992: 15). State forma-tion processes – which differ from state building efforts to create an apparatus of control – are thereby rendered non-teleological but historical, without a pre-es-tablished pathway but with multiple trajectories (Hagmann and Hoehne, 2009). Analysing these processes "impels us to reconsider the mechanics of rule and wor-kings of power" and "enables us to examine the dispersed institutional and social networks through which rule is coordinated and consolidated, and the roles that 'non-state' institutions, communities and individuals play in mundane processes of governance" (Sharma and Gupta, 2006: 9). Moreover, state formation processes are inherently conflictive and contested (Hagmann and Péclard, 2010: 557).

The geographical starting point for this study is the Guéckédou borderland, a remote space between coastal and savannah West Africa, approximately 700 kilo-metres southeast of Guinea's capital. Thus, it addresses a rather remote town and its rural fringes to understand youth–state relations. By doing so, this research brings a perspective one rarely encounters in youth studies and research interes-ted in the state. Generally, youth studies focus on the urban spaces of major cities and young unemployed men trapped in inactivity, tending in contrast to avoid the peripheries of the state. In addition, research interested in political transforma-tion processes often neglects the state apparatus as an important site for political imagination. It concentrates instead on regional contexts where the state as an institution is weak or has vanished altogether. Hence, this monograph asks for the research agenda for African youth studies to be broadened to remote areas such as the Guéckédou borderland and to manifold arenas including the state as an institution.

This study also aims to bridge the research gaps in the scientific treatment of Guinea. Although youth has always been a subject of state formation processes, it was not until the mid-2000s that social scientists interested in Guinea started to recognise youth as a subject worthy of study. In particular, McGovern's and Stra-ker's exceptionally rich contributions on the postcolonial Guinean state's relation toward the youth figure prominently among the key references for this study (cf. McGovern 2004; 2012b, Straker, 2004; 2007a; 2007b; 2009). Both authors focus particularly on Guinée Forestière and the socialist state, which came to an end in 1984. Thus, their writings serve as the bedrock for my own investigation into youth and the state in Guinea.

Besides asking what it means to be young in the Guéckédou borderland, this research also aims to understand how the state is done and re-done or un-done in the locality, and how young people negotiate and participate in state formation processes. To answer these questions, I find it crucial to consider the making of the Guéckédou borderland and therefore include a historical perspective in the analysis. In addition, understanding youth is closely related to answering questions that address the changing shape of youthful identities and the management of generational relations. While looking at young people in relation to both past and present state formation processes, it is also crucial to understand the state in its local manifestations. Therefore, this monograph also takes a closer look at different political actors or power brokers, as well as encounters with formal political institutions. Finally, taking a closer look at crucial arenas for negotiating the political within and outside the state as an institution offers additional insights into young people's agencies and socio-political imaginations. These arenas refer not only to the street or to the taking up of arms but, as this study will show, include public crossroads, rice fields, the *Maison des Jeunes* or assemblies of youth associations. In all these arenas, which are perceived as relational and contextual, young people establish, shape and terminate various sets of social relations. I consider it crucial that youthful practices are not automatically associated only with what we may perceive as progressive attitudes or revolutionary ideas beyond the family and/or the state – a fact that the sociologist Mannheim underlined years ago while he studied "the problem of generations": "biological factors (such as youth and age) do not themselves involve a definite intellectual or practical orientation (youth cannot be automatically correlated with a progressive attitude and so on)" (Mannheim, 1997: 297). This does not, of course, mean that there are no confrontations between elders, the political elite and young people (Bangura, 2018, Philipps, 2013).

2.   A territory near or at a border

According to its geographical position in the far southeast of Guinea on the border with Sierra Leone and Liberia, Guéckédou town and prefecture can be described as a "territory at or near a border", thus as "borderland" (Newman, 2003: 123). Hence, throughout this book I also use the description 'Guéckédou borderland' to describe my research site.

In addition to describing the geography of the research site, "borderland" also hints at the fact that the region comprises different socio-ethnic relations, crossroads and interactions, referring to so-called "dynamic migrant spaces" (Park, 2010: 461). The national borders that characterise the Guéckédou borderland can be seen as both a resource for and a restriction on local agency, identities and state formation processes. As Wast-Walter writes, "[o]ver the course of history, the functions and roles of borders have continuously changed" (Wastl-Walter, 2011: 1). Accordingly, borders and borderlands can only be understood within their context – and this is equally true of Guéckédou. Borderlands are therefore not only spatial or geographical phenomena informed by the demarcations of the sovereign territories of states, but also refer to "social, political or economic expressions either of belonging or of exclusion within state territories" (Wastl-Walter, 2011: 2).

To understand state formation processes in the Guéckédou borderland, I, like McGovern (McGovern, 2013: 3), perceive four states to be relevant: that of Almamy Samory Touré, whose late-nineteenth-century state encompassed much of the region, the French colonial state, the postcolonial socialist state headed by Ahmed Sékou Touré (1958–1984) and the post-socialist government which began with Lansana Conté (1984–2008). This study in particular focuses on the period between 2000 and 2010, thus it includes the turbulent period before and after Conté's death in 2008. Despite political actualities, however, a nuanced understanding of the past is important to grasp youth–state relations in the Guéckédou borderland. Hence, although this monograph concentrates on more recent political transformation in postcolonial Guinea, references to the past are included in various chapters.

Guéckédou town

Guéckédou centre or town is one of ten sub-prefectures, together with Bolodou, Fangamandou, Guendembou, Kassadou, Koundou, Nongoa, Ouéndé-Kénéma, Tekoulo, and Temessadou. Together they made up Guéckédou prefecture, which belongs to the Guinée Forestière, along with Kissidiougou, Kerouane, Beyla, Macenta, Yomou, Lola and N'Zérékoré prefectures.[2]

Guéckédou town lies approximately 700 kilometres from Conakry, Guinea's capital. In terms of infrastructure and economy, the main road, the National 2, connects Conakry via Mamou, Faranah and Kissidougou to Guéckédou and thereafter continues to Macenta and finally to N'Zérékoré. Hence, this highway is key to Guéckédou's national economic integration. The "forest" part of the main road (running from Kissidougou to N'Zérékoré) was, at the time of this research,

---

2 Guinea has four regions in total: Guinée Forestière, Guinée Maritime or Basse Côte, Moyenne-Guinée or Fouta Djallon, and, finally, Haute-Guinée.

full of contradictions. Whereas the road to and from the Guéckédou area was in a terrible condition, with patchy tarmac and often impassable during the rainy season, the final part to N'Zérékoré was one of the newest and best-designed roads in the entire country. Likewise, electricity in the Guéckédou prefecture depends on private generators and back roads on international donors or community efforts. N'Zérékoré, however, seems to profit far more from border trade and is a busy, sprawling town. All in all, the Guinée Forestière is rich in contrast, not only in terms of infrastructure, economic life and urbanity, but also in terms of its residents, and its ethnic and religious groups.

The latest census (2014)[3] indicates that Guéckédou town has a population of 66,761.[4] It can be described as a scattered settlement with 21 *quartiers* or neighbourhoods and covers a relatively extended area. The city centre encompasses the neighbourhoods of Sandia, Macenta Koura and Sokoro and is the liveliest part of the town, containing the main market, the taxi rank, the offices of the police and the gendarmerie, the prison, the Catholic Church, various mosques and most of the administrative state and community buildings such as the prefectural building, the *Maison des Jeunes* and the municipal building. As a result of my research interest, I spent a lot of time in this central part of town. However, as I myself lived in the Carrier neighbourhood and used to visit my diverse dialogue partners at their homes, in the end I got to know at least seven neighbourhoods quite well, among them Carrier, Nyalinko, Madina, Mangala, Heremakono, Solondoni and Waoutoh. In addition, I regularly visited Guéckédou-Lélé, a rural area some distance out of town centre. I could reach this area quite easily by crossing one of the rivers close to my home in a pirogue ferry and then walking for twenty minutes through gardens and rice fields.

The main road directs most of the traffic through Guéckédou town; side roads lead off to different neighbourhoods and the countryside. In addition, the Oueou, Boya, Ouoya and Wau rivers and their tributaries and bayous meander through the settlement, dividing the town into the various neighbourhoods and, a short distance out of town, mark the national border with Liberia. These streams flow into the Makona, the river which forms the border, and then finally into the ocean on Sierra Leonean territory where the river is called the Moa.

---

3 https://www.citypopulation.de/php/guinea-admin.php?adm1id=82 (accessed 28.03.2019).

4 In 1996, Guéckédou town was officially said to have 85,457 inhabitants. In 1983, the official census stated that the town had 2800 inhabitants (Bidou and Toure, 2002). The population growth between 1983 and 1996 is first and foremost related the presence of Liberian and Sierra Leonean refugees, which in 1996 consisted of 400,000 in the prefecture, bringing the total to 611,753 inhabitants (D'Urzo, 2002). Most of these refugees have in the meantime left the region. The rate of growth has, accordingly, completely changed (Bidou and Toure, 2002).

In everyday discourse, Guéckédou town is, in contrast to its surroundings, an urban space, attracting villagers to the market on Wednesdays to do business, to the hospital for treatment or simply to take a taxi to other major towns. It is also the capital of the prefecture and so for administrative purposes you have to come to town – although certain everyday matters can be dealt with at the local level or at the sub-prefectural headquarters. However, Guéckédou lacks many of the amenities one might expect of an urban area, for example an electricity and a water supply, area-wide cellphone coverage, and regular access to national newspapers. Also economically speaking, Guéckédou is hardly appealing. The main employer is the state, which offers job opportunities in different institutional settings, for instance in the administrative or security sectors, as well as in the education or agricultural sector. Apart from the state, where employment is determined by official recruitment drives and/or good connections, there is no large business that exerts an irresistible economic attraction or provides many formal jobs. However, important seasonal trade does include the cross-border kola market and the distribution of the new rice crop. Both businesses provide seasonal work on various scales and contribute to the income strategies of numerous families. The region's prosperity is based mainly on the fertility of its soil – and people are well aware of this. Accordingly, many activities and comings and goings are determined by the rhythms of farming. The hilly landscape and the region's rainy climate allow the cultivation of rice, palm oil, coffee and bananas, to mention just a few of the most important agricultural products. Farming activities shape the villagers' lives as well as everyday life in Guéckédou centre, which is surrounded and traversed by rice fields, small gardens and cultivated land. Thus, many inhabitants of Guéckédou town not only maintain an interest in farming in their home villages and go there to help out during the harvest season, but also cultivate land on the urban periphery or fallow land. In addition to flooded rice, urban farmers grow cassava, peanuts, yams, maize, and sometimes fonio.

With regard to the national borders close by, one must also consider economic activities that benefit from the location between three different administrative regimes (Guinea, Sierra Leone and Liberia) and rumours of diamond and drug smuggling and related fortunes are part of everyday life. People said for instance that one of the few guesthouses in town – a spacious, multi-storey hotel with conference facilities, a swimming pool, a billiard saloon and a weights room – was financed by a prominent local man involved in drug trafficking. To think of Guéckédou as a border boomtown, however, would have been misleading at the time of research. In general, people described the area as being quite calm, almost paralysed compared to former times, when Guéckédou held the largest market in the entire country, selling merchandise from the entire Upper Guinea Coast. The civil wars in Liberia and Sierra Leone (also known as the Mano River War) and, finally, the rebel attacks on Guéckédou itself had led to a shrinking economy and to many abandoning the town, excepting for market day on Wednesday.

Because of the Mano River War, Guéckédou can also be described as a small hub for different humanitarian aid projects, at least during the 1990s. At the time of the research, most of the projects had left the area or switched from humanitarian to development aid projects. Consequently, the stream of cash had dwindled and several local NGOs or associations that originated in the realm of development aid struggled to obtain financing. Nevertheless, most job seekers, including those who were already employed, for example within the state bureaucracy, longed to work for an NGO financed by an international development agency.

Pays Kissi

Along with the neighbouring Kissidougou prefecture and the bordering regions in both Sierra Leone and Liberia, Guéckédou prefecture forms part of the so-called *pays Kissi*, in reference to the dominant ethnic community in Guéckédou centre and prefecture, the Kissi-speaking people.[5] The Kissi-speaking people generally describe themselves as farmers and particularly rice growers; accordingly, I will critically reflect on both descriptions in subsequent chapters. I will also discuss the relations with other ethnic communities living in the area, like the Malinké, Peul or Soussou, and discuss the various past and also more recent population movements and the religious affinities in this particular region. In all the chapters I use the ethnic notations as my Guinean interlocutors used them when talking to me in French. I thereby use only the singular term (e.g. I will speak of the Kissi referring to the ethnic community of the Kissi-speaking people who describe themselves as *les Kissi*, although, in grammatically correct Kissi language, it would be *Kissia*) to keep it as simple as possible.

Some notes on the three largest ethnic communities present in Guinea: The Malinké, also known as Mandinka or Man(d)inko are one of the largest ethnic groups throughout West Africa and belong to the linguistic group of the Mande. The Soussou or Susu, Soso, are also a Mande-speaking community but live primarily in Guinea. The Fulani or Ful-speaking people, also known as Fulbe, Fula or Fulani, are like the Malinké spread over many countries. In Guinea, they call themselves Peul or Pulaar-speaking people and claim to hold the majority.[6] Ho-

---

5   Guinea is a multi-ethnic country, in which Mandé- and Pulaar-speaking communities are the most numerous, together making up around 80 to 90% of the population. Thus, if one accepts the framework of the nation-state, the Kissi, like the other Forestières, can be described as national minorities.

6   I use "Peul" and "Pulaar-speaking people" to address the ethnic Fulbe.

wever, the staging of numbers can also be seen as a political strategy and must be interpreted with caution (Arieff and McGovern, 2013).

Although I use the different ethnic labels I am well aware of the artificial character of most of these attributions. Thus, I am aware that "the Kissi", or "the Peul" do not exist as closed entities but are social constructions; I will elaborate on this further on in this book. Generally speaking, the making of various identities and, for instance, ethnic consciousness, is contextual and refers to open and thus incomplete processes (Förster, 1997: 46).

Importantly, the research site for this study includes different communities from different religious backgrounds. The latter aspect is rather uncommon in Guinea, which is generally described as having a Muslim majority (Camara, 2007).[7] Moreover, the dominant ethnic community living in the research area, the Kissi-speaking people, describe themselves as the autochthons who inhabit a cross-border space.

Postcolonial historical background

Guinea became an independent state in 1958.[8] Guinea's independence was characterised by a massive rejection of membership of General Charles de Gaulle's *Communauté française*: On 28 September 1958, the population voted overwhelmingly for complete and immediate independence from France – 85% of registered voters participated with 94% favouring immediate independence (Schmidt, 2005: 1). At the forefront of the Guinean nationalist movement was the Guinean branch of the RDA (*Rassemblement Démocratique Africain*), the *Parti Démocratique de Guinée* (PDG), although often both abbreviations were used: PDG-RDA. However, "the most visible player in Guinea's startling rise to nationhood" was Guinea's first president Ahmed Sékou Touré (Straker, 2009: 5). He was the nation's charismatic leader from the advent of independence until his death in 1984. Born in 1922 in Faranah, he was 36 years old when his presidency began and 62 when it ended. McGovern declares that the material on Guinea immediately after independence and during the First Republic had but one author – Sékou Touré himself (McGovern, 2004). Thus, "[t]he puzzle of Guinea and the puzzle of Sékou Touré are inextricably linked" (McGovern, 2004: 31). McGovern also recognises other important political actors, but Sékou Touré always managed potential political rivals: "He [Touré] obviously worked through colleagues and intermediaries, but so many of these were eliminated along the way, from Telli Diallo to Fodeba Keita, that

---

7   Most Guineans practise relatively orthodox forms of Islam (O'Toole and Baker, 2005: 115).

8   As a supplement the interested reader will find an extended chronology in Appendix I which includes important events and names from 1895 to 2012. For an insightful recent publication on the history of Guinea since World War Two, cf. Camara (2014).

only a few lasted more than ten years close to power" (McGovern, 2004: 31). During his presidency, Touré and his cadres established a socialist state with various institutions at national and local level to confirm the state's sovereignty. The PDG monopolised the political, judicial, administrative and technical authority and controlled state functions and public affairs. In the course of his presidency, Touré declared the socialist Cultural Revolution and Demystification Campaign, "vowing intensified transformations of national economic and cultural processes" (Straker, 2009: 7). Touré placed particular importance on youth; young people were considered the key supporters of the socialist revolution. They were therefore organised into various youth groups which were incorporated into the one-party state. Guinée Forestière and thus the Guéckédou borderland during that time was one of the main sites of Touré's state building efforts.

Although Touré reorganised the economy, especially agriculture and secondary industry, the one-party state struggled with financial hardship and international isolation (Rivière, 1977). Touré nevertheless maintained some relations with other socialist countries such as Cuba and the Soviet Union. However, in the course of his presidency Touré grew more and more despotic, which resulted in state violence against various individuals, social groups and ethnic communities. Many people died under suspicious circumstances, some ethnic communities were marginalised and exiled, and others lost their religious heritage owing to the pervasive nature of the socialist state's iconoclasm. According to an ICG report, Sékou Touré's authoritarian rule "was characterized by paranoia about plots, state violence unprecedented in Africa and the country's isolation in the context of its nationalist and socialist stance" (ICG, 2007: 1). Consequently, when Touré finally died a natural death in 1984, he left behind a devastated country.

A few days after the death of Sékou Touré, Lansana Conté together with a group of officers seized power in a coup. Lansana Conté's presidency, which was to last 24 years, was characterised by economic reforms and political democratisation processes. Thus, the Guinean government also solicited the support of the International Monetary Fund (IMF), the World Bank and major donors and introduced a constitution and a multiparty system (Smith, 2006: 418). In 1993, Guinea finally held its first presidential elections. Conté, however, "always kept a firm grip on power and never entertained the possibility of losing any election organized under his tutelage" (ICG, 2007: 1). Conté won the elections in 1993, 1998 and, finally, in 2003. In 2001 he also organised a constitutional referendum that gave him the opportunity to become president for life – removing restrictions on the number of presidential mandates and the age limit (70) and extending the term of office from five to seven years (ICG, 2007: 2).

By the late 1990s, Guinea was surrounded by civil wars in Sierra Leone, Liberia, Guinea-Bissau and later Côte d'Ivoire (Arieff, 2009: 338). The Mano River War – the civil wars in Sierra Leone and Liberia – affected the Guéckédou borderland considerably. Accordingly, many international observers warned that Guinea was at serious risk of civil war or a military coup. But Conté managed these conflicts to his benefit (Arieff, 2009: 339). In 2006 and 2007, the situation again became tense after a trade union confederation called for several national strikes. They finally proved to be an effective force for mobilising the opposition and Conté appointed a new prime minister, Lansana Kouyaté, who enjoyed the support of the trade unions. Thus, 2007 seemed to hold promise of political change (McGovern, 2007), but only a few months later the situation changed; Conté took back power and finally dismissed Kouyaté in May 2008 (Engeler, 2008).

In December 2008, after 24 years in power, President Conté finally passed away. Only hours later, a group of soldiers took power in a bloodless coup. The military junta was organised as the *Conseil National pour la Démocratie et le Développement* (CNDD) and declared Captain Moussa Dadis Camara as their leader and the country's new president. After a turbulent year, the military regime culminated in the violent oppression of a political party rally on 28 September 2009; Dadis Camara was shot by one of his military allies and had to leave the country for medical treatment in Morocco. By January 2010, after a political agreement known as the Joint Declaration of Ouagadougou signed by Dadis Camara, Blaise Compaoré and Sékouba Konaté, the latter became interim head of state and thereafter formed a "government of national unity" and organised presidential elections (Arieff, 2010: 1). These elections took place in June 2010. It was "the first national election in Guinea's history organized by an independent commission, and the first not to feature an incumbent government candidate" (Arieff and Cook, 2010: 9). Two candidates won the most votes in the June poll: Cellou Dalein Diallo of the UFDG (*Union des Forces Démocratiques de Guinée*), and Alpha Condé of the RPG (*Rassemblement du Peuple de Guinée*). In November 2010, Alpha Condé won the second round and has been president of Guinea since December 2010 (Ammann and Engeler, 2013).

3.   Listening, experiencing, observing

This monograph integrates and interprets fieldnotes that were developed using various methods. In the following chapters I will, for instance, include personal descriptions of public events or discussions, integrate information I obtained from semi-structured or life history interviews, refer to data from more informal conversations and, finally, take account of my own experiences and reflections. Methodologically, my data collection, analysis and interpretation were inspired by the circular research methodology of grounded theory and related approaches.[9]

---

9 The analysis process was supported by CAQDAS, thus by Computer Assisted/Aided Qualitative Data Analysis Software.

In order to make data collection reasonable, all upcoming chapters include information regarding the data basis. I therefore take account of varying challenges depending on the topic and/or the actors focused on and add further information regarding my research approach. Moreover, I hold the interpretation and analysis of my data up to scrutiny and allow the reader to make a methodologically more informed reading of the chapters throughout this monograph.

In what follows, quotes from semi-structured or life history interviews are in quotation marks, followed by a footnote indicating the date and with whom the conversation was held.[10] For easier reading, I translate all French statements into English, but add the French version in the footnote for good measure. All of the names used are pseudonyms in order to preserve my communication partners' anonymity.[11] Some of the more public figures, however, remain recognisable, as there were for instance only one prefect and only one mayor in Guéckédou at the time of research. As a supplement to the information in the text, a list of all the key informants is included in Appendix II.

Approaching the field

As both resources and time were limited, this research project is based on approximately fourteen months of anthropological fieldwork undertaken in Guinea. The fourteen months were divided into different periods. The first period, January and February 2008, may be called a preliminary field trip, since it served to develop the research topic and a local network. I also had the chance to make a brief visit to the Guinée Forestière and decided that Guéckédou should be my primary research site. The second field trip was dedicated particularly to coming to grips with the Guinean state apparatus and presence nationally. I visited Conakry for the festivities to mark the 50th anniversary of independence and learnt about how the state tried to be represented in public. During this second stay I also established further personal contacts in and beyond Guinea's capital city. The following two visits between 2009 (September to January) and 2010 (June to November) were spent mainly in the town of Guéckédou and other small towns and villages in Gué-

---

10   Data collection was done with the help of a digital recorder. Thus, whenever possible, I recorded the conversations and the semi-structured or life history interviews. However, I also made notes following all the discussions and social interactions I observed, no matter whether they were recorded or not. After all, I did not always feel comfortable with recording, especially with elderly people or during informal meetings. However, taking out my small notebook, among other things, to clearly indicate my identity as a researcher was never a problem.

11   While choosing a pseudonym I tried not to change the name's resemblance to a particular social, ethnic or religious community. Thus, I replaced a Christian name with another Christian name and so forth.

ckédou prefecture[12] and beyond.[13] This is how the main body of data was collected. My last stay in 2012 (January to February) can then be labelled as a closing field trip during which I collected further data from other regions, not least to compare with my own findings, and also updated the data I had collected on people's life trajectories, everyday life and the socio-political situation in and beyond Guéckédou.[14]

This division of fieldwork had several advantages. Amongst other things, it enabled me to follow specific political processes, case studies and life courses over a longer period of time. In addition, I could take stock of the material regularly and was therefore able to continuously reflect on how to proceed. On a more personal level, I felt more at home each time I arrived in Guinean territory and could build on an ever more familiar local network of people.

I could count on various people who facilitated and supported my research during the fieldwork. One of my most important assistants for the main research in Guéckédou was Augustin Tamba Koundouno. At the time of research, Augustin was completing his studies at the *Supérieur des Arts de Guinée* (ISAG) and was based in the city of Dubreka, Guinée Maritime. However, he spent much of his time in Guéckédou and agreed to become my research assistant. We got to know each other through a mutual friend who knew that we were both intending to do some research in the area: at the time Augustin had completed his master's dissertation on local conflict resolution strategies in Guéckédou prefecture. Accordingly, we had similar interests and I also accompanied him to some of his appointments, during which he talked with local elders about conflict within families or between different ethnic groups and was particularly interested in how people managed to resolve the conflict. Among other things, he described mediation procedures, joking relationships or mutual pacts for non-violence as typical strategies for conflict resolution in the *pays Kissi* (Koundouno, 2009: 6ff).

Regarding my own research, Augustin featured as a gatekeeper to the many youth groups active in Guéckédou and also knew most of the important power brokers in and around Guéckédou – or at least had no problem with simply knocking on their doors. When visiting these actors and institutions, Augustin served, whenever the conversation was not in French, as a translator and also as a companion who would introduce me to the people and help me to ask my questions.[15] Usually, the conversations would lead on to more informal discussions du-

12 I made day trips to the following villages in different Guéckédou sub-prefectures: Nongoa, Temessadou, Kouakoro, Beindou Boodou, Koundou and Mongo.

13 Other towns I visited in Guinée Forestière include Kissidougou, Macenta, N'Zérékoré, and Lola.

14 I got to know Mamou and Dalaba in Fouta Djallon, and Kouroussa and Kankan in Haute Guinée.

15 Almost all of the semi-structured interviews or more informal conversations were carried out in French. This has consequences in that some of the nuances of the local languages such as local expressions or meanings were lost in translation processes.

ring which Augustin also participated. Thus, besides being my research assistant, Augustin became himself one of my key informants, allowing me to understand being young and growing up in the Guéckédou borderland.

In addition to Augustin, I could count on the help of many other people, who assisted me a great deal with my research and also helped me to overcome some of its challenges. Most of those people lived in the same neighbourhood as I did and simply became friends, with whom I shared the everyday life of going to the market, preparing food, drinking coffee and, whenever the political situation was tense, listening to the radio and waiting for news from Conakry. Some of these people where not originally from Guéckédou but described other Guinean regions as their ethnic origin. Accordingly, they extended my view on the Guéckédou borderland by introducing me to religious and ethnic communities other than those introduced by Augustin, who is Christian and part of the Kissi-speaking community. This extended view actually proved to be an important source for understanding the making of local identities and the subjectivities of first-comers and latecomers in the Guéckédou borderland, as well as to have a more differentiated view on being young and on the political turmoil at the time of the research.

My neighbourhood was not only important in broadening my views of different ethnic or religious communities, however; it also proved to be very important for grasping the everyday lives of young women from whichever community. Through these daily interactions with my young female neighbours, during which we simply cooked or did our hair, I was able to learn a great deal about their lives, their worldviews and the way they manoeuvred through the local socio-political terrain. This generated a no less valuable but different data set to the one I was able to assemble with male youngsters. Among other things, the sheer number of female informants was lower and the fieldnotes I wrote about the long periods I spent with female friends included many more personal issues about family and financial problems for instance.

Life history interviews and shared experiences

After the preliminary field trip and an exploratory period spent in Guéckédou, during which I organised my research and familiarised myself with the surroundings, I decided to approach the relationship between youth and the state by focusing on three aspects: firstly, on the everyday life of the youth; secondly, the organisation of young people into different social groups; and thirdly, on the political terrain with its diverse state and non-state institutions and actors.

To grasp youths' everyday lives and their agency I carried out life history interviews and participated in parts of their lives, going to the market and preparing food, sitting outside different homes making and drinking tea, visiting small video clubs to watch football games, visiting people's gardens, or spending time in small mobile phone repair and charging shops, just waiting for the next client and talking about anything and everything. Very often these shared activities allowed for a more embedded interpretation of the data I gathered through interviews. Another part of the fieldwork involved the workings of several different social groups. Semi-structured interviews, focus group discussions and more informal conversations were carried out with the young members and founders of these groups. In addition to talking to them or interviewing them, I also participated in their weekly meetings or visited their offices or project sites, if these existed. I was interested in youth associations and cooperatives as well as in young vigilante groups, the motorbike taxi union and religious groups such as the Scouts. I was thus able to include not only a particular milieu – for instance students – but also other youngsters living in and around Guéckédou. As I conducted most of my interviews in French, my informants had to have a certain level of education. Moreover, most of my interlocutors who were commonly described as young were between 18 and 34 years old, so they were no longer children but rather meandering through the youth/adult nexus.

The decision to focus on, among other things, the way young people were organised socially was closely related to my interest in former socialist youth groups, which were, as I learnt from many local elders, closely linked to the state. Accordingly, the focus on contemporary youth groups provides an important lens through which to research youth–state relations sensitive to history and socio-political change.

To research the third aspect – the political terrain – I talked to political actors and local power brokers such as local authorities, various public servants, NGO activists and mapped out political institutions representing or related to the state apparatus in Guéckédou, for instance the state administration bureaus, the municipality, or the council of elders. Again, life history interviews provided crucial insights into the political actors' career trajectories and various perspectives vis-à-vis the state. In addition, observations of state orchestrated events allowed for multifaceted insights, not only regarding state imagery but also regarding state–society interactions. Finally, I also traced settlement histories and researched the way in which elders perceived their own youth, which resulted in important background knowledge to understand socio-political changes and continuities against the backdrop of past and contemporary youth, youth groups and state–society relations.

All in all, one of the key methods besides participation and observation was the life history approach, which included not only life history interviews but also more informal conversations, discussions and observations of everyday life which, in combination, helped me to grasp people's life trajectories, their past career moves and future plans (Engeler, 2011). As Atkinson notes, "[i]n the telling of a life story, we get a good sense of how and why the various parts of a life are connected and what gives the person meaning in life. There may be no better way to answer the question of how people get from where they began to where they are now in life than through their life stories" (Atkinson, 1998: 20).[16] Thus, while I tried to approach the field sensitive to local concerns, meanings and categories, the life history approach proved to be an important method that provided me with insights into the ways in which personal experiences and life trajectories were shaped by social dynamics, as well as by socioeconomic and political changes. I am aware that the life history interview can, besides providing space for remembering and reflection, also provide a stage for image cultivation (Svasek and Domecka, 2012: 122). Moreover, as Crapanzano writes, people not only remember or stage particular life episodes during life history conversations but also imagine alternative trajectories and interpretations (Crapanzano, 1980: 10).

Besides life histories and, more generally, besides simply asking people what matters to them I followed Emerson and co-authors who suggest: "Writing ethnographic fieldnotes that are sensitive to members' meanings is primarily a matter not of asking but of inferring what people are concerned with from the specific ways in which they talk and act in a variety of natural settings. Thus, interviewing, especially asking members directly what terms mean to them or what is important or significant to them is not the primary tool for getting at members' meanings. Rather, the distinctive procedure is to observe and record naturally occurring talk and interaction" (Emerson et al., 1995: 140).

Thus, I perceived the sharing of parts of daily life and the experiencing of, for instance, the same sorrows and fears because of the complex political situation, as crucial additional methods.

Challenges and lessons learnt

Researching youth and the state in Guinea was accompanied by various challenges. Obviously, the political circumstances at the time of the research complicated my life as a researcher and significantly affected my data collection and analysis: In late 2008, the country's long-term President Lansana Conté passed away and hours later a group of soldiers took power in a bloodless coup. In 2009, when the military junta was still in power the militarisation of everyday life with its numerous roadblocks and over-zealous soldiers restricted travel and at times also generated anxiety and uncertainty. On certain days it was better to stay at home and wait for news from Conakry or, paradoxically, from friends in Switzerland, who

---

16 Many authors discuss the life history approach. I thereby perceive Bjarnesen's "mobile life story-approach" as very useful for grasping young people's life trajectories (Bjarnesen, 2007; 2009). However, other approaches are as helpful, cf. amongst others (Svasek and Domecka, 2012, Anderson, 2011, Atkinson, 1998, Bertaux, 1981, Heinz and Krüger, 2001, Luttrel, 2005).

had much more information about what was going on in Guinea from the Internet than we had in Guéckédou, where we were often cut off from the Internet, thus depending predominantly on *Radio France Internationale* and *BBC Afrique* for news of the regime. Accordingly, my neighbours and I soon formed some sort of information centre as we all had different sources supplying us with the latest news. I generally felt safe while we were sitting together and sharing the news, whether good or bad, in large part thanks to my host family. I only found out later that the mere fact that I had stayed in Guinea during the CNDD regime was for many people evidence of my strong commitment to the country and its residents and opened more than one door when I returned to Guéckédou in 2010.

During the transition period preceding the presidential elections in 2010, I was put on the spot by the intensified ethnic conflict, resulting in serious disputes between people I had previously known as friendly neighbours. All of a sudden I realised how much it mattered to many of my friends where they went for water or food, with which taxi driver they drove and which mosque they visited for prayer. And even if they did not care, others did and could make an issue out of it. As the political circumstances affected both my data collection and my data reading and interpretation, I will return to that issue several times in this monograph.

Another challenge of doing research in the Guinean forest region was related to the hierarchies of withheld knowledge. Fairhead and Leach relate this practice to the region's power societies and the politics of secrecy (Fairhead and Leach, 1996: 15). According to them, there are "limits of knowing" because: "As researchers, the way villagers located us in their politics of knowledge has certainly circumscribed the information and understandings accessible to us. Furthermore we cannot know the extent of these limits, since withheld knowledge or the extent of ignorance is integral to the politics of secrecy" (Fairhead and Leach, 1996: 18).

Similarly, Knörr and Trajano Filho (2010) state with reference to "the underneath of things" analysed by Ferme (2001): "Another feature associated with the political culture of the Upper Guinea Coast is the widespread culture of secrecy. Secrecy is a salient feature of political culture and we have to look at the "underneath of things" (Ferme, 2001) to understand secrecy's meaning for processes of integration and conflict in everyday life as well as in situations of strife and warfare" (Knörr and Trajano Filho, 2010: 10).

McGovern further relates the culture of secrecy or discretion, as he frames it, to the scare tactics of the socialist state: "In Guinea, the cultural emphasis on discretion that is so pronounced in Forestier societies was compounded by the culture of paranoia cultivated by Sékou Touré's government" (McGovern, 2013: 200).

Generally speaking, I tried to accept the limits of knowing and could also see some advantages to it. As ordinary Guineans are in general also confronted with some of these limits, I could understand their perspective and shared some of their experiences, for instance when asking for a particular service from the state administration. Very often state bureaucrats answered my questions indirectly so that in the end I did not know whether, for instance, there were no statistics on the town's population at all, whether I should offer some money to get more information, or whether the respondent simply did not want to help me with the matter. At the beginning of my research I was often very frustrated by these experiences but later realised that many of my dialogue partners faced similar problems in their everyday encounters with the state, as well as with some of the local elders and other authorities. I then started to appreciate these instances of talking without getting information, of endlessly waiting for people with whom I thought I had an appointment, or of getting answers to different questions to those I had asked. Mostly, these experiences taught me about issues which proved to be as important to my topic as the initial questions I wanted to ask. I learnt, for instance, about the sensitivity of putting what I considered banal questions to trade unionists in times of political tension. I took on board the fact that when talking to an elder it was not recent political transformation that was important but the Kissi-speaking community's origins and early migration movements. And I learnt that I was the only one who thought that the simultaneous presence of pictures of Mao, Marx, Sékou Touré and Jean-Marc Télliano (the local candidate for the 2010 presidential elections) in a village chief's living room was a contradiction of different political imaginations; for local people they formed an acceptable unity. Finally, this concurs with McGovern's finding regarding methodological problems in Guinea's Forest region: "there is more to be gained by watching, listening, and considering, than by talking" (McGovern, 2013: 200).

As previously mentioned, I also had to deal with other challenges. I had to be careful to listen not only to young men but to include the often less forceful voices of young women. Thanks to a few close female friends I was able to enter the world and perspectives of young women, although not as often as for young men.

Finally, my own age was both an advantage and a disadvantage. In the eyes of almost all of my conversation partners I was a young woman who had not yet attained adult status. This was related to the fact that, at the time of fieldwork, I was not only a student but also unmarried and childless. Of course this was a door-opener for researching youth – but also a difficulty when entering some of the political arenas. However, in retrospect these circumstances allowed me to get a better grasp of youths' everyday life in Guéckédou, as the youngsters I talked to often could not enter the political terrain that easily either.

All in all, I do not claim "to know the other" (Jackson, 2006) but tried to approach the emic perspective as best I could. Thus, as young men and women are at the centre of this study, I simply tried to follow them and accompany them in order to grasp parts of their different life trajectories, to understand their future dreams and everyday problems, and to see things through their eyes to further understand youth and the state in Guinea.

Grounded theory

This research project applied a grounded theory methodology. Hence, data collection is, as Silverman puts it, "only half the battle". Data analysis and writing-up are "the name of the game" (Silverman, 2007). Hence, I agree with Emerson and co-authors when they write: "Ethnography is an active enterprise. Its activity incorporates dual impulses. On the one hand, the ethnographer must make her way into new worlds and new relationships. On the other hand, she must learn how to represent in written form what she has come to see and understand as the result of these experiences" (Emerson et al., 1995: 15).

While developing this "written form", I considered it important that data collection, analysis and interpretation in the grounded theory tradition form a circular process. Accordingly, my own data analysis started directly following the first visits to the field and continued over the years. In addition, I continued memo-writing throughout the research and analysis process and established the analysis against the backdrop of several rounds of coding and analysing. In addition, I followed Emerson and co-authors (1995) by devising thematic narratives that were closely linked to the fieldnotes and organised around a specific topic or event (Emerson et al., 1995: 170). During these processes of identifying relevant stories and writing thematic narratives – related to a second round of more specific coding – I drew my inspiration from, among other things, my memos. However, I also tried never to lose contact with my data and re-read my fieldnotes over and over again. Nevertheless, in moving from fieldnotes to writing the ethnographic text, I turned away from local scenes and their participants, "from relations formed and personal debts incurred in the field" (Emerson et al., 1995: 169). Instead, I started to compare the narratives with youth studies and the anthropology of the state. Finally, my interpretations emerged from these processes of rereading fieldnotes and intertwining them with scientific discourses.

In general, I agree with Emerson and co-authors who write that "data are never pure; they are ripe with meanings and always products of prior interpretative and conceptual decisions" (Emerson et al., 1995: 167). Thus, even the process of data collection, which I have called "listening, experiencing, observing", was influenced by theory and did not simply spring from nowhere.

4.   Book outline

In reflecting on this research focus and the related questions, this monograph is organised into nine chapters and one concluding reflection. All the chapters are grounded in empirical evidence and include references to different scientific discourses related to the topic and the argument. The timeframe concentrates on post-revolutionary Guinea, in particular the period from 2000 to 2010. This period emerged from the data analysis and represents the temporal context in which most of my young interview partners located themselves. However, references to the more distant past were frequent. Accordingly, I also outline the making of the Guéckédou borderland with references to early population movements, to the impact of colonialism and to colonial boundary demarcation in West Africa. In addition, a couple of chapters address revolutionary Guinea, as a thorough awareness of this period is crucial in order to understand present-day social and political circumstances in Guinea, in particularly in the Guinée Forestière. Moreover, the legacies of the socialist period were very present in people's accounts, especially when talking about the state administration or the relationship between youth and the state.

The book is organised as follows. This first introductory chapter has sought to provide an understanding of youth and the state and has introduced the reader to the research site and research approach. The second chapter examines the making of the Guéckédou borderland and local ethnic and national identities. The next chapter is particularly interested in looking at Touré's state-building efforts in Guinée Forestière, which included the creation of revolutionary youth and inter-generational confusion. Chapter four, then, addresses state re-making processes after 1984. Besides looking at governmental changes and continuities, this chapter takes a closer look at how and by whom the political is shaped in the context of the local state in post-revolutionary Guéckédou. The next couple of chapters address young lives in relation to the youth–state nexus in the Guéckédou borderland. I initiate the discussion by first reflecting on being young and growing up and then referring to the meandering everyday lives of the youth in that particular region. I then write about what for most of my young interlocutors was an extremely crucial time: the rebel attacks in the 2000s and the young vigilante group that was formed in response to the increasing insecurity. The following chapters introduce the post-war period and discuss the political terrain that unfolded by examining youth-state relations in particular within the context of various social groups such as unions, associations and branches of religious movements. I perceive the members of these groups as interesting actors who navigate the local political terrain and create room for political participation – not only through street protests or by violent means but also by building up complex negotiating arenas, characterised by relationships to various actors such as civil servants, religious authorities and NGOs.

All the chapters of this study may be seen as complementary clusters. However, the different chapters also tell their own story, which will be discussed in the last paragraph of each chapter. The final chapter completes this book on youth and the state in the Guéckédou borderland by summarising the most important aspects.

II. At the crossroads
The Guéckédou borderland in the making

"In the Borderlands
you are the battleground
where enemies are kin to each other;
you are at home, a stranger,
the border disputes have been settled
the volley of shot have shattered the truce
you are wounded, lost in action
dead, fighting back;
to survive the Borderlands
you must live sin fronteras
be a crossroads"
(Anzaldua 1999 quoted in [Aitken and Plows,
2010: 327]).

In September 2009, after heavy rainfall across the entire Guinée Forestière, the rivers that meandered through Guéckédou before finally flowing into the river near the border between Liberia and Sierra Leone broke their banks. A number of neighbourhoods were heavily affected. The town's centre and buildings, including the market area, the stadium and parts of the *Maison des Jeunes*, were under water. My own neighbourhood was greatly affected by the high water; families lost their homes and many of their belongings. Fortunately, none of my neighbours were hurt or died, for there had been flood warnings in the previous couple of days and most people who lived close to the rivers had left their homes to sleep elsewhere. During this time, my neighbours talked about the official delegates from Conakry who were expected to reach the town soon to inspect the damage and discuss assistance with the local authorities and NGOs, as well as telling me stories about the rivers that wind they way through the town. On one of these afternoons when the water level was still quite high, Albert, one of my Kissi-speaking friends, visited me and we started chatting out on the veranda. Boubacar joined us soon after. His family is part of the Peul community but Boubacar was born in the Guéckédou borderland. Both Albert and Boubacar were in their late twenties.

After some small talk, Albert started telling us a story about a crocodile that lived on one of the nearby river bends. The crocodile, Albert explained, was not just any crocodile but used to be a human being. Decades ago he was one of the founders of the settlement we today call Guéckédou who, after he died, turned into a crocodile and lives in the river to this day. He posed no threat to autochthons, Albert said, but the crocodile did not like foreigners. Boubacar and I kept silent during the story and when it ended Boubacar went home, as it was the hour of prayer.

Albert, however, continued to think about the rivers and the nearby hills and expressed his embarrassment, for according to him some of the names of the rivers' and hills meant nothing in the Kissi language. He concluded that other peoples who had lived in the region before the Kissi must have named them. "But then who is the crocodile", I asked, "it must be dangerous for the Kissi community too, no?" Albert had no answer to that.

As described previously, Guéckédou forms part of what is commonly called the "country of the Kissi" or, in the local French, *le pays Kissi*. The country of the Kissi unites Kissi-speaking people in Guinea, Sierra Leone and Liberia. Thus, although the borders between the countries produce different political cultures and administrative identities, the people describing themselves as the Kissi perceive their community as at home across the entire border region. Linguistically, the *pays Kissi* represents an island in the wider Mande-dominated region. Moreover, they describe themselves as the autochthons, not least as a political strategy.[1] Questions regarding the origins or ancestry of the Kissi-speaking people are, however, more or less unanswerable, as many of the Upper Guinean Coast societies "have been so intermingled that their genesis is a conundrum" (Hair 1967, in Knörr and Trajano Filho, 2010: 5). Nevertheless, the "mystery" around the origins of the Kissi has been widely discussed in a range of scientific contributions.

The aim of this chapter is to take a closer look at the oral histories and ethnic identities of the inhabitants of the Guéckédou borderland. The chapter sheds light on three interrelated issues that are organised as follows. First of all, I introduce the reader to the pre-colonial and colonial background of the Guéckédou borderland. Especially during the colonial period, local ethnic identities became increasingly clear. The border with British-ruled Sierra Leone and independent Liberia marked the boundary between different political cultures and administrative

---

1 Interestingly, McGovern discusses autochthony as a cultural resource in the Guinée Forestière, especially in relation to the social and political life of the Loma (McGovern, 2013: 65ff). He defines autochthony as "the relation of a particular territory with a defined group of persons with rights in that territory" (McGovern, 2013: 69). Furthermore, he importantly states that "concepts such as autochthony have been fundamental to establishing hierarchy, legitimacy, and effective power" (McGovern, 2013: 112).

identities.[2] However, by referring, secondly, to the founding myth of the Guéckédou settlement, I stress that "the ethnic other" is formed not only by distinctions but also by relations, what must be perceived as important for processes of local identity formation, generational relations and political imagination in the contested and ever-changing border environment. This will become more evident by, thirdly, writing about so-called secret or power societies and the management of regional integration and generational relations. Thus this chapter shows that local perceptions of "being Kissi" include both integrative and delimitative characteristics. Times of political and economic crisis, however, boost the drawing of boundaries. In addition, colonial administrators and ethnographers, as well as Guinean politicians, have all contributed at times to contested border demarcations.

This chapter is based on various kinds of source material. On the one hand, it reviews different ethnographic accounts that write about the ethnic background of the Guéckédou borderland, the Guinée Forestière and the Upper Guinean coast. This material is interlinked with references to literature that provides a more general conceptualisation of borderlands. On the other hand, the chapter includes qualitative data derived from interviews with local elders in which I sought to trace the settlement history and the origins of the Kissi ethnic group. Thus, I have tried to grasp how Kissi-speaking people imagine and discursively construct their ethnic and territorial identities in present-day Guéckédou.

The very first paragraph is meant as a personal prelude, reflecting on my journeys to and from Guéckédou.

1.   Journeys to and from Guéckédou

When I travelled to Guéckédou for the first time in September 2009, I profited from the Air Passenger Services provided by the World Food Programme (WFP) which allowed me to overcome some of the 800 kilometres from Conakry to the town in Guinea where I wanted to conduct my research. Thanks to a development aid agency and a short visit to the WFP offices I was allowed to book the flight. I arrived at the airport in Conakry early in the morning but had to wait for hours until the flight was ready to leave. On boarding I realised that we were only two passengers. It was a small plane that did not fly at high altitude. I therefore had a perfect view and could see Conakry clearly from above. Shortly after leaving the urban area I was especially impressed by the deltas of the Soumbouga, Morébaya and Forécariah rivers and their meandering courses. We continued northward, flying over countless villages of varying sizes, connected by thin pathways and interspersed with forests. The wonderful hilly landscape calmed me down and I forgot about the anthropological mission that awaited me in Guéckédou. Before landing I could see the small villages and individual houses of the Guinée Forestière. We landed outside Kissidougou, which is still a three-hour car journey from Guéckédou. En route to Guéckédou it was raining but I could still see rice fields, palm oil plantations and village streets.

Arriving at Guéckédou, I was very tired and missed the smells and sounds of slash and burn agriculture I remembered from my first time in Guéckédou, when I was there for my preliminary field trip in January 2008. It was another season – January is hot and dry while it still rains in September. In addition, not only was the weather different. A lot had changed in Guinea in the past eighteen months; the old President Lansana Conté had died a natural death in December 2008 after a reign of 24 years. Shortly thereafter, a group of young army officers carried out a coup d'état. This military junta, called the CNDD (*Conseil National pour la Démocratie et le Développement*), made one of these officers, Capitain Moussa Dadis Camara, the new president. He promised to hold free and fair elections but changed his attitude soon after taking office. Therefore, he and the military were still in power when I arrived in Guéckédou.

Apart from the worries about the political situation I personally felt much better in the field than a year earlier; in 2008 I had been unwell and my voice was hoarse. I remembered the visit to the local state administration when I had said, whilst talking to the prefect, "I lost my voice". He looked at me with big eyes and asked "where?" I did not have an answer. However, on arrival in Guéckédou this time I was in a good mood and joked about my memories of the previous visit. In retrospect being ill had had a psychological dimension: first contacts are never easy.

In the following months I established myself in Guéckédou – but since this short prelude is about journeys to and from Guéckédou, I will fast forward about four months to when I left Guéckédou for the first time and travelled back to Conakry. The political situation had changed a great deal in the interim. President Moussa Dadis Camara had tinkered with the idea of presenting himself at the planned elections, although he had originally promised not to do so. Political parties, civil society groups and trade unions were disappointed and called on their supporters to meet in Conakry. This meeting at the end of September 2009 started as a peaceful reunion in the city's stadium but ended as a massacre with many deaths, women raped and people displaced. In Guéckédou, we got the information via friends, mobile phones, BBC Afrique and Radio France International: an estimated 157 people had been killed and more than 1000 injured. Soldiers were stabbing people with bayonets and gang-raping women and girls. Dadis told the media that some elements of the army were "out of control". Accordingly, the following months were politically difficult, unsettled and unpredictable. Thus, when I travelled back to Conakry, I was quite happy to accept a lift: I had the chance to travel in a four by four (4x4) belonging to one of the development agencies, whose local staff were still working in the region although the expats had left following the September unrest.

The two-day trip was comfortable and I could again enjoy the landscape. I was impressed by the condition of the road once we had left Guinée Forestière: no more huge potholes the size of a motorbike! Nonetheless I was also confused, mainly by the small villages I saw during these two days. Depending on the region I saw round houses with thatched roofs built in various ways. In front of the houses women and children were cooking, pounding spices and washing clothes. Old men were sitting in front of their homes watching the passing cars. I was familiar with these scenes from Guéckédou, and I was also used to no electricity or running water. But after all, Guéckédou is – I had never realised this so clearly before – a small town with a market, some shops, a hospital, a lycée, and a youth centre, whereas the people in these small villages did not have much beside their community and their small houses. What was it about this life? Most of my friends and informants in Guéckédou had close relationships with the villages, had grown up in one or spent parts of their lives there. They went back to their home villages to assist with harvesting the crops, for celebrations or in times of personal crisis. Hence, they were used to moving between a profoundly rural and a (semi-)urban environment, which to me seemed so different and little related at the time although actually forming one integrated living environment.

After two days on the road we arrived in Conakry. It was extremely hot, noisy and smelly. All the traffic, the exhaust fumes and the people impressed me but I already missed small but calm Guéckédou. After a short stay in Conakry I left again for Guéckédou, this time by public transport. The journey with the bush taxi turned out to be very difficult. It was very uncomfortable and after 17 hours of driving I had stopped thinking about the pain in my limbs. Even more of a nuisance than the physical pains were the military roadblocks, of which there were around 25 before arriving in Guéckédou. The soldiers were looking for Aboubacar "Toumba" Diakité, the man who, on 3 December, had shot President Moussa Dadis Camara in the head, ostensibly because the junta leader planned to hold Toumba solely accountable for the September atrocities. The soldiers at the roadblocks stopped most of the vehicles, asked for passports and, when they saw my white face, for my vaccination card. These stops were often difficult because the soldiers' behaviour was unpredictable, at least for me. Moreover, the taxi passengers repeatedly provoked the uniformed officials and the atmosphere became quite tense. During the drive the passengers discussed the assassination attempt over and over again, deliberated on whether the president would recover and about the whispered mystic forces of Toumba. After all of this, I was happy to arrive in Guéckédou. It was 3 o'clock in the morning, the full moon the only light. But I had arrived safely and was among friends again – I felt at home.

The wounded president was recovering from the assassination attempt in Morocco. Rumours about his health reached the veranda of my Guéckédou home and for my neighbours the country's future appeared to be uncertain. They were afraid of war and remembered the brutal conflicts in Liberia and Sierra Leone. Some of my Kissi friends still supported the absent president Dadis. They were sure that as a Forestière the bullet could not have wounded him seriously. My friends who spoke pulaar were also waiting for news from Morocco but hoped for a change in government. Whatever the case, they were all hoping for peace and steady development.

In January 2010, I travelled again from Guéckédou to Conakry en route to Switzerland. Again I passed the 25 military checkpoints in a bush taxi. During the road trip, I saw a man standing at the rear of his car, where the letters CNDD were emblazoned in big black letters. I then realised that he was covering them with a fresh layer of paint. Today I think he must have known that it would only be weeks before the CNDD would be out of fashion. However, at the time, I reflected on the fact that only a few soldiers were asking for money or were otherwise behaving improperly when we passed the checkpoints. In fact, most of the soldiers were very young and seemed uncertain when trying to read the passports. Like the first time I had passed through the roadblocks, the other passengers provoked them and laughed at their inability to read. A military regime with shy and friendly soldiers? However, shortly before reaching Conakry I had to revise my interpretation; 36 kilometres outside the city, the soldiers went crazy. They stopped the traffic from midnight to around 6 o'clock in the morning and then proceeded to collect their "toll" from the tired drivers and passengers. Equipped with arms and bags they collected money aggressively. They claimed their dues from the hundreds of cars, buses, trucks and other vehicles pushing toward the city centre. "Ici, c'est la frontière" one soldier screamed as I hesitated to hand money over to him. Having lived close to the Liberian and Sierra Leonean borders during most of my stay in Guinea I was confused about this statement but finally gave him what he asked for.

Some days later I was back in Switzerland. Soon after Dadis went into exile in Burkina Faso, the junta minister of defence, Sékouba Konaté, was made interim leader and finally organised more or less free and fair elections. No member of the CNDD or the transition government was allowed to run for office.

After a year of absence, I returned to Guéckédou in January 2012. In the meantime, Alpha Condé ruled the country. Hardly any roadblock delayed our journey but the passengers in our bush taxi were packed together like sardines. According to my fellow passengers, this was because of the change of regime: whereas Dadis had tried to reorganise and control the traffic, I was told, the new president did not look at such issues. However, I myself preferred the sardine can to the "militarised" roads. When I arrived in Guéckédou I forgot about much of the political issues. I was just back among friends. And although many had left for Conakry or other towns to look for jobs or to be reunited with family members, I met many of my dialogue partners. Some had married, others had brought children into the world, and others still had died or become seriously ill. However, I could still find some of them on the very same corners and crossroads, waiting for taxi passengers, selling coffee or bread, awaiting new customers in order to repair their mobile phones. My visit was only a short one but I managed to see many people – most of them were very happy to see me again. For me it was a sort of farewell, as I knew that my research project would be finished quite soon. And here it started: nostalgia for Guinea, coupled with the certainty of returning whenever possible.

2. Political relations, population movements and colonial boundary marking

The Guéckédou borderland has a turbulent history; competitive political relations, trade and warfare, and associated population changes and movements had a formative impact over centuries. Fairhead and Leach write the following about the neighbouring Kissidougou prefecture: "These movements in the pre-colonial period, overlaying subsequent movement, interpretations and boundary-drawing under colonial rule, account for the broad distribution of population, languages and forest islands within Kissidougou today and are important, in turn, in comprehending present ethnicity and its relationship to vegetation" (Fairhead and Leach, 1996: 95).[3]

Thus, the present-day ethnic imprint in the region must be seen as a (never-ending) process, involving constant relational movements and changes that started a long time ago and will continue to shape the region. Accordingly, one has to perceive the local ethnic groups not as people with a separate, independent or autonomous past, but as constructed entities that arose out of diverse social crossroads, keeping in mind that "people have undoubtedly been more mobile and identity less fixed than the static and typologising approaches of classical anthropology would suggest" (Gupta and Ferguson, 1992: 9).

Different ethnographic accounts describe the Guinée Forestière as inhabited by the "Forestières", which included the Kissi, the Toma/Loma, the Guerzé/Kpel-

---

3 I consider the research and publications of Fairhead and Leach as an important reference for understanding the Guéckédou area. Their research focused especially on the Kissi-speaking people in Kissidougou prefecture, just north of Guéckédou prefecture (Fairhead, 2010, Fairhead and Leach, 1994; 1996; 1997; 2002).

le and certain other minor ethnic groups (Germain, 1984). Various authors stress that the Kissi language is not part of the Mande language group, which includes most of the other Forestières, but rather part of the Atlantic language group: Greenberg classifies the Kissi language within the Mel sub-branch of the West Atlantic language group, properly called Kissié (Greenberg, 1966: 8). The online tool multitree.org however talks about 'Southern Kisi' regarding the Guéckédou area, subordinating it to the Kissi, the Bullom-Kissi, the Mel, and then the Southern Atlantic/Atlantic-Congo/ Niger-Congo language family. Germain, on the other hand, classifies the language within the Senego-Guinean subgroup of the North Atlantic language group (Germain, 1984: 44). For the purposes of this book, however, the most important statement is that the Kissi language is not part of the Mande language group but of the Atlantic language group.[4] Thus, linguistically speaking, the Kissi communities are quite isolated and are primarily surrounded by Mande speaking people. As a result, the origins of the Kissi-speaking people have been widely discussed in different ethno-linguistic and ethnographic accounts, and also reflect the main scientific discourses and perspectives of specific time periods. Some argue that the contemporary Kissi heartland in Guinea, which corresponds approximately to today's Kissidougou and Guéckédou prefectures, has been inhabited by Kissi speakers since 1630 at least (Fairhead and Leach, 1996: 100). Others argue that a different ethnic community populated the cross-border region before the influx of the Kissi. These authors especially refer to stone statuettes found in the area. Paulme, for instance, could not find anybody capable of sculpting such statuettes during her field stay in the Guéckédou borderland and accordingly argues that another ethnic group must have made them (Paulme, 1942; 1954: 2). Schaeffner and Germain deploy fairly similar arguments and think there must have been some sort of 'original people' that once inhabited the region (Schaeffner, 1951, Germain, 1984). Katzan again challenges these assumptions and argues for a more relational perspective, viewing "Kissi origins" as more flexible and related to different societies and migration periods (Katzan, 1998: 50). Similarly, Knörr and Trajano Filho more recently argue that the wider region (the Upper Guinea Coast)[5] should be described as a crossroads of diverse migration movements from both savannah and coast (Knörr and Trajano Filho, 2010). The

---

4 Pulaar, the language of the Peulh, also belongs to the Atlantic language group.

5 Knörr and Trajano Filho define the Upper Guinea Coast geographically as follows: "The Upper Guinea Coast refers to that part of the West African coast located between the south bank of the Gambia River and a vaguely defined area along the coast of present-day southeastern Liberia. Along the horizontal axis, the Upper Guinea Coast is bordered by the Atlantic Ocean in the West, with its eastern-most confines placed somewhere in the Futa-Jalon highlands and in the mountains of N'Zérékoré, both in the Republic of Guinea" (Knörr and Trajano Filho, 2010: 2). So they use this geographical label to place and correlate cultural, linguistic and social phenomena and processes in the entire region.

region is therefore "home to a large diversity, with languages belonging to three African language families (West Atlantic, Mande, and Kruan)" (Knörr and Trajano Filho, 2010: 3).

Knörr and Trajano Filho perceive the Mande expansion as formative for people living on the edge of the Atlantic forest and the savannah. From the thirteenth century onwards, the expansion included conquest and assimilation, resistance and the accommodation of local inhabitants. The authors distinguish between three different waves of migrants. The first wave comprised "agriculturalists in search of land", the second included "Islamized groups of Mande traders, who exchanged salt, clothes, and iron tools they brought with them from the savannah and from the Saharan region for forest products such as kola, nut, ivory, and dyes", and, finally, the third wave comprised "state-builders, Manding warriors who were pushed out of the centers of the Sudanese states by its centrifugal forces" (Knörr and Trajano Filho, 2010: 4). Besides the Mande expansion, the arrival of the Portuguese on the Guinean coast in the mid-fifteenth century can be perceived as having a wide impact not only on the coastal region but also on its hinterland. Again, in the words of Knörr and Trajano Filho: " [...] the arrival of the Portuguese on the coast in the mid fifteenth century brought about a long-term West African-European encounter which was to cause substantial change in the social configuration of the Upper Guinea Coast" (Knörr and Trajano Filho, 2010: 4).

The slave trade influenced regional trade networks in particular and initiated major socio-political restructuring in the Guinean forest region (Fairhead and Leach, 1996: 93). D'Azevedo accordingly writes that between the seventeenth and the nineteenth century, when the slave trade was at its peak, fighting over control of trade routes and the acquisition of slaves dominated communal life in the Guinée Forestière (D'Azevedo, 1962: 535). However, Fairhead and Leach accentuate that the forest–savannah transition zone was affected by trade and related struggles and conflict even before the Europeans established coastal trading opportunities (Fairhead and Leach, 1996: 93, cf. also Brooks, 1993).

The Atlantic slave trade would have a major impact on the demography, the agriculture and the development of local political institutions in what we today know as Guéckédou prefecture (Peters, 2010: 326). The slave trade, Peters writes, "tended to consolidate the power of the chiefs and armed merchants" (Peters, 2010: 326, cf. also Goerg, 1986: 188). Accordingly, the situation at the turn of the nineteenth century and the first years of colonisation can be described as the aftermath of a period of intense struggle and warfare.

In addition to the slave trade, a further powerful figure was crucial in the making of the Guéckédou borderland. By 1888, the Mande warrior Samori Touré had built a huge empire, which incorporated the regions around today's Kissidougou and Guéckédou prefectures (Fairhead and Leach, 1996: 96). Samori Touré's empire resisted French colonisation attempts for a number of years. In addition, the empire further promoted local chiefs and armed merchants involved in the slave trade. Shifting loyalties gave rise to various regional conflicts and violent clashes within the empire. According to Massing, the related political transformation processes marked the definitive end of the Kissi's organisation as a segmentary society (Massing, 1980-81). [6] He writes, "[a]t the end of the nineteenth century, the dispersed Kissi villages and hamlets were incorporated into the larger territorial federation of Samori and war chiefs, who owed him allegiance at the periphery of his empire" (Massing, 1980-81: 2). Thus, the villages, the key social entity of the Kissi-speaking segmentary society, lost their independence and were incorporated into Samori's empire. One of Samori's allies was Mori Soulèmani Savané who created a small realm on Kissi territory in the 1870s and finally federalised with Samori Touré (Goerg, 1986: 192, Person, 1963: 125). In 1893, however, the French colonial army arrested Samori Touré, and his empire and associated regimes disintegrated after years of political and military manoeuvring.[7]

Thereafter, the colonial powers of France and Great Britain fought for regional hegemony and over the demarcation of the border (Bah, 1998, Katzan, 1998, Massing, 1980-81). Regional warlords formed changing alliances with the French or the English, which made the forest region around Guéckédou a fuzzy borderland with shifting boundaries. Finally, the French colonial state introduced a civilian administration to Guéckédou in around 1917, hence much later than in Kissidougou, where it was established around 1893. According to Iffono, the French merged existing villages or districts (Wonkissi and Sandia) into one town (Iffono, 2010: 165). As part of the colonisation process in the region, a Christian mission with a mission school was founded in 1910 in the village of Mongo west of Guéckédou, influencing not only faith but also education across the entire region. Thus, France finally cemented its regional hegemony by implementing both administrative and religious institutions in the – in their perspective – remote Guéckédou borderland.

An old man I once met in the border town of Nongoa, very close to Sierra Leone, remembered it thus: "My grandfather already lived here and my father also lived here. They did not know national borders. Then de Gaulle came and we started to call the other side of the river England."[8]

---

6 The Kissi-speaking people can be described as a segmentary society. The village, patrimonially and patri-locally organised, was the key social entity (Paulme, 1954: 95).

7 For further details on Samori Touré's empire and his life see the multivolume work by Person (Person, 1968-1975). To understand the economic changes and trade networks around that time, Goerg is very helpful (Goerg, 1986).

8 "Mon grand-père était déjà ici, mon père, lui aussi il vivait ici. Eux, ils n'ont pas connu la frontière. Mais après, de Gaulle est venu et on a commencé à dire que l'autre côte du fleuve, là-bas, c'est l'Angleterre", 16.09.2010, interview with an old man living in Nongoa, a border town in the Guéckédou prefecture situated close to Sierra Leonean territory.

Iffono, who recently published a book on the region's colonial past, stresses Kissi resistance to these colonial influences (Iffono, 2010).[9] He mentions many traumatic experiences for the local population during that time and refers to forced labour, economic and social exploitation, and the recruitment of soldiers for European battlefields as having a considerable influence on the socio-political fabric of Kissi communities in the Guéckédou borderland (Iffono, 2010: 214f, 259, 268f, 278). Goerg also highlights local resistance by Guinean forest communities to French occupation, which lasted, according to her, until 1911 (Goerg, 1986: 233). According to Goerg, the French finally consolidated their colonial authority by appointing local chiefs, generally without regard for former authorities or powerful lineages (Goerg, 2006a: 9). This affected local power relations: "Chieftainship as an administrative institution was attractive to a good number of the colonized. It involved the development of a new category of local dignitaries, who achieved legitimacy within the colonial system. This resulted in the bureaucratization of the function and in setting the incumbent on a career path with a potential for social mobility defined by the colonizers: chiefs were distinguished according to grade and class, and a training period was introduced before tenure was granted" (Goerg, 2006a: 21).[10]

One may conclude that in the course of the colonial period "when early administrators mapped out ethnic boundaries, when anthropologists mapped out ethnic cultures, and when historians sought to map out ethnic origins" (Fairhead and Leach, 1996: 114), identity and ethnicity became related to the national border and, together with language and origin, gained great significance for local power relations.

---

9 Iffono, who was born in the Guéckédou area, is both a historian and a Guinean politician. Hence his writings also follow a fairly political agenda. Accordingly, I perceive Iffono's attempt to especially stress Kissi resistance to the French invaders not only as historical analysis but also as part of a political strategy to create a strong and unified Kissi community/entity through a historical narrative.

10 Goerg examines colonial times in Guinea with a focus on urban areas; cf. (Goerg, 1990; 1998; 2006a; 2006b). Mauri further discusses the colonial legacy within Guinean politics (Mauri, 2007). For references to low-level African colonial intermediaries cf. Osborn (2003), and for military conscription, Summers and Johnson (1978). For further details on economic transformation during the colonial period (e.g. the establishment of a rail network from Conakry to Kankan), cf. Goerg (1986: 249ff), and on changes in political imagination from pre-colonial to colonial times in the Milo River Valley (Haute Guinée), cf. Osborn (2011).

3.   Narratives on Kissi origins and Guéckédou's founding myth

The making of ethnic identity is reproduced as part of contemporary narratives about Kissi origins and Guéckédou's founding myth. Thus, present-day local narratives of "being Kissi" delineate their group identity using both essentialist perspectives (understanding "the Kissi" as a closed entity) and more open perspectives that refer to their multiple origins. Thus, like other ethnic groups, they constantly modulate their frame of reference. Discourses on group identity remain highly contextual, "establishing complex relationships between identity, origins, neighboring groups and languages" (Berliner, 2010: 255), as described in Berliner's insightful paper on identities among the Bulongic, a people living on the Guinean coast: "Paradoxically, Bulongic people define their society as based on migration and heterogeneity [...] Depending on the context, people hover between 'identity as invented *mélange*' and 'identity as given *pureté*'" (Berliner, 2010: 269).[11]

In the following section, I briefly relate local narratives about Kissi origins and the foundation of the Guéckédou settlement as a couple of local elders described them to me. I do not claim that these narratives represent 'the truth' or the one and only 'founding myth' that is told in Guéckédou. I am also well aware that these narratives have a political dimension, for instance indicating who has the right to be part of the local council of elders, further discussed in Chapter IV. Accordingly, other interlocutors would probably mention other names and lineages. However, the idea is to echo some of the accounts, which refer to how my interview partners imagined and reproduced the Kissi's origins and Guéckédou's settlement history.[12]

The account I have heard briefly tells that the Kissi came from the Fouta Djallon. As a result of Islamic pressure, one of my informants told me, they left the area in the eighteenth century and finally settled in the forest region. In some narratives, the Fouta Djallon was represented as just one stop in a much longer journey which started in Kenya, where the Kissi lived close to the Luo ethnic group. They then left the area and arrived in the Guinean coastal region in the eighth century. In the fifteenth century, however, they fled from the coast towards Fouta Djallon to avoid the slave trade and the related insecurity.

This account is similar to the one reproduced in publications by Iffono, who has published several articles on the origins of the Kissi-speaking people (Iffono,

---

11 The Bulongic people, a small group of 6000 rice cultivators, are affiliated to the Baga people. They live on the Guinean coast and are located on the edge of the area in which the Poro and Sande secret societies are found (Berliner, 2010). Ethnographically, they are quite unknown. The Kissi and the Bulongic people can be compared against the backdrop of the Guinean nation-state as both of them live at the edges of the state and represent national minorities.

12 For a similar approach regarding oral narratives about the past in Guinea, see Emily Lynn Osborn's very insightful book (Osborn, 2011).

2011; 2010, Iffono and Kamano, 1975). In his writings he claims that the Kissi first came from the Sahara but migrated towards the southern coast as a result of climate change (some time before the fifteenth century), and then changed direction again because of the increasing dangers related to the slave trade, starting with the arrival of the Europeans in the fifteenth century. The Kissi then settled down in the Fouta Djallon, but Islamisation forced them to move to the region where they live today (Iffono, 2008).

After all, both narratives – Iffono's and the one people told me – forge the Kissi-speaking people into a strong ethnic entity, united by centuries of flight and migratory movements.

Interestingly, the founding myth of Guéckédou tells a slightly different story. Regarding local discourses, the town that is now known as Guéckédou was founded around 1730 by the establishment of a village called Sandia. The founding family was from the Komano line. Following a visionary's advice they resettled their village on the other side of the River Wau and renamed the settlement "Kpekodou, the place where people came to satisfy their needs", according to one of the sons of the Komano I talked with.[13] According to another of my dialogue partners, the town known today as Guéckédou thus united three different villages founded by three different lineages. The three founding lineages were the Komano, the Leno and the Dembadouno. The latter were said to have come from Mali, where the families had fled local wars and conflicts and migrated southwards. They finally settled down and "became" Dembadouno, a Kissi family name. Finally, all three families are said to be the founders of modern Guéckédou. Consequently, all three families have the right to head the council of the elders. Thus, this narrative stressed that the founding families that are known today as having Kissi origins or as representing "the autochthons" initially came from different regions, including the Mande world to the north.[14] This account diverges from the narratives on the Kissi origins in Fouta Djallon and emphasises the Kissi's diverse origins and, just as crucially, the possibility of someone "becoming Kissi" even if he/she is originally from a different region.

This integrative notion may seem astonishing in the context of present-day discourses on the sharp and clear separation between, for instance, the Kissi and the Malinké or the Kissi and the Peul. In everyday discourses about the present

---

13 „Kpekédou, l'endroit ou les gens viennent satisfaire leur besoins", 18.09.2010, communication with a representative of one of Guéckédou's founding families.

14 Schaeffner (1951) also indicates that some Kissi families claim to have Mande origins. However, he assumes that they are simply trying to relate to a more "noble race" to compete with their Malinké neighbours: "Quelques familles kissi se prétendent d'origine Mande. Ce passé soudanais pourrait être en partie imaginaire. Vis-à-vis les Malinké, les plus proches voisins venus du nord, ne songerait-on qu'à se targuer d'une égale noblesse de race?" (Schaeffner, 1951: 5).

difficulties between Peul herders and Kissi agriculturalists, however, many people remember the (violent) expulsion from Fouta Djallon. Members of both ethnic groups also accept some sort of relationship between their ethnic groups. I was often told that their relationship to each other could be explained by affinity, as "the Kissi and the Peul had the same mother, but not the same father."[15] Against this background people also explained political party affinities or alliances in the context of the 2010 presidential elections.

Finally, these contradictions provoke at least the following question: How was it possible to "become Kissi" even if one came from a completely different region? Berliner argues regarding the Bulongic-speaking people that "language must be seen as one of the most essential pillars of groupness, and that its maintenance seems a necessary condition for group continuity" (Berliner, 2010: 266). Others, like Paulme or Fairhead and Leach, refer to the modes of life and the geographic conditions, which, according to them, unite the Kissi and the Malinké, but distinguish them from the Peul cattle-breeders (Paulme, 1954, Fairhead and Leach, 1996). Finally, as Barth wrote in his famous book *Ethnic groups and boundaries*, ethnic identities are often established at the "boundaries" of different modes of life (Barth, 1970 [Repr.]). And, as Dobler appropriately adds, "[t]his is, of course, not only true for ethnicities. It is as important for more institutionalized political entities, not the least for modern states" (Dobler, 2010: 22).

4.   Secret societies and generational relations

As the narratives on the founding of Guéckédou show, people not only reproduce narratives of closed ethnic entities and boundaries but also refer to the possibility of "becoming" Kissi and thereby becoming integrated into the ongoing making of the local socio-political organisation. Different authors stress the importance of so-called secret or power societies for past (and present) socio-political relations in the Upper Guinea Coast.[16] These authors mostly refer to the Poro and Sande ty-

---

15 *"Les Kissi et les Peuls, c'est la même mère mais pas le même père"*. Interestingly, people did not stress language relations, although both languages, Pulaar and Kissi, form part of the Atlantic language group.

16 Regarding the "secretness" of these societies, cf. Förster (1987; 1990) and De Jong (2007). Förster describes the Poro type of secret societies amongst the Senufo in Côte d'Ivoire. Like the Kissi, the Senufo are surrounded by different Malinké groups. In addition, they live between important trading routes leading from the north to the coast. Thus the secret societies do not only practice in secret but also very openly, in public, and this is what finally lends them their power (Förster, 1987: 192). McGovern adds in his writings about the Loma people and their power associations that these institutions were rather about knowing what must not be said or broached directly than about secrecy *per se* (McGovern, 2004: 16, McGovern, 2013: 199).

pes of secret society into which either men (Poro) or women (Sande) were initiated (cf. Højbjerg, 2007). D'Azevedo thereby argues that these societies have a political and economic role in the entire Upper Guinea Coast, knitting together, as he sees it, culturally diverse and mobile groups in the forest–savannah transition zone (D'Azevedo, 1962: 516). The Kissi-speaking people also have these kinds of secret or power societies or associations to make and remake their communities (Paulme, 1960: 76); the same is true for many of the neighbouring ethnic groups within Guinée Forestière and along the entire Upper Guinea Coast (cf. among others Förster, 1987; 1990, Little, 1965a; 1966, Højbjerg, 2007). Importantly, Förster for instance indicates that these societies in the context of the Senufo in Côte d'Ivoire not only represent age groups but are also responsible for economic redistribution between different generations (Förster, 1990).

Interestingly, different authors suggest that the Kissi-speaking people actually borrowed or appropriated the Poro and Sande societies from the neighbouring Loma-speaking people (Fairhead and Leach, 1996, Højbjerg, 2007, Schaeffner, 1951). McGovern and Højbjerg are two anthropologists who describe the secret societies in the context of the Loma-speaking people, who live just to the east of the *pays Kissi*. They describe the societies as associations that used to be particularly relevant to local and regional power figurations (McGovern, 2004: 83ff; 2012b, Højbjerg, 2007; 2006; 2002; 1999). Accordingly, one may suggest that the same must be true for the Kissi community. Eberl-Elber wrote in 1939 about Kissi speakers living in Sierra Leone: "All social life is based on the Poro" (Eberl-Elber, 1939: 163).[17] And Ellis concludes with more hindsight, "initiation societies and oracles were of crucial importance for the organization of power" (Ellis, 2010: 191).

However, the aim of this section is not to fully review literature on secret or power societies, but to hint at their importance for regional integration – also beyond national borders and ethnic boundaries – into local politics and generational relations in the Guéckédou borderland, at least in the past: Thus, secret societies can be described as a political strategy employed both within and beyond people's own communities and therefore also vis-à-vis external societies. Non-native societies would get together with the host society through the act of initiating the children of mixed marriages between strangers and hosts into the hosts' initiation society (Fairhead, 2010: 84). Initiation into Poro or Sande secret societies therefore had an integrative character and so fixed local identities, affiliations and belonging in the borderland. In regard to generational relations, however, secret

---

17 These early writings emphasised that Poro and Sande institutions were of importance not only in religious, political and economic affairs, but also in education and medicine (Eberl-Elber, 1936, Little, 1965a; 1966).

knowledge separated initiated elders from non-initiated youths.[18] Thus, secrecy, according to Murphy, who worked on the Kpelle/Guerze-speaking people in the Guinée Forestière, offered the possibility of a second world alongside the manifested one (Murphy, 1980: 195). Unlike settlements, the forests were the areas of greatest secrecy, privacy and mystery – referred to as *les forêts sacrées* in local French. The youngsters could only be initiated into this world through initiation camps. Initiation thereby intensified respect for the elders and their apparent knowledge of the mystical powers. The elders in turn maintained barriers to knowledge to protect their social control (Murphy, 1980: 200). In his writings on the Kpelle secret societies, Murphy concludes: "The resulting image of Kpelle elders is not one of benevolent, wise old men who pass on hallowed cultural traditions to the young. Rather, it is one of calculating elders who withhold more than they teach and use claims on withheld knowledge to keep the young under their thumbs" (Murphy, 1980: 204).

5.   Integration and conflicts

This chapter summarised population movements and political transformation processes in relation to the making of ethnic identities and local generational organisation in pre-colonial and colonial times. The Kissi-speaking community of the Guéckédou borderland formed the ethnographic starting point for grasping the processes of identity formation, intergenerational relations and political imaginations. The chapter has therefore provided certain background knowledge that will be crucial to a further understanding of youth and the state in the Guéckédou borderland. This borderland can be described as a crossroads, as it hosts the Kissi people who emigrated as a result of various pressures related both to the slave trade and to the increasing Islamisation of the northern parts of the Upper Guinean Coast. The politics of ethnic identities became more and more concrete during colonial times and is still reproduced today. However, as local myths about origins and settlement history show, group identities are not only fixed by demarcations and the drawing of boundaries but also by integration and relations. Thus, the secret societies were crucial institutions for regional integration and local gerontocracy, mainly because of the way they regulated the transition from youth to the adult world. To what extent Poro and Sande secret societies still shape local identities, integration and generational relations in present-day Guéckédou is a

---

18 Different anthropologists discuss the topic of initiation in terms of age groups, thus age transitions or rites of passages in the context of different societies. A classic is Evans-Pritchard's book *The Nuer*, in which he describes initiation as the very moment in which age cohorts become created (Evans-Pritchard, 1960 [reprint]).

difficult question that is related to colonial and postcolonial state interventions. The Demystification Campaign and the Cultural Revolution launched by Sékou Touré changed the social fabric of the Forestière communities immensely, and this is the subject of the next chapter. At this point, however, I would like to hint at Højbjerg's statement regarding secret societies and their practices in contemporary Loma communities: "Today most Loma are still being initiated, Catholics included, though it is not at all unusual for young men to create their own household before initiation" (Højbjerg, 2007: 241).

In colonial times, the Guéckédou borderland remained a remote and conflict-ridden area characterised by local resistance and the contested hegemony of various actors. Thus, the territory was a major platform for the struggle for supremacy by France and local insurgents like Samori Touré and his aides, and, later, of the colonial powers of France, Great Britain and independent Liberia. Finally, the national borders became more and more institutionalised as state boundaries but even now they are porous. Accordingly, what people now know as the *pays Kissi* describes a physical space straddling the national borders with Sierra Leone and Liberia. This transborder space is not so distinct in terms of national identities but is disassociated from the predominantly Mande-speaking ethnic surroundings. However, later chapters will show that the perception of national and ethnic identities remained in a constant state of flux due to postcolonial state formation processes.

All in all, this chapter pointed out the sensitivity and historically determined nature of the politics of ethnic identities in the Guéckédou borderland. Local identities are shaped by ethnic affiliations "across" national borders and ethnic boundaries, but are also related to colonial and early postcolonial state formation processes (Højbjerg et al., 2017). As the next chapter will show, the drawing of boundaries by colonial powers was crucial, but postcolonial state interventions and institutions also played a considerable part in shaping not only local ethnic and national identities but also local social and generational organisation in the Guéckédou borderland.

III. Get the state to work
State iconoclasm and revolutionary youth

> "Now the people themselves create culture, and through it achieve self-realization. The sacred forests have delivered up their secrets, the spirits and witch-doctors have gone to the ground, the devil no longer has any place in society.
>
> Art has become a weapon in the hands of young people and throughout Guinea has brought enlightenment, awakened the consciousness of the people, laid the foundations for tomorrow's world and established a new value system"
>
> UNESCO Cultural Policy in Guinea (1979) quoted in Straker (2009: 179).

Guinea became an independent nation-state in 1958.[1] Early postcolonial nation and state building processes in Guinea were predominantly characterised by the political work of Ahmed Sékou Touré, the country's first president. He was "the main ideological force for the nation-building project in Guinea to date; his speeches were recorded, broadcast and printed, hailing not only the one-party state and the socialist revolution, but also the unity of the Guinean nation, which was portrayed as the basic condition for prosperity" (Schroven, 2010b: 663). The remote Guéckédou borderland – and the entire Forest region – became one of the centre stages of his revolutionary state and nation building efforts. Thus, I agree with

---

1 On the specifics of the Guinean road to independence and Guinea's early postcolonial period compared to other West African countries, for instance Côte d'Ivoire (cf. (Du Bois, 1970, Coleman and Rosberg, 1970). Revolutionary Guinea represents a strong revolutionary-centralising trend, Côte d'Ivoire by contrast a pragmatic-pluralistic type – both tendencies had consequences for their relations to non-party groups (Coleman and Rosberg, 1970: 7). Countries like Revolutionary Guinea thereby tended towards a complete fusion with all other associations or groups, as well as an assimilation of party and governmental structures throughout society (Coleman and Rosberg, 1970: 6).

Christensen, as well as Das and Poole, who indicate that a borderland is not as such detached from the political centre or marginal to central state formation processes, rather, it is often essential to these processes and their understanding (Christensen, 2012, Das and Poole, 2004).

With the help of the Demystification Campaign and the Cultural Revolution, Touré launched a vast campaign against what he considered old-fashioned and colonial socio-political structures. Shaping a "unified and embedded youth" was the foundation for overcoming regional ethnic peculiarities and for the revolutionary state to emerge.

This chapter starts by discussing "the osmosis" between the political party and the state apparatus under Sékou Touré, which manifested in different national and local state institutions and the ideological background to the state. Touré's one-party state thus proclaimed its authority not only over the political but also over the religious and cultural development of its people, especially its young citizens. The chapter then addresses the Demystification Campaign and the Cultural Revolution as state interventions aimed at overcoming socio-political practices introduced during colonial times and by secret societies. Further, I introduce the reader to Sékou Touré's plans for creating a "revolutionary youth" by embedding young people in the newly established party structure and look at the way in which today's elders remember their youth. Among other things their memories make clear that they perceived "being young" in the Guéckédou borderland not as being isolated or marginalised but as being part of a nation-state in the making, which related them to the wider socialist world. All in all, I argue that the ethnic identity of Kissi-speaking people gained an additional, more national identity, providing the basis of a strong historical generation describing a cohort of people of approximately the same age, and a political generation, well aware of their uniqueness and shaped by shared experiences (Mannheim, 1997: 301f, Bellagamba, 2008: 238).

This chapter provides the reader with some basic knowledge about Guinea's socialist past. The main sources for this chapter were various historical publications on Guinea and Guinée Forestière. In addition, I used the data I had gathered from interviews with local elders living in Guéckédou during my research. In these interviews, I asked both men and women of around 60 years of age how they remembered their youth and became aware of the great importance of state-orchestrated interventions and institutions such as socialist youth groups. While I was analysing this data set from the interviews and more informal discussions and conversations with various people, I recognised some of the key aspects many people mentioned about the past. I am thus aware that "present conditions, values, and interests affect the way in which people remember – or fail to remember – past experiences" (Schmidt, 2005: 13). Moreover, as McGovern insightfully hints at, people often prefer to remember good things or things they enjoyed, for instance things related to the ballets and orchestras of the socialist period in Guinea (McGovern, 2013). Consequently, one has to be careful with the rhetoric that portrays the revolutionary period as being without problems (McGovern, 2013: 272). Personal accounts of the past are nevertheless of enormous value, as these memories also shape the present, both through the narratives of the witnesses of times past and through the everyday discourses of subsequent generations.

Unlike Schmidt's experiences in Guinea in the early nineties, people did not hesitate to explain their memories and perspectives concerning the Touré regime to me (Schmidt, 2005). Schmidt attributes people's hesitations during her field-work to the repressive regime of Lansana Conté, who was afraid of plots and mass mobilisation and therefore also suppressed glorifying memories of Sékou Touré and his socialist regime (Schmidt, 2005: 14). As a result, people rarely mentioned his name in public or spoke freely about the revolutionary movements. During most of my own fieldwork, however, Lansana Conté was already dead and the country's political orientation was not clearly defined but rather under construction. I thus had the impression that people were not afraid of talking about the socialist past and about Sékou Touré in particular. By contrast, conversations about the present-day political situation were much more difficult. I generally learnt that most Guineans, no matter what their ethnic background and no matter what regime they talked about, out of respect do not openly denounce specific leaders or powerful men, especially if they are deceased. Reading between the lines, however, I learnt that Touré's legacy was a controversial topic and also fostered ethnic friction. According to Kaké, "*Si la vie de Sékou Touré est exceptionnelle, c'est qu'il est de ces rares hommes dont on n'a jamais fini de parler: en bien ou en mal*" (Kaké, 1987: 246), also quoted and reflected in Pauthier (2013).

1.   The postcolonial state apparatus and political ideology

Before talking about the early postcolonial state apparatus and its political ideology, I briefly discuss Sékou Touré's background. Touré was born of peasant parents in Haute-Guinée around the year 1922 (Johnson, 1970: 350). He was from the Malinké ethnic group and claimed to be related to Samori Touré, the "great warrior and partisan" who has been mentioned in previous chapters. It is especially important to remember Sékou Touré's ethnic background, as it still has a strong influence on contemporary Guinean politics, which often negotiate which ethnic group has "the right" to come to power and which ones have already "had their turns". This discussion was particularly influential during the 2010 presidential elections, during which the Peul claimed to be the legitimate successors to the presidency, as the Malinké had had their turn with Sékou Touré.

However, back to Revolutionary Guinea and its main orchestrator, Sékou Touré, who was always described as a self-made and self-taught man, "something which is virtually unique among the members of the political elites which have ruled West Africa in the last decade" (Johnson, 1970: 350). In the years following independence, Touré and his cadres – who were generally from the same ethnic group as Touré himself – established various national and local state institutions to enforce the state's sovereignty.[2] The PDG and Touré himself monopolised and controlled the socio-political landscape, since the party's general secretary was at the same time prime minister and president of the Republic. The PDG's highest authority and executive organ, the national politburo (*Bureau Politique National* or BPN), managed "all questions involving appointments to the bureaucracy, the management of state enterprises, the delimitation of administrative regions, economic planning, international relations and the like" (Rivière, 1977: 95). At village level, the *Pouvoir Révolutionnaire Local* (PRL) constituted the party's base and replaced former village or urban district committees (Du Bois, 1970: 200ff). To be elected to the PRL directorate, a candidate had to be a party activist. Rivière calls this interrelationship between the political party and the administrative state apparatus "an osmosis" that was justified as a means to perpetuate the socialist revolution: "The very uniqueness of the single party and the osmosis between the political and administrative functions were justified by the need to preserve the revolution's dynamism, make the anti-colonial struggle effective, and economize on cadres in a country as underdeveloped as Guinea" (Rivière, 1977: 97).

Thus, the PRL closely linked the local administrative staff to the ruling party and the state, "breaking down the potential boundaries between state and society at the ideological level" (Schroven, 2010b: 663f). The party's control over all institutions in every domain and the lack of any separation of powers brought about an "over-politicisation" of society and created a vast bureaucratic apparatus whose maintenance demanded many of the state's financial resources (Rivière, 1977: 100). According to Du Bois: "The vigorous pursuit of this [Sékou Touré's] policy and the pervasiveness of party life in Guinea have induced a degree of political involvement which is matched in few nations, except, perhaps, in those of the Communist world. The national government and, more importantly, the party control the country's economy, its educational system, and its health facilities, and instigate any change that comes to Guinea. Thus they dictate the fortunes of the people. For the vast majority, government-com-party offers virtually the sole hope for advancement. In such circumstances the government and the party tend to elicit an almost total commitment on the party of the individual citizen" (Du Bois, 1970: 200).

---

2 For further details on the state's economic reorganisation after independence, especially of agriculture but also of secondary industry, cf. Rivière (1977). One of the few case studies that discusses economic change in Guinea from colonial to socialist and post-socialist times on the basis of a brewery, cf. Souaré (1995).

Touré's one-party state was particularly influenced by Marxist-socialist ideas.[3] According to Camara, immediately after independence the regime encountered difficulties in its attempts to legitimise the one-party state with the country's elite, mainly because of Touré's pursuit of a Maoist brand of party authority (Camara, 2007: 160). However, Touré then turned to the Eastern Bloc for economic aid and resorted to Marxist interpretations of history. Touré had already encountered Marxism in the *Cercles d'Études Marxistes* (CEM), which French leftists had organised in the 1940s to train "revolutionary elites" throughout the French Empire, including on the African continent (Camara, 2007: 160). In any case, according to Camara, Touré adopted socialism because of his views about the socialist nature of African societies in which "family, village, and clan are the primordial parameters for any meaningful expression and understanding of individuality", and not because of the influences of French leftists (Camara, 2007: 160). Johnson adds that Touré's personal path through trade unionism also strongly influenced his socialist thinking (Johnson, 1970: 351).

This socialist ideology also got Touré into trouble in Guinea-based religious circles, among them the Christians (particularly the Catholic clergy that had been present since colonial times) and in Islamic circles.[4] However, through the invention of the National Islamic Council, Touré successfully integrated the latter into his state-building project. Thereby, the secretary general of the council became at the same time the Minister of Islamic Affairs and head imam of the Great Faisal Mosque in Conakry. Thus, Touré succeeded in connecting the newly born nation-state with the religious community. According to Camara: "The state immersed Islamic faith in a sea of ideology, thus utilizing its most effective asset to efficaciously connect with the Muslim world at large and benefit substantially from the global auspices of Islam" (Camara, 2007: 170).

The Christian churches and associated organisations came under a great deal of pressure from the socialist regime. As early as 1959, the Guinean state decided to nationalise the private Catholic schools and all non-Guinean missionaries had to leave the country by 1967 (Kamano and Sagna, 2010: 22). Many Guinean Christians experienced extreme state violence and some of the leading figures were jailed in the infamous Camp Boiro (Vieira, 2005), to which I shall return in the next paragraph. This persecution affected the Guinée Forestière in particular, the region where Christian missionaries had been especially active due to colonial

---

3 A large body of literature is devoted to Sékou Touré's politics and ideology. Not all of this is free of the authors' own political preferences, however, to mention just a few, cf. (Diallo, 1990, Maier, 1990, Sorry, 2000, Johnson, 1970, Du Bois, 1970). Touré himself also published extensively about his state and nation-building ideas (see for instance (Touré, 1961; 1963).

4 For further information regarding the conflict between Marxism and Islam in Guinea's nation building history, cf. Camara (2007).

attempts to mark the (also ideological) borders between French and Anglophone West Africa. As I learnt on a visit to the parish of Mongo, in the Guéckédou borderland, which was one of the first Catholic missions in the region, missionaries and congregants were confronted with increasing state restrictions during socialist times. Finally, the foreign missionaries had to leave and local priests took over responsibility for the parishioners. However, it was not until the 1990s, when religious freedom was re-established, that Mongo and other Christian denominations could fully re-establish their institutions and communities. This prosecution of Christians left its mark on the collective memory of the Catholic community and their youth groups, a topic I will come back to in Chapter IX.

The Guinean state ideology and apparatus of power generally clashed with religious practices and ideas and was also directed at actors from specific ethnic groups like the Peul or at social milieus like academics or members of trade unions, with lasting political consequences to this day. Usually, opposing actors and institutions were simply incorporated into the one-party state.[5] However, many of these suspected opponents also ended up in Camp Boiro, a former military barracks converted into a political prison: "People accused of a wide range of misdeeds from lacking identity papers to spying for foreign governments were locked up there, and many of the inmates were tortured or executed. According to international human rights organizations, some 50,000 people lost their lives in Camp Boiro and other prisons" (Conrad, 2010: 357).

McGovern gives examples of political opponents who were accused of being part of conspiracies and were imprisoned in Camp Boiro to get them out of the way (McGovern, 2004: 413). In fact, the atrocities committed behind the walls of the Camp Boiro are still hotly debated to this day, as most of the crimes were never publicised and the prisoners seldom came back. Those who survived, however, and the relatives of some of the victims have written books, including biographies, and they continue to demand a national inquiry into the past.[6] Moreover, some milieus and ethnic groups attempt to make collective political capital out of it: some Peul politicians, for instance, combine narratives of past victimisation with contemporary claims to power or are at least accused doing so. Arieff and McGovern discuss that in more detail (Arieff and McGovern, 2013).

As his presidency wore on, Sékou Touré became more and more despotic and lived in fear of assassination attempts by his political opponents. One may conclude that Sékou Touré's authoritarian rule "was characterized by paranoia about plots, state violence unprecedented in Africa and the country's isolation in the context of its nationalist and socialist stance" (ICG, 2007: 1). This was highlighted by the fact that many Guineans left the country not only for economic but also

---

5 On the close union-party intimacy in Guinea after independence, cf. Berg and Butler (1970).

6 Many of these attempts are documented on the webpage www.campboiro.org.

for political reasons; Bah and his co-authors estimate that there were two million Guineans living outside the country in 1984, the year Touré died, taking the one-party state with him (Bah et al., 1989: 22).

The next section of this chapter will take a closer look at the socialist state's attempt to "nationalise" the entire Guinean territory through iconoclasm, i.e. the profanation of sacred or secret objects.

2.   The Demystification Campaign and the Cultural Revolution

Early on, Sékou Touré's postcolonial state proclaimed and enforced not only its authority over people's relations with Islam or Christian missions but also over their cultural development, especially in the remote south-eastern forest prefectures bordering Sierra Leone, Liberia and Côte d'Ivoire, which were well known for their secret societies and "backward" culture (Conrad, 2010, Straker, 2008). With the help of the Demystification Campaign and the Cultural Revolution, Sékou Touré and his cadres aimed to set the stage for Guinea's "new citizens".

As Sarro has accurately observed, there is some confusion among scholars as to when exactly the Demystification Campaign began (Sarro, 2007: 219). Straker probably provides the solution when he writes that the Demystification Campaign went through several phases and that its transformative processes for demystifying local practices such as secret societies and beliefs had started long before Touré's nation and state-building project (Straker, 2009: 110f). Thus, the moral and material foundations of the elders' power were challenged even before independence, mainly through the presence of the colonial state and mission schooling, as well as religious movements headed by Muslim preachers. As an example of the latter, Asekou Sayon, an iconoclastic jihadist figure who appeared in 1956, may be mentioned: "Sayon was a Muslim converter, a witch-finder, a fetish destroyer, and RDA sympathizer, an unsatisfied people's leader, among other things" (Sarro, 2007: 217). According to Sarro's insightful paper, Sayon's movement marked a turning point in the history of the Upper Guinea Coast (especially its coastal peoples such as the Baga) and promoted demystification processes before the declaration of independence (Sarro, 2007). In the forest region, similar transformative processes started long before Sékou Touré's politics of demystification. Straker accordingly writes that demystification is merely the final step in a gradual demise of traditional mechanisms of gerontocratic authority in the forest region that had reigned for centuries before colonial penetration (Straker, 2009: 110).

In postcolonial times and during Guinea's First Republic, Straker describes three phases of demystification campaigning that were important in the forest region and lasted from 1959 to 1961 (Straker, 2009). The first phase was a more or less local affair and had its roots among PDG militants in the Macenta region adjacent to the Guéckédou borderland. Straker explains this by referring to the particularly long-lasting initiation rituals of the Loma-speaking communities that lived around the Macenta area. They practised Poro initiation rites lasting seven years. In the course of the campaign, the local PDG militants collected hidden masks and other secret objects and showed them to non-initiated women and youth. According to Straker, these "opening acts" provoked profound changes in local intergenerational and gender relations (Straker, 2009). Young men perceived the campaign as granting them access to growing social, economic, political and cultural opportunities: "Direct involvement in assaults on "fetishism" was an essential obligation of young *forestiers* aspiring to climb to positions of responsibility and respect within the broader revolutionary nation-building project" (Straker, 2009: 113).

Thus, the Demystification Campaign in the end implied that for Loma youth the "old customs" of initiation rites were no longer the best option, even for their life trajectories and social development. Instead, schooling became much more important to them: "Schooling and forest initiation were thus framed as starkly antithetical and antagonistic pedagogical domains – the former generating progress and freedom, the latter sustaining gerontocratic custom and stagnation" (Straker, 2009: 113).

Demystification also had an impact on young girls and women. For the first time ever they saw specific ritual figures, musical instruments and other secret objects. Nevertheless, access to school was reserved mainly for boys.

During this first phase of demystification in Guinée Forestière, as Rivière reminds us, the campaign did not cause all the inhabitants to break with their erstwhile beliefs (Rivière, 1971). The PDG representatives for instance still allowed short-term initiation camps during school vacations, and local beliefs and practices were not totally banned. Following Straker (2009), who also refers to Rivière (1971), a second phase of demystification started soon after a certain event in Guinée Forestière. This was the detection of a human sacrifice in Macenta. It was said that in the course of initiation preparations local *"fetisheurs"* sacrificed a young woman. When some local party members discovered the body, they communicated the news quickly to Conakry. As a result, local rituals and religious practices were harshly condemned and perceived not only as morally intolerable but as criminal acts. This reaction finally changed the state's practices towards the Forestière communities and "demystification transmuted into an overtly systematic and comprehensive crackdown on fetishists themselves" (Straker, 2009: 115). Thereafter, the campaign became state-orchestrated national police action. Its management was no longer left to local cadres and militants but to central state authorities with the intention of nationalising the entire country – including the remote forest areas: "Demystification assumed the guise of a law-and-order project designed to bring wild and wayward forest communities into line with normative social and legal structures that ought to govern all localities of any modern nation-state" (Straker, 2009: 115f).

State authorities arrested a number of people in the forest prefectures and reinforced the demystifying attempts – if necessary, with violence. This second phase of the Demystification Campaign was accordingly the most aggressive and left strong memories of violent state-building practices in all forest communities (McGovern, 2004; 2012a; 2013, Straker, 2009).

Finally, the campaign shifted again and became much more of an educative or pedagogical project, relying particularly on state media such as radio and television, which became the "voices of the revolution" (Camara, 1996: 155ff), and on state-monitored militant theatre (Straker, 2007a). The latter was designed to replace ritual initiations, which became appropriated by the state with the purpose of creating a new national folklore and tradition with masks and objects from various regions (Sarro, 2007: 220). Young people in particular were mobilised for various dance and ballet performances.

Officially, the campaign ended in 1961. But, as Straker helpfully reminds us: "Demystification as a nationalist ideological theme and goal flourished throughout the entire revolution, continually influencing outsiders' notions of forest difference, as well as *forestiers'* perceptions of their unique, deeply complicated cultural 'belongings' and potential roles in the development of the Guinean nation-state" (Straker, 2009: 116). Demystification thereby also became part of the socialist Cultural Revolution, launched on 2 August 1968 and inspired by the Chinese example. Sékou Touré explained the Cultural Revolution as follows: "The Cultural Revolution had to attack fetishism, charlatanism, religious fanaticism, any irrational attitude, any form of mystification, and any form of exploitation, with the aim to liberate the energies of the People and engage them in the consolidation of the rational bases of its development" (Touré 1978: 33, translated by Sarro 2007: 219).

With the help of this state iconoclasm, Touré aimed to create a new nation. In the words of McGovern: "These undertakings were strong and most used some degree of coercion. This was not the inexorable pressure of Foucaultian governmentality, but the radical and violent rupture of social engineering" (McGovern, 2004: 11).

One should keep in mind that, at least according to Højbjerg, some of the Forestière communities also resisted state iconoclasm, and certain religious practices persisted until the declaration of religious freedom in the early 1990s, after which they could be practised more openly again (Højbjerg, 2002). Højbjerg describes these mechanisms as religious or cultural robustness, which exists even in the context of massive state interventions like the ones during the Touré regime (Højbjerg, 2002: 71).

3.   Revolutionary youth

Early on, Revolutionary Guinea enforced its authority over the political development of young people. Accordingly, Sékou Touré embedded young people from
the beginning in the emerging new political structure, which was especially
shaped by the one and only political party, the PDG. Back in 1959, he created the
official youth wing of the PDG, the JRDA (*Jeunesse du Rassemblement Démocratique Africaine*) (Straker, 2009: 85) and thereby stressed the increasingly important
role of youth in the revolution (Johnson, 1970: 364). During this party structuring,
young people became organised into different party sub-branches. The numerous
members of these institutions met weekly and were organised into various sections, federations, commissions and congresses. In this way the Guinean state
apparatus tried to keep (young) people's political lives under close supervision.
Thus, different youth groups became embedded in the party structure, not least
because the state wanted to manage the potential threat of barely controllable
youths with opportunistic or rebellious ideas. As a result, non-state youth groups
established during colonial times – for instance Christian youth movements or
student organisations – were forbidden. In the words of Rivière: "*il (le gouvernement) a supprimé purement et simplement tous les mouvements qui ne faisaient pas
partie de la jeunesse RDA.*" (Rivière, 1969: 70). Rivière describes how the Guinean
state finally aimed to create one single youth that was "organically and spiritually"
embedded within the party structure: "*Pour éviter que des organisations multiples de
jeunesse ne deviennent des partis de jeunes réformistes en marge du parti unique, la solution la plus facile et la plus efficace était leur absorption pure et simple dans une jeunesse
unique, intégrée organiquement et spirituellement dans le P.D.G.. A l'heure actuelle, le
Parti est la plus importante des forces ambiantes qui modèle la conscience de la jeunesse
guinéenne et en dirige les activités politiques, économiques et socio-culturelles*" (Rivière,
1971: 159). I will come back to this topic in the course of subsequent chapters of this
book, which will address present-day youth groups. Finally, one may state that
the political leaders of the PDG created and imagined youth as a social category
in order to control and manage potential threats, as well as to create the future postcolonial nation and its new citizens. As in other socialist countries, youth
"was imagined by state leaders as the decisive constituency in sustaining revolutionary momentum" (Burgess, 1999). The revolutionary youth organised within
the JRDA, while being a single grouping consisted of multiple sub-branches and
various divisions. Accordingly, Rivière describes the JRDA as having two divisions,
the "sport division" and the "general division", of which the latter was made up of
six departments (Rivière, 1971: 171). The six departments included the department
of young women, of youthful socioeconomic action, of culture and art, of school
and university, of civil defence and, finally, of pioneers (Rivière, 1971: 172). Straker
describes the last-mentioned as a "Scout-like" organisation, which may be seen as

part of Sékou Touré's revolutionary education project (Straker, 2009: 83). Thus, the pioneers were a state-monitored education project peculiar to the last phase of the Demystification Campaign. The various branches were also related to different ages – the pioneer movement was for youngsters aged between 7 and 18, the civil defence or people's militia for youths between the ages of 20 and 30, while the JRDA encompassed them all (Mignon, 1988). The socialist state also defined youth in terms of a specific age bracket.

Besides defining, disciplining and controlling youth, however, I argue that these diverse state-controlled youth institutions also allowed young people to become part of pre-colonial state and nation-building processes. Thus the politics of generation that mobilised youth for national purposes also allowed young actors to participate officially in politics – at least partially. As McGovern describes, youths also gained "considerable power over their elders through such role-reversing movements", and he concludes that "this is one of the important ways that the state sometimes became an ally of those skilful enough to use it to their advantage (McGovern, 2004: 173).

Overall, the Guinean socialist political elite considered young people as important to realising the formation of both the postcolonial Guinean state and its new citizens; they attributed strategic importance to the youth. Nguyen argues that many socialist or Marxist-Leninist countries considered young people as "'blank sheets of paper' on which everything can be printed [...] Thus they do not possess any political and ideological stance and therefore are able to be molded and persuaded to work for the communist party's objectives" (Nguyen, 2005: 5). In other words, the party-state has to mobilise and educate its youth in order to help them find the revolutionary truth, in sharp contrast to the "colonial lie". In Guinea, these attempts were also linked to the party-state's idea of fighting against and wiping out what they considered to be backward traditions and customs especially endemic to the forest communities.

By inventing "youth", the state not only tried to manage its juniors but also gave them official status with the formation of youth groups attached to the PDG. Thus young people became both the henchmen of and the key actors in Guinea's self-designated revolutionary era. Johnson assumed back in the '70s that Sékou Touré "has written off the present generation of office holders and civil servants as irredeemably corrupted by colonialist ideology; hope lies with the younger generation who have come to maturity in the twelve years since independence" (Johnson, 1970: 363). In other words, while Sékou Touré's nation-building programmes exploited the youth, the youth were also able to disassociate themselves from their parents' generation, gain power and participate in the political landscape – sometimes even to the present day. Lastly, I argue that youth–state relations during that time were not merely typical but constitutive of the Guinean one-party state of Sékou Touré. Thereby, the state not only created its youths but the youths created the state – something that will also be addressed in the next section, which concentrates on the narratives of witnesses, often former JRDA members and/or pioneers.

4.   Remembering the days of youth

At the time of the research, many witnesses of the Sékou Touré era were still alive. When I spoke to these older people about their youth they had many stories to tell. Many of these narratives were at one point or another directly or indirectly linked to the socialist state institutions and interventions of Revolutionary Guinea, and I got the impression that almost all of them formed part of one or other group, be it the JRDA, the pioneers or an orchestra and performance group. The following paragraphs will address these narratives in more detail.

One aspect many talked about was the organisational structure of the different youth movements. Accordingly, the elders I spoke to explained the different organisational units and hierarchies within the JRDA or the pioneer movement in some detail. Some emphasised age and experiences, others told me that the youth groups were very well structured in village-level offices moving right up to regional levels and, finally, national headquarters. The organisational structure of the JRDA was also remembered as being strongly interlinked with the PDG party structure, and the young people who had been active in the revolutionary youth movement learnt about the party's setup and its institutions. The main message was that both the youth and the country were organized through the sole party. Personal accounts accordingly explained that "Touré had organized the country starting with Independence. The revolutionary youth was very organized".[7] In general, this idea of structuring was not linked to skills for self-organisation but to the state's successful efforts in supervising young people. The elders generally drew this picture as being in sharp contrast to present-day realities where they perceived young people as no longer being supervised by the state.

There were some especially vivid memories related to national and international integration and the recognition of the revolutionary drama groups, dance teams and orchestras. A former dance master told me stories about young men and women from Guéckédou who travelled as far as Cuba for performances, concerts and courses. Born in 1937, he told me he had received his dance training in the initiation camps of the *forêt sacrée* but later fell in line with the revolution and became an accepted dance teacher in the JRDA structures. In his narratives he depicted his fairly steady progress from former societal institutions like the secret

---

7   *"Touré a organisé le pays, ça commençait avec l'Independence. La jeunesse révolutionnaire était organisée"*, 10.07.2010, communication with an elderly man about his youth.

societies and initiation camps to socialist state institutions such as the JRDA dancing classes. Everyone had "the intention to teach the young", and "[t]he JRDA and its cultural education had replaced the *forêt sacrée*, but the intention was still the same: to teach children and youths".[8]

At the time of the research the former dance master was still a well-known promoter of local culture and had recently been given a national award from the national Ministry of Culture. He proudly showed me pictures of the ceremony at which he received the medal in honour for his engagement in national arts and culture.[9] He was very proud of this official recognition of his artistic talent and waxed lyrical about the golden days of the past.

Other elderly people particularly remembered the various educational youth gatherings that were held in Cuba or the Soviet Union. One man surprised me by still having active Russian language skills and talked about his experiences as an exchange student in the Soviet Union. One elderly woman told me that the Guinean airline was still in use under the socialist regime and she once flew from the forest region to Conakry, from where she travelled on Cuba to participate in a dance festival. Broadly speaking, these narratives did not talk about Guéckédou's or Guinea's marginality but about national and international integration. In their (certainly glorified) recollections, the past ballets africaine and orchestras of Guéckédou had enabled young people to visit other parts of the (socialist) world and to show pride in their own nation-state.

Other accounts of revolutionary times and their youthful activities emphasised physical memories. Some of my interlocutors particularly remembered distant and often exhausting hikes from one village to another to learn about their region and its geography. In each village elders told the children and youths about the history of the settlement and the birth of the Guinean nation. They "learnt about the community, the village, and the nation", the elders told me. During the breaks they shared food rations provided by the different participants' families and relaxed around campfires. They also memorised party slogans and revolutionary songs and slogans. Other physical activities included plays as well as parades. During these parades my informants remembered that both young men and women were dressed in uniform. Girls and boys donned the same costumes with different coloured scarves, according to rank and age. They also described marching and drills, and many compared these actions to military training and discipline.

---

8   "*La JRDA et l'éducation des arts avaient remplacée l'éducation dans les forêt sacrée. Mais c'était comme avant pour éduquer les jeunes et les enfants*", 09.07.2010, communication with Mr Oussa.

9   He received this award in 2008, shortly before Lansana Conté's death, from the then Minister of Culture, Arts and Leisure Aly Gilbert Iffono, who is also originally from Guéckédou. Iffono is a historian and has published much about the Guéckédou borderland and its people, cf. Chapter II.

Finally, many of my interviewees remembered their activities and their engagement in the JRDA and the pioneer movement not as something they had been forced into but as an opportunity to participate in the country's development. This development was closely linked to the party-state and the JRDA, and the pioneer movement was recalled as a "state service" or even as the state itself.[10] This tight nexus between the youth and the party-state was perceived as a means of gaining responsibility, even authority and political power. As one of my informants told me: "The pioneers became leaders."[11] Of course not all children and youths active in the JRDA or the pioneer movement were later lucky enough to find a job in the public service or become important policy-makers – but the people I talked to in retrospect at least perceived it as possible. Therefore, being part of the revolutionary youth movement could open the door to a political career within the socialist state apparatus and the political party. Trained after independence, these former youngsters perceived themselves as a "new type of man" with a different educational background to the one their parents had had during colonial times.[12] Hence, my dialogue partners perceived their youth as an active time in which they could participate in a range of state building activities. The state's effort to "make youth" was also about "youth making the state"; in their memories of the past, the elders often did not highlight the partially forced participation in the different youth groups and institutions but instead stressed the advantages of being an active part of the nation-state. Nevertheless, the "embodied state" of long hikes and parades also provides a reminder of the physical and psychological force and, in this case, at least the structural violence of the socialist state.

5.   Continuity and interruption

Youth-state relations during socialist times were characterised by one-sided mechanisms of control and influence that sought to invent, organise and frame youth and its potential oppositional energy. The Guinean state with its educational projects became the ultimate patriarchal authority. In other words, there was little to negotiate between youth and the state. At the same time, however, young people built the heart of Revolutionary Guinea and were considered to be its new citizens – thus, they formed the bedrock of a new national identity. The parades, theatre

---

10   *"La JRDA, c'était une service de l'Etat. La JRDA, c'état l'Etat"*, 20.09.2010, communication with Mr Maoumou, a former JRDA member and today civil servant.

11   *"Les pionniers, ils sont devenu des chefs"*, 21.11.2009, communication with Mr Millimouno, former JRDA and present-day parliament member.

12   *"On* était *des hommes types nouveaux"*, 21.12.2009, communication with a former member of the pioneer movement.

and ballets gave youths a sense of "official" status, of recognition and, finally, gave them a place in the global communist community. Accordingly, they experienced an international integration and a kind of spatial mobility (often related to social mobility, though), which, at the end of the regime and for the following generations, would remain wishful thinking. This created a strong generational identity and is, in retrospect, was also linked to the specific agency of this generation, which indeed formed both a historical generation, describing a cohort of people of approximately the same age, and a political generation, well aware of their uniqueness and shaped by a commonality of experiences (Mannheim, 1997: 301f, Bellagamba, 2008: 238, Whyte et al., 2008: 5f). Against this backdrop, membership and engagement in the JRDA or the pioneer movement represented important arenas that allowed for political participation and enabled access to different jobs and/or political bureaus. Moreover, the newly born nation-state was dependent on its "new young citizens" to co-create and maintain the socialist state apparatus beyond what the political elites perceived as "colonial ideology". Burgess argues similarly in the context of Revolutionary Zanzibar and states that youngsters "were exposed to a range of experiences unique for their time, which fundamentally influenced the narratives of their lives. They were hailed as the vanguard of a new order – and potentially also its saboteurs" (Burgess, 2010: 233).

The contradiction of a totalitarian state is also reproduced in the memories of the witnesses, as they perceived the state's influences not necessarily as cultural disruption but rather as continuity. In addition, they remembered themselves as being active participants in these past Guinean state formation processes. In the local arena, the national identity took on greater significance. However, as a matter of course the local ethnic identity had not vanished; on the contrary, people managed to have multiple identities at the same time. Accordingly, the transnational space of the *pays Kissi* endured.

Overall, one may state that Revolutionary Guinea was not simply about the state introducing a new national identity by inventing its youth but also about young people who were co-making the state and who were successfully managing various types of identity. Thus, one can describe the youth–state relations in Revolutionary Guinea as complex dialectical interplay allowing space for agency and different kinds of identities, also in seemingly predetermined conditions. However, the Demystification Campaign and the Cultural Revolution also had a lasting effect on local intergenerational relations and the integration of the "ethnic other", formerly institutionalized in the Poro and Sande secret societies. These institutions did not simply disappear during the revolutionary times but they did come under serious attack. In this context, Højbjerg states with regard to the Touré regime: "local religious practices were outlawed during this period of harsh dictatorship, when all forms of political opposition were suppressed and Guinea became isolated from the outside world" (Højbjerg, 2007: 234). Through my investigation in the field I would argue that the politics of secrecy, and the cultural repertoire and spoken discourses of secret societies, are still in use in contemporary Guéckédou. Thus, the still vivid mémoires regarding these institutions preserve some relevance, also for the young Kissi living in the Guéckédou borderland. However, I suggest that secret societies have nevertheless lost much of their power with regard of regional integration.

IV. I am the state
Re-making the state in post-revolutionary Guinea

"L'État, c'est moi. Le gouvernement, c'est moi. La justice, c'est moi",
Lansana Conté quoted in Seck (2007).[1]

When I visited Guinea in 2008 I experienced an interesting historical moment; on 2 October 2008, Guinea celebrated 50 years of independence. My intention was to get an idea of representations and imageries of the state and of state-society relations more generally while experiencing these festivities in Guinea's capital, Conakry.[2] The official programme for the *cinquantenaire* started with a presidential address on the eve of Independence Day, followed by fireworks in the evening. Independence Day itself opened with the raising of the national flag at the *Palais du Peuple* and the arrival of honoured guests like the presidents of neighbouring countries. At midday, flowers were laid at the *Place des Martyrs*, followed by a parade by the *Forces Vives de la Nation* in the afternoon. Shortly afterwards, invited guests were given lunch (*Déjeuner du cinquantenaire*) in front of the *Palais du Peuple*. In the evening, the programme promised a *Banquet d'Etat* and a cultural evening in the hall of the *Palais du Peuple*.

As I could not be present at all these events, in the following section I briefly describe some aspects of one of the main events intended for the public at large, the *Défilé des Forces vives de la Nation* along the Boulevard du Commerce, one of the main axes in the administrative centre of Conakry. Scheduled for around twelve noon it did not start until 2 p.m. However, as many of the participants were already in place around 11 a.m., I was able to spend time visiting the various delegations

---

1 Seck quotes then President Conté who in January 2007, after having liberated a business man accused of misappropriation of public funds, said that the accused person has absolutely no problem with the state, the government or the judicial apparatus as he himself represents the state, the government and the judiciary.

2 On the 50 years of independence festivities in Guinea and in other African countries, see amongst others Engeler (2009), McGovern (2010), Pauthier (2013), Förster (2012), Lentz (2010), Lentz and Budniok (2007) or the edited volume of Bierschenk and Spies (2012).

and groups that had been invited to participate in the procession. Amongst others, I recognised different trade unions and civil society groups, youth groups like the Scouts, as well as comedians, orchestras, ballet companies, the Guinean Olympic team, cycling teams and soccer teams. A few groups represented the country's different regions and carried masks, usually identified as "traditional" and representative of a particular ethnic background. To my surprise there was also a small group of young men wearing t-shirts, belts and caps in the style and in honour of Ernesto "Che" Guevara. One of them even carried a framed picture of the Cuban revolutionary leader (Engeler, 2009).

The majority of the parade's participants, however, were uniformed and armed units of the army, the police and the gendarmerie. In particular I noted the cadets who had been mobilised to march. While waiting for the march to start they proudly took pictures of each other, posing with proper uniforms and serious faces.

My overall impression of the event was that it was a very youthful parade. One got the impression that the idea was to represent a young and strong nation on the move. Thus, the organising committee had made use of a specific image of youthfulness to convey a dynamic Guinean nation-state. The TV commercial that was broadcast on the occasion of the Independence Day festivities used the very same image when showing young people working on diverse construction and mining sites. Moreover, one could see trucks and large diggers in the clip, accompanied by the slogan of the festivities' "ensemble pour bâtir" – "together to build". President Conté referred to the same image in his presidential speech, exhorting the youth to be hardworking citizens helping to create the economic future of the country. One gained the impression that the state's representation of the youth preferred to present an image of young people as respectful, obedient and hardworking, rather than incorporating youths as active political members of the Guinean nation-state – an impression that was reminiscent of Revolutionary Guinea. This representation also, however, eschewed the glorification of the past. During the entire parade I only saw one picture of Sékou Touré, for instance, and this picture showed him as very young – as if they preferred to forget about the "old Touré", who became increasingly despotic and tyrannical.

When the parade finally started, I realised that few people were attending the spectacle. Even before the event many of my dialogue partners had expressed great disinterest in the festivities. It happened that Independence Day coincided with the end of the Ramadan and I got the impression that religious and family celebrations were far more important to most of them. In the aftermath of the cinquantenaire many people complained about the poor organisation and implementation of the events. One of the moments which gave rise to discussions was the laying of flowers at the Place des Martyrs. People explained that the president should do this, but as he was absent from the entire festivities his first wife, Henriette Conté, performed the ceremony – and not the prime minister or the president of the national assembly. The fact that no officially recognised state actor was doing the president's job was perceived as shameful. In addition, by this gesture people were reminded of the fact that the president's family and entourage were favoured over the republican state structure (McGovern, 2010). Accordingly, *le Lynx*, a much read satirical newspaper in the capital, declared the Independence Day festivities as *"la fête de la défaite"*, hence, the "feast of the defeat".[3]

In retrospect, the controversial festivities were not only the occasion of Conté's last appearance but were also a suitable introduction to state–society relations in post-revolutionary Guinea, further discussed in this chapter. First of all, the chapter addresses the Second Republic's administrative de-concentration and political decentralisation attempts. This provides the basis for an understanding of the local state apparatus in post-revolutionary Guinea. The next paragraph explores one of the decrees introduced after 1984 which officially acknowledged the council of the elders as local power brokers. In Guéckédou, these elders have an important role to play with regard to conflict resolution and land allocation. Additional important actors that are shaping the Guéckédou borderland are the national and international NGOs and their representatives. These elements have only been active since 1991; Guinea did not previously allow the intervention of foreign or international NGOs apart from humanitarian operations. Next, I will discuss some additional power brokers and especially hint at their career trajectories. My study will show that these actors can be described as nodes in networks, combining the efforts of projects directed at economic and political joint action (regarding Big Men and networks, cf. Utas, 2012a; 2012b). However, they also form a specific political and historical generation that has constantly been making the state in the Guéckédou borderland since socialist times.

I used various methods to gather the data for this chapter. Personal fieldnotes, descriptions of the local political terrain and the mapping of state and government institutions and actors were key sources for this chapter. The chapter on the council of elders includes data gathered through a variety of conversations and observations. Talking with members of the council of the elders did not always prove easy, however. In general, the different members of the council did not keep to pre-arranged appointments and I started to visit their homes unannounced, just to try my luck. I thereby got the impression that these elderly people were often very busy compared to some of my younger interlocutors. During conversations with these elders, I also often got a feeling of general mistrust and rejection. Thus, while talking to some of them I often became trapped in the role of either a young female outsider to whom they did not intend to talk about internal issues or was the white European who could be accused of her colonial past. I nevertheless consider my insights about these power brokers to be important, as they also re-

---

3 *Le Lynx*, 6 October 2008.

present the fuzzy logic of the Guinean state and its various, at times contradictory, actors, images and practices in different local arenas.

The paragraphs that portray some of the local power brokers build on life history interviews collected over the entire research period. Talking with these political actors was just as tricky to as discussing things with the elders. However, the life history approach turned out to be useful for obtaining additional information on these actors' career trajectories and their political becoming and imagination. Thus, it seemed to me that these actors in most cases loved narrating their personal social becoming and career trajectories, whereas talking about politics was often not so easy. The biographies of political actors and of the state are strikingly closely intertwined: both persons and states are not stable figures but, as Spencer suggests, protean entities subject to growth, change and also death (Spencer, 2007: 100). Accordingly, biographies and career trajectories can reveal much about political practices and imaginations and provide some stimulating insights for a more distinct understanding of the local state in the making.

1.   The Second Republic: administrative changes and reforms

When Sékou Touré died in 1984, a group of soldiers led by Lansana Conté seized power in a bloodless coup d'état. Soon after, Conté proclaimed the Second Republic and declared himself the new president of the Guinean nation-state. In the context of economic liberalisation and greater religious and political freedoms in the 1990s, Conté and his entourage started to reform the country. These reforms led to an administrative reorganisation of Guinea, and the state's powers were decentralised. These reforms were part of several attempts at an internationally recognised democratisation process and were also linked to the introduction of a constitution and a multiparty system. The following paragraphs will address these reforms in more detail.

To begin with I briefly describe the territorial fragmentation and the administrative changes from colonial rule to the First and Second Republics. During colonial times, Guinea was divided into administrative *cercles*, which were in turn subdivided into *cantons* headed by chiefs. Sékou Touré's one-party state reorganised the newly independent nation into *arrondissements*, an administrative level between the regional and local levels. President Lansana Conté rearranged the country into eight provinces headed by governors. These provinces were divided into prefectures, sub-prefectures and districts known as quarters in the cities (*préfectures, sous-préfectures, districts* and *quartiers*) (O'Toole and Baker, 2005: 100). At the time of research, there were a total of 33 prefectures and one special zone, Conakry. Most of the prefectures – former *arrondissements* – reflect the French administrative *cercles* (O'Toole and Baker, 2005: 46, Schroven, 2010a: 115).

The town of Guéckédou is the capital of the prefecture and also hosts the prefect, the direct representative of the country's president, cabinet and all other government in the prefecture (Schroven, 2010a: 117). The president chooses the prefect from among the highest-ranking civil servants or senior army and police officers: "He [the prefect] is nominated by the president to safeguard the execution of decrees and uphold the law" (Schroven, 2010a: 117). The prefect manages the deconcentrated branch units of ministries (Pinto, 2004: 270), for example the prefectural department of education (*Département Préfectoral de l'Education*, DPE) or the prefectural department of youth (*Département Préfectoral de la Jeunesse*, DPJ). Two secretaries assist the prefect: one is responsible for the *collectivités décentralisées*, thus for the local authorities (*collectivités locales*), and the other for administrative issues. The Guinean president nominates both of them.

In the 1990s, in the context of economic liberalisation and opening up politically to the influences of the international financial development institutions, Conté started to implement a programme of administrative deconcentration and political decentralisation (Schroven, 2019). Thus, the territorial fragmentation of the country into different provinces/prefectures/sub-prefectures was linked to the central government's attempt to deconcentrate its power and to establish a variety of local state institutions (Pinto, 2004: 264). In the context of decentralisation, councils and mayors were elected to represent the *collectivités locales*, the local authorities. These authorities consist of the rural development municipalities (*Communautés Rurales de Développement*, CRD), which are subdivided into districts (*districts*), and urban municipalities (*Commune Urbaines*, CU), which are subdivided into neighbourhoods (*quartiers*). Their councils consist of elected district counsellors and *chefs de quartier*. Municipal councils elect their own president, who is effectively the chief executive of the municipality or mayor. Upon election, they become civil servants employed by central government (Pinto, 2004: 269).

The intention of this decentralisation process was for mayors and town councils to take over certain public services, technically assisted and supported by the deconcentrated state institutions. Around the time of the first municipal elections in the mid-1990s, the state organised several workshops with the help of international and national NGOs to try and emphasise citizenship, participation and the public ownership of political decision-making processes (Schroven, 2010b: 665). After a transition period, the decentralised institutions were expected to take over public services such as electricity, health, education and security.

However, the relations between the state administration and the municipalities often remained hazy, as the municipalities' authority was defined in a complex and un-codified body of legislation. Schroven adds that most financial resources and communication channels remain in the hands of the state administrations, which hinders the evolution of mayors and councils into effective local institutions (Schroven, 2010b: 666). Pinto furthermore hints at the Guinean state's attempt to exert strong territorial presence and control (Pinto, 2004: 269). Thus, according to him, the local state administration is closely tied to the national security apparatus and the Guinean government's motive for deconcentration and decentralisation can be described as merely a way of ensuring a central government across the entire national territory. All in all, the municipalities remain an ambiguous political and institutional entity, and their legitimacy has also been called into question.

At the time of the research, the *chefs de quartier* were named by the prefect and no longer elected – a sign of the balance of power between the deconcentrated state and the municipalities, i.e. the decentralised local powers. In other words, public services are supposed to be guided by communal authority, but the reality can actually be quite different. According to Schroven, this can formally be explained by a decree in the 1992 constitution stating that prefects and sub-prefects are entitled to suspend all decisions taken by CRDs and municipal councils if they contradict any law or proceedings that do not "correspond with the official fashion" (Schroven, 2010a: 118). We may conclude this section with the finding that the local manifestations of the state in Guéckédou receive strong guidance from the prefect and his staff, who represent the central state and very often the leading political party. A closer look at the landscape of public buildings in Guéckédou at the time of research further illustrates the changes from the First to the Second Republic and hint at important actors and institutions: "A construct such as the state occurs not merely as a subjective belief, but as a representation reproduced in visible everyday forms, such as the language of legal practice, the architecture of public buildings, the wearing of military uniforms, or the marking and policing of frontiers. The ideological forms of the state are an empirical phenomenon, as solid and discernible as a legal structure or a party system" (Mitchell, 1999: 81).

Public buildings in Guéckédou

The newly constructed prefectural building in Guéckédou is located on a hillock above the city centre and can be seen from most parts of the city. The prefecture was at the time of the research one of the newest buildings in Guéckédou and one of the few with several floors, mirrored windows and a spacious interior. Because of the building's location, the prefecture staff had a perfect view over the downtown area, some of the neighbouring quarters and the rivers running through the settlement. "The authorities see everything" an informant once remarked on the location with a laugh.[4] The building housed various offices and services of the local state administration including the prefect's secretaries' offices and the heads

---

4 *"Les autorités voient tout"*, 15.09.2009, communication with Moïce, with whom I visited the prefect and the prefectural building several times.

of the different units. In addition, it contained the prefectural press agency, the statistics agency and some conference facilities. The nucleus or heartbeat of the building was the prefect's office; when he was around, everybody was busy. But since he was often away on duty, the activities in and around the prefecture were kept within certain limits. Nevertheless, one could on an everyday basis observe comings and goings by different civil servants and civilians looking for a service or for some information during office hours. While visiting the area several times, I soon learnt that two wooden benches in front of the building and right next to the main entrance were important meeting points. A newcomer would find it hard to distinguish between civil servants and common passers-by. The rash Western idea that the civil servants would be inside the building and the common people outside turned out to be utterly wrong: both administrative staff and townspeople usually sat on the benches chatting or waiting for an appointment.

The youth department of the local state apparatus, the DPJ, was not based in the prefectural building but located in a different building which defined the state's imagery in Guéckédou: the *Maison des Jeunes*. This was an old pink building with a greenish roof and a large two-storey structure with a number of wings and entrances. It was located downtown, close to the main market, the bus station and the taxi rank. Hence, in contrast to the hilly, serene location of the prefecture, the *Maison des Jeunes* was completely caught up in the various business activities that surrounded every part of the complex, be they small second-hand clothing shops, hairdressers with their clients, or leatherworkers on the job. Accordingly, I almost failed to notice it in the early days of my field trip, as I was too busy watching the fascinating bustle around it. However, in one of these embedded corridors one could find the two offices reserved for *Monsieur le Directeur*, the head of the DPJ, and his staff and aides.[5] Besides the two offices of the DPJ, other institutions, groups and persons also used the rooms in the *Maison des Jeunes*. One room close to the DPJ's office was the workplace of the president of a local youth association, which will be further discussed in Chapter VIII. In another second-floor wing one could find the town council offices, housing the mayor himself, the general secretary, the representative in charge of youth, and some other aides. This corridor offered a nice view over the marketplace. Accordingly, the staff and passers-by were often to be found watching and listening to the diverse activities and goings-on in the town centre. A little further downstairs, the association of *anciens combattants* (former soldiers of colonial France) had their office. The most impressive and, at

---

5 Not all the *Maison des Jeunes* are located so prominently in the town centre as in Guéckédou, though. In the city of Kankan, Haute Guinée, for instance, the *Maison des Jeunes* was located far from the busy market. In addition, most of the offices seem to be deserted and this meant that they were very quiet. Only the community hall looked like it was in use when I visited the place in 2012, as the walls were covered in election and campaign posters.

times, most vibrant part of the *Maison des Jeunes* was the huge community hall with its large stage. There, the prefect welcomed central state representatives, international NGOs celebrated World AIDS Day, political parties held their election meetings and campaigns, and youth groups organised sporting or musical events.

The *Maison des Jeunes*, in contrast to the newly constructed prefecture, perfectly symbolises "the past in the present", as it was built during the presidency of Sékou Touré. The *Maison des Jeunes* was one of several monumental construction projects undertaken during the socialist state era. Another was the *Palais des Peuples*, which was built with the help of Chinese architects and donors (Brygo, 2006). The *Maison des Jeunes* in Guéckédou was commonly said to be the second construction project after the *Palais*, making it the biggest party headquarters and youth club in the whole of Guinea. It served as a *"permanence"*, referring to the office and headquarters of the local PDG branch and its associated youth groups and cultural institutions. Thus, the building nicely delineates Touré's ideology and state building projects. At the time of the research, people often called the *Maison des Jeunes* the *"ex-permanence"*, in memory of its past. According to local discourse, the exceptionally large building complex was a gift to the population and an acknowledgment of the pioneering role played by Guéckédou's agriculture, orchestra and ballet. "Guéckédou as pilot federation"[6] recalled the collective memory of Guinea as the *Etat pilote* for the whole of Africa – the first nation that decided to say "no" to colonial hegemony (Gigon, 1959). The monumental building therefore mirrors the socialist state era and the intended close connection between the state, the party and the local youth during this time. Similar institutions or party headquarters existed all over Guinea. At the end of the socialist regime in 1987 all of them were transferred to the Ministry of Youth, Sports and Culture and thereafter renamed *Maison des Jeunes*. In 1993, the Conté regime implemented a national youth policy but cuts in resources and ongoing reorganisation of the ministries, together with shifting regimes and power relations, has complicated effective youth-centred work in the past few years. The reorganisation, management and re-equipment of the numerous *Maison des Jeunes* – also in Guéckédou – were often entrusted to international donors and their development agencies.

To conclude: the architectural state projects of Sékou Touré can be read as efforts to create and introduce imageries and spaces for collective life under a new, postcolonial ideology. Nowadays, these socialist relics and artefacts are re-embedded in a post-war cityscape, which is particularly characterised by development-aid sponsored building projects. This new masonry of the state represents the economic and political opening of post-revolutionary Guinea and hints at potentially new images and spaces for collective life. However, they have also rede-

---

6 *"Guéckédou comme fédération pilote."*

corated the state, which uses them in the same way as the socialist buildings. Thus, the architectural landscape may reflect the shifting but interrelated past and present political discourses and imaginations of the local political terrain. From this perspective I follow Humphrey, who in her article reminds us that political practices and ideologies are not only to be found in texts or speeches but are also manifested in constructions and material objects (Humphrey, 2005: 39). Architecture, she further states, can be seen as one of the key political arenas. Thus, state buildings can be read as "a pronounced intention of the state to make use of the materiality of dwelling to produce new social forms and moral values" (Humphrey, 2005: 39f). Of course, social reality often differs from the state schedule, and state constructions may have their own dynamics besides the intentions of the state. Furthermore, the underlying politics of architecture is often hidden from the population and does not necessarily interact with the imaginative and projective inner feelings of the people (Humphrey, 2005: 40).[7]

Nevertheless, the location and history of these buildings can give us food for thought while trying to understand changing state–society relations and political transformation processes from socialist times to present-day Guéckédou. Moreover, these buildings can be read as places of memory, which create a sense of continuity from the past into the present and, in the case of Guéckédou, stake out a socialist presence in the political terrain of today (Till, 2003: 289).[8] Finally, Crapanzano reminds us that such buildings also have a history that is continuously in the making, and "their histories remind us of the 'mutability' of the events they commemorate" (Crapanzano, 2003: 170). Thus, they are sites of continual reinterpretation.

The prefect's changing uniforms
and the variously printed t-shirts in Guéckédou

As written earlier, the Dadis regime and the subsequent transition and presidential election period under the guidance of Sékouba Konaté strongly informed both the data collection and interpretation for this book. During that politically turbulent time, the constitution was dissolved and the state administration was

---

7 According to several anthropologists, post-socialism infrastructure in (post)socialist societies has to be approached from a Marxist materialist perspective: "That is as both physical-material-economic entities and also more abstractly as entities on which the sociocultural superstructure is being erected" (Dalakoglou, 2012: 14).

8 There is a huge body of literature that addresses the relation of memory to different places and/or buildings (cf. amongst others Till (2003), Young (1992), Berliner (2007), and Crapanzano (2003). On the relation of memory and political identity in Africa, cf. De Jorio (2006), Werbner (1998). These contributions also remind us of the importance of state-promoted commemoration of the past as a strategy for legitimating state hegemony and power.

seriously paralysed. However, the state institutions remained on standby and the local political actors adapted to the new power structure, which was later characterised by presidential elections and party mobilisation. In other words, the political turmoil at the time of the research provided crucial insights into the workings of political life, the related manoeuvring of certain actors and the physiognomy of national political change on the ground.

To illustrate, I would like to make two brief observations; firstly, the prefect's changing uniforms and, secondly, the different printed t-shirts in a local studio.

When I first met Guéckédou's prefect in January 2008, he welcomed me dressed in a fine suit to the old prefectural building, which was visibly war-damaged and badly in need of renovation work. When I came back to Guéckédou more than a year later in 2009, the very same prefect was still in office. This could not be taken for granted; long-term President Conté was dead and in the meantime the military CNDD junta had taken over, not without changing their machinery of power at the local level. However, *Monsieur le Préfet* in Guéckédou was still in office and proudly holding audiences in the new prefectural building which had been sponsored by international donors. He enforced the image of having successfully managed international development aid to strengthen the state's presence in the local arena – at least as far as architecture went. This time the prefect welcomed me at his home and was, to my surprise, dressed completely differently than in 2008. Sitting on his veranda, together with a handful of other supplicants and many children, I met a very relaxed man in the uniform of a high-ranking officer. In 2010, after several political intermezzos and a turbulent phase of transition in the run up to the presidential elections, the prefect had successfully managed to host various political campaigns in town despite increasing ethnic tension. He was still in uniform. When I met him again in 2012, however, he was dressed as a civilian again and preparing to visit the newly elected President Alpha Condé in Conakry. He told me that he had retired from his military duties and was toying with the idea of becoming ambassador to a European country. As I found out from my local friends he also became an RPG (*Rassemblement du Peuple Guinéen*) party member, the political party led by Alpha Condé.

All in all, the chameleon-like prefect knew which dress was appropriate for which regime. In 2007 and 2008, politics had been shaped by popular Prime Minister Lansana Kouyaté, who was always dressed properly. Between 2009 and 2010, however, the military set the agenda and the prefect cast off his civilian clothes, only to slip back into them again after the elections and the return to civilian rule. As one of my informants commented with regard to the situation in 2009: "Last year, with Kouyaté, you needed a tie. This year a military uniform might be helpful."[9] Interestingly, these local facets of political transformation and changing state imagery neither surprised anybody nor provoked rash comments. Rather, the perception was that authorities counted very much on their ability to adapt quickly and successfully to remain in power.

The prefect was not the only one who knew which dress was appropriate at which time; local businesses also readjusted again and again during the time of the research. During each field trip to Guéckédou, I would drop into two ateliers, Bongoe Decor and Fat décor, at least once. I discovered them by chance when visiting my research assistant's neighbourhood. Both studios offered calligraphy and serigraphy, however what caught my eye was not so much their range of services but their wide range of printed t-shirts.

When I had arrived in Guéckédou in September 2009, the t-shirts showed Captain Moussa Dadis Camara with the heading "Hope of the Youth" (*Espoir de la Jeunesse*) and the subheading "President of the Guinean Republic" (*Président de la République de Guinée*). To my surprise, close to the Dadis t-shirt another one fluttered in the wind, this time with a picture of Ahmed Sékou Touré. The subheading read "PDG-RDA, 1922–1984." Lansana Conté, Guinea's president between 1984 and 2008, was however nowhere to be seen. In July 2010, the presidential elections gave rise to different printed t-shirts representing the nominated candidate of various political parties: Alpha Condé, Cellou Dallein Diallo, Jean Marc Telliano and Aboubacar Barry. Crammed in between them you could also find Bob Marley and Emanuel Felemou, who at the time of the research was bishop of Kankan, Haute Guinée. They looked as if they were keeping peace in the multiparty system.

Some months later, at a time when everybody in Guéckédou and the whole of Guinea were waiting for the second round of voting, only two t-shirts were left hanging. Both represented the political alliances that had been created in the meantime. One figuratively united Alpha Condé with Jean Marc Telliano and El Papa Koly Kourouna, the other Cellou Dalein Diallo with Abe Sylla and Sidya Touré.

More than a year later, in 2012, the elected president Alpha Condé was the only politician who still decorated one of the t-shirts in front of one of the studios; the other seemed to have closed in the meantime. Apart from that there were lengths of cloth for sale. A difficult time for business, I guessed, as the political reorientation period under the CNDD and later the transitional government came to an end or at least paused for an indefinite period of time.

---

9 "*L'année passée, avec Kouyaté, c'était les cravates. Cette année, c'est la tenue des militaires qui peut aider*", 15.09.2009, communication with Moïce, one of my key informants working for local branch of an international NGO.

2.   Recognising the elderly: *conseils des sages*

Besides administrative reorganisation, in 1985 the Second Republic issued a decree officially recognising the previously suppressed *Conseils des Sages*, i.e. the councils of elders (Rey, 2007: 56).[10] In the light of state iconoclasm and the making of revolutionary youth described in Chapter III, I perceive this decree to be extremely valuable, as it brought the elders back into the official political arena of the state.

After 1985, councils of elders were re-established and/or strengthened throughout Guinea and usually consisted of members of the towns' founding families. According to the decree, the elders were to organise religious festivities and ceremonies, engage in conflict resolution within and between families, preserve local traditions for children and youths, and control land distribution (Rey, 2007, Koundouno, 2009). Due in particular to this last aspect, the elders remain highly influential in Guinea, at least in more rural areas. After all, most of the land in Guinea is unregistered and primarily governed by so-called customary laws that are strongly interlinked with the council of elders (Schroven, 2010b: 666). In other words, the land officially belongs to the state but, at the same time, the state has to some degree recognised customary laws and allows the land to be used accordingly (Black and Sessay, 1997: 603). All in all, current land tenure law is so ambiguous that most people do not really know that "their land" still officially belongs to the state. A more recent land tenure policy passed in 2001 lacks application texts and is, according to USAID, not functioning (Usaid, 2008: vi). This ambiguity regarding land rights can be described as characteristic of many aspects and policies of the post-revolutionary Guinean state. The following two vignettes provide further insights into the work and reputation of the councils of elders in Guéckédou, Beindo Boodo and Temessadou, all of them (small) towns within the wider Guéckédou borderland.

Providers of the past and the present

Meeting the council of elders in Guéckédou was one of my primary tasks when I was settling in. Together with one of my first local informants, a young motorbike taxi driver, I went to see the president of the council and finally met him in the small annex close to his family home. [11] The single room appeared to be a combi-

---

10 Pascal Rey's thesis is one of the few accounts that in detail analyzes the councils of the elders and its relations to the Guinean state, cf. Rey (2007).

11 I will come back to the motorbike taxi drivers in Chapter VII of my study. At the time of my first visit to the council's president I was not aware that most motorbike taxi drivers were former vigilantes and therefore had a particular relationship with the local authorities and the coun-

nation of a reception room and living room and was furnished with several chairs, some of them quite simple and made of wood, others upholstered armchairs. They were arranged along two sides of the room and lined the back wall where the president of the council had his seat and his table. My companion introduced me to the president and two other elderly men who were present in the room (we obviously interrupted their meeting) and I was asked to introduce myself too. After a short presentation about myself and my research project, in which I described my interest in young people and recent political transformation processes, the president reacted with a long speech about the pre-colonial history and how people back then organised themselves. This was my first opportunity to learn something about local perceptions of the Kissi community's origins (cf. Chapter II). In a few sentences the old man told the history of the Guéckédou borderland as a series of invasions and conflicts, starting with the Mande people coming from the north and ending with the Europeans and their priests and companies. More recent political transformations such as the takeover by the military junta he legitimised with references to peace and stability. According to him, political parties were not familiar with local realities and a multiparty system was not the best way to govern Guinea and the Guéckédou borderland. To back up his argument he pointed to the political system in China, which was, according to him, very successful in organising a huge country and showed strong economic progress as well.

I later learnt that such statements did not prevent the council from hosting and supporting political parties during the 2010 multiparty presidential elections. Accordingly, posters of different presidential candidates began to decorate the elders' domiciles as well approximately a year after my first visit. I observed this not only in Guéckédou but also in Beindo Boodo, a village in Temessadou sub-prefecture: In the local council of elders' meeting room I noticed a poster showing the presidential candidate from the Guéckédou region, which dated from 2010. Yet another wall was decorated with very old posters showing Mao, Marx and Sékou Touré alongside each other.

Harmonising and conflictive relations

Once, the president of the Guéckédou council of elders told me that he perceived today's young people to be very dynamic and full of initiative. He said that he therefore supported many of the youths in town. He described the collaboration between the council of elders and the young people of Guéckédou as follows: "The young inform us about the latest problems in the town. They are like our arms,

cil of elders. Accordingly, like so many times during my field stays, I was simply not aware of the "underneath of things", to use Ferme's words, but only started to understand this several months later (Ferme, 2001).

our legs and our eyes."[12] Thus, he perceived the young and the old to be part of the same body but with different functions. The elders accept and respect youths' initiative and physical strength and see themselves as the intellectual mind of the social body.

On a visit to Temessadou, the rural capital of Temessadou sub-prefecture, I learnt that the relationship between councils of elders and the rest of the community is not necessarily always harmonious. I had accompanied my research assistant, Augustin, who was conducting interviews for his master's dissertation. He was very interested in local conflict resolution and became very excited about the means and tools applied by the councils of elders (Koundouno, 2009). We soon realised that the elders in Temessadou were unwilling to answer the questions he had prepared. Although we managed to meet them in one of the public buildings, we could not really talk to them. Instead, we were confronted with mistrust and accusations of being useless students. So we stopped our investigation and just walked around the settlement. By coincidence, we met and talked to another resident of the village and learnt that the elders were very angry at the time because they had been accused of witchcraft by some local youths. These accusations were, in addition, related to a matter of money. Herders from the Peul ethnic group had paid the money in compensation for damage caused by their cattle crossing areas under cultivation. The farming villagers claimed that the local authorities, among them the elders, had taken the money instead of distributing it to the affected peasants. Our conversation partner concluded by saying that the police that should now settle the conflict. He concluded by saying that "dealing with the modern and the traditional authorities is like dealing with a disease. First of all, you have to go to the modern doctor who will give you medicine. After that, you go to the traditional healer; he will give you a product to neutralise the medicine. Finally, you will need both to achieve balance and to recover from your disease."[13]

---

12 *"Les jeunes nous signalent les problèmes dans la ville. Ils sont nos pieds, nos bras, nos yeux"*, 08.10.2010, communication with Mr Komano, president of the council of the elders at the time of the research.

13 *"Avec les autorités traditionnelles et modernes, c'est comme avec une maladie. D'abord tu visites les docteurs modernes. Ils vont te donner des médicaments. Après ça tu es obligé d'aller chez le guérisseur traditionnel, lui aussi il va te donner des produits pour neutraliser les médicaments. C'est pour la balance. Finalement tu as besoin de tous les deux pour recouvrer la santé"*, 02.11.2009, communication with a resident of Temessadou.

3.   New and old actors: *forces vives*

Some relatively new actors who are shaping everyday state–society relations in the Guéckédou borderland are international and national NGOs and their representatives. These elements have only been around since 1991 – Guinea did not previously allow the intervention of foreign or international NGOs beyond humanitarian operations. Compared to other regions in Guinea, Guéckédou has had quite a lot of experience with international NGOs, mainly because of the close links to the Mano River War, which started in Liberia in 1989 (Hoffman, 2011a). Like several other prefectures along the Sierra Leonean and Liberian border, for example Forécariah prefecture depicted by Schroven (2010a: 109) and Kissidougou prefecture of which Agier (2010) gives an impression, Guéckédou became a minor hub for different international NGOs in the late 1990s. During the civil wars in Sierra Leone and Liberia, these organisations were especially concerned about the stream of refugees arriving from the various battlefields of the West African conflict zone.[14] The international NGOs cooperated with local authorities and government representatives, and many local NGOs emerged to build a growing civil society.[15] In Guinea, the term "civil society" is generally employed for these national NGOs, which became, as Schroven argues, a valid and accepted institution (Schroven, 2010a: 135ff). These civil society organisations are often grouped together in the *forces vives*, comprising the national NGOs, and include long-standing trade unions, opposition parties and religious leaders. Whereas the NGO representatives refer to themselves as apolitical, the others became prominent political actors in 2006 and 2007, when the trade union confederation USTG-CNTG called for several national strikes (Engeler, 2008, McGovern, 2007, Schroven, 2010b). The trade unions thus proved to be, for the first time since independence, an effective force for mobilising opposition in many towns across Guinea, including Guéckédou. People described the events during the national strikes and the demonstrations in 2007 as relatively minor in Guéckédou, but I also learnt that one of the local police stations and the municipal building had been destroyed in the course of events.

However, the local civil society groups, and first and foremost among them the local NGOs, should not only be perceived as a counterweight to the state but also as strongly tied to local power brokers and governmental institutions. Thus, a sharp distinction between so-called civil society and the local state would be too

---

14 Chapters VI and VII will further discuss the context of the West African conflict zone in relation to local youths.

15 Schlichte calls the interactions between the government and international NGOs, which often resulted in internationalised post-war policies, the "internationalization of rule" (Schlichte, 2008). Although he describes the case of Uganda, his analysis is also useful for understanding the situation in post-war Guéckédou.

artificial and, as in other countries, the non-government character of these NGOs must always be questioned. The reason for the blurred boundaries between civil society and the state is not least their common language; all the actors, whether they claim to be "state", "non-state", "political" or "apolitical", use the same development vocabulary as international donors. Thus, through their language but also through their practices and relations, the different actors are a blurred mix of the state, the government, political parties and civil society organisations. In addition, a closer look at the actors representing the institutions in Guéckédou showed that most of them were simultaneously involved in a whole array of institutions. Thus, most of the actors were wearing several hats at the same time and were not only working for an NGO but also worked, for instance, for the state administration.

4.   Mayor, civil servant, politician or NGO activist?

In the preceding paragraphs we have met several actors making, shaping and representing state–society relations in post-revolutionary Guinea, be they local NGOs or members of the council of elders. In the following section I would like to add some detail to this perspective by looking at three political figures. The three portraits include one woman and two men. I start with the female actor. All of these actors described themselves as part of the Kissi-speaking people.

I changed into trousers

Madame le Maire, as she is commonly called, is a trained teacher and worked for several years in different regional schools.[16] Thus, her education and job made her a *fonctionnaire* from very early on.[17] During the 1990s, she got a job with the state

---

16 I got to know Madame le Maire in 2009 while researching the *Jeunes Volontaires*, further discussed in Chapter VI. Thereafter I visited her several times in her office at the DPE, close to the main prefectural building.

17 The term *fonctionnaire*, a French colonial legacy, "encompasses all hierarchical levels possible in state employment and therefore designates a very heterogeneous group in terms of family or educational background, social standing, income or influence on decision-making processes. The prefect, his driver, the nurses in hospital or the secretaries to the mayor are all subsumed under this term" (Schroven, 2010b: 662). Lipsky calls them, or at least the lower-level civil servants, "street-level bureaucrats" (Lipsky, 1980: 3). Civil servants generally originate from different regions and only stay for certain number of years in a specific prefecture, where they usually form a very specific milieu, cf. Bauer (2005: 496). In Guéckédou, however, most of the *fonctionnaires* (with the important exception of the prefect) I met were born in or near by Guéckédou prefecture and did not form a segregated community in town. Nevertheless, one could

administration and occupied a post in the prefectural department of education, the DPE (*Département Préfectoral de l'Education*). In 2000, however, she was elected town mayor and agreed to take on the office. This was, as she told me, not an easy decision, and she initially wanted to refuse the honour of becoming mayor and only accepted the post after persuasion from her parents and local elders.

So Madame le Maire finally agreed to become the town mayor. Her term in office was characterised by exceptionally turbulent times due to having to deal with refugees from neighbouring civil wars and then the rebel attacks on Guéckédou territory at the end of 2000 and the beginning of 2001. Unlike the prefect and his staff, she stayed in the town during the fighting and was closely involved in building up a local civil defence force to protect the town from a rebel takeover and looting. In her own words, she "changed into trousers and stayed at the military camp" to fight and protect the town.[18] Together with youth representatives, the military and community elders, she successfully defended the national territory and became widely viewed as a war hero. I will come back to these relations in Chapter VII.

However, Madame le Maire's term of office ended in 2005 and she received another post in the DPE. At the time of research she was responsible for civic education projects across the prefecture.

Don't see me as 100% political

Mister Kamano also became mayor at one point in his career, although he was previously active in Sékou Touré's one-party state and was elected as a youth representative onto the local politburo, the PRL or *Pouvoir Révolutionnaire Local*.[19] He did not mention that he was an active party militant, but it is conceivable that he was one, as almost all Guineans became party members and usually only active party militants could be elected. Instead, he emphasised that he had been elected because of his commitment to local sports, especially soccer. Hence, he organised regional soccer games and mobilised local youths to participate. During the subsequent political transformation from the socialist one-party state and his institutionalised youth work in the decentralised state apparatus, he successfully managed to become neighbourhood counsellor and finally *chef du quartier*. In this

---

at times distinguish them from others according their dress; they often wore cloth pants and a chemise in the same colour, usually blue or brownish, cf. the description in Bauer (2005: 500).

18 "*J'ai mis un pantalon et je suis restée dans le camps des militaires*", 11.08.2010, communication with Madame le Maire, a former mayor and, at the time of research, a civil servant.

19 I met Mr Kamano several times at his home as well as at his father's place, which was closer to the centre of town. In fact, he became one of my regular dialogue partners, and my research assistant and I simply dropped in when we were in the neighbourhood. I also got to know his son and other family members. Sadly, Mr Kamano died in early 2012 after a long illness.

way, he forged a smooth path into the newly established or reorganised state institutions and became part of the local authorities. Finally, he was elected major in 1995 for a five-year term. In 2000 he claimed that he had been cheated and another person got the position – the aforementioned Madame le Maire.

However, he explained that he did not complain, as "he never had debated power affairs."[20] During the rebel attacks he then left Guéckédou for Kissidougou and became involved in various development projects initiated by a range of international agencies. He returned to Guéckédou four years later and, although he did not openly admit it, he contemplated standing for mayor again. It would therefore seem that he tried to extend his repertoire and resources to achieve power with the help of development aid. He subsequently stood for re-election, styling himself as someone capable of attracting different donors and international agencies, thus implying that he was part of the development world. However, he was not very successful and someone else was elected. Subsequently, he reoriented himself towards another business connected to political party engagement. He became a PUP (*Parti de l'Unité et du Progrès*) member, he explained, and was thus a member of President Conté's political party. Recent political transformation processes had caused him some personal political uncertainty, however, and Mr Kamano seemed to be uncertain about how to cope with this turbulent political terrain. In 2009, during one of our first interviews, he mentioned that he was an UFDG (*Union des Forces Démocratiques de Guinée*, the opposition party) member but stressed that he was a friend of the military, as his father was also a military man and he himself has grown up in various military camps all over the country. He struggled with the term "opposition party" and tried to avoid mentioning it. When we met again after the military regime had lost a lot of its power and reputation in the forest region, he felt more comfortable and said that he had recently become head of the local UFDG branch. Like Madame le Maire, he emphasised that others had asked him to take this leadership position and that he had agreed only after his mother confirmed that he had to because it was the will and wish of the community. To my surprise, he repeatedly stated that I should not take him as "a 100 percent political man" and that he would actually prefer to have a different job.[21] As if wanting to broaden his repertoire and his image once more, also with regard to me, he also presented himself as a devout Catholic, who spent a lot of time praying. Later I found out that he had fallen seriously ill, which he attributed to the mistrust and curses of his neighbours and political opponents.

---

20 *"Moi, j'ai jamais discuté les affaires du pouvoir"*, 18.12.2009, communication with Mr Kamano, a local political party leader and former mayor.

21 *"Ne me prenez pas pour un homme politique à 100 pour cent"*, 23.11.2009, communication with Mr Kamano, a political party leader and former mayor.

At the time of political campaigning in 2010, Mr Kamano finally became a proud follower of Cellou Dalein Diallo, the leader of the UFDG and one of the most promising presidential candidates. Thus, Mr Kamano became prominent in local campaigns, finally representing himself as a political party member and becoming visible as such in public at the local soccer arena, where campaigning usually took place.

Only two years later, in early 2012, Mr Kamano died. His funeral can be read as the final twist in the making of a local power broker, since the ceremony united the whole of Guéckédou, no matter what their religious background. On that occasion everyone came to show respect for this "son of Guéckédou and great political man", as one of my local informants described him. There were also rumours of witchcraft, which confirmed my earlier guess that people perceived plotting a (successful) political career in the Guéckédou borderland to be a very dangerous undertaking.

Peace comes first

Mister Milimouno was born and grew up in Sierra Leone but came Guinea and to Guéckédou, which he described as his town of origin, as a young student in 1961.[22] During his student days he became active in the local pioneer movement. This movement awoke his interest in party politics – "There I acquired a taste for politics", he explained – and he finally became involved in the youth activities of the PDG-RDA and, thus, an active member of the JRDA.[23] In the JRDA he became a representative of and worked at the village, prefecture and regional levels. He accordingly saw revolutionary education as the transfer of knowledge – knowledge about the history of his people, the villages and the cities, as well as about the country's political landscape – and he got to know the various authorities, the party structure and the nation.

Interestingly, he explained the death of Sékou Touré by referring to a personal crisis related to his wife's infertility. At the time of Touré's death in 1984, he recalled that he and his wife had left the area to get treatment in another part of the

---

22 Mr Milimouno lived very close to my research assistant's home. Accordingly I got to know him quite well and I during my field trips used to see him almost every week. He always insisted that I should take out my recorder and interview him "properly", which I did several times, although not on the more "informal visits".

23 "Là j'ai commencé à prendre goût à la politique de parti unique qu'on avait ici, le PDG-RDA, et j'ai commencé avec le JRDA", 01.12.2010, communication with Mr Millimouno, a former JRDA member, a deputy and NGO activist. It must be noted that when talking about the JRDA or the pioneers I often had the impression that people did not differentiate between the different revolutionary educational projects or used their names interchangeably. They would refer to the entire education efforts undertaken in the socialist state. For further information, cf. Part I.

country. He did not return to the Guéckédou region until after his daughter was born. Thus, Mr Millimouno, an active party member committed to the socialist one-party state, framed the end of an era with a personal narrative recounting a long absence from both his residence and his political duties. He only returned to Guéckédou shortly before 1992, at the time when President Conté introduced the multiparty system. He then became a member of the local PUP branch (the political party of which President Conté was leader) and even claimed to have been one of the founding members of the party's local branch. After the first parliamentary elections in 1995, he became a deputy in the General Assembly and was successfully re-elected to the second parliament in 2002. Simultaneously, he started to get involved in various development projects launched by the international development aid agencies that had moved into the war-effected region in the 1990s. In the aftermath of the regional conflicts, he was one of those who assisted with the Mano River Union and engaged in peace-building projects across national borders.

His political engagement underwent a significant change with the death of President Conté and the suspension of the constitution in 2008, as he lost his seat in parliament. During this time he also tried to deny or downplay his relationship to the past regime and the president's party. However, he did not seem to be too bothered by this and busied himself instead by supporting certain smaller development projects for peace and reconciliation. He used to tell me that "peace comes first", and he was very active in promoting his NGO.[24]

Mr Milimouno went back into party politics shortly before the presidential elections in 2010, this time supporting the local Guéckédou RDIG candidate (*Rassemblement pour le Développement Intégré de la Guinée*).

5.   A flexible political generation

Many of the power brokers active in Guéckédou borderland politics were born around the 1960s and started their professional and political career within the one-party state, usually as members of the pioneer movement or the JRDA. Thus, these actors can be described as a historical and political generation (Mannheim, 1997: 267ff).[25] Their (political) careers did not end with the death of Sékou Touré but continued after a short period of reorganisation. Most of these actors therefore successfully navigated the changing political terrain and obtained a new

---

24 "*D'abord la paix*", 09.11.2009, communication with Mr Millimouno, a former JRDA member, deputy and NGO activist.

25 For further explanation of the concept of historic and political generation, cf. Braungart and Braungart (1986), and the contributions of the reader edited by Alber et al. (2008) and Steele and Acuff (2012).

position or duty within the post-revolutionary local state, either in the local state administration within the decentralised institutions, or as a politician in the political party landscape.

Concurrently, in the 1990s, these Guéckédou-based power brokers started to engage in NGO business, which flourished because of the new political ideology and, in the case of the Guéckédou borderland, because of the Mano River War, the refugees and the rebel attacks. Thus, by using and adapting to different repertories and resources – or, as Lentz described it in regard to Ghana, by "combining various fields of action" (Lentz, 1998: 64) – most of the local power brokers could readjust to new political situation.[26] For instance, by describing themselves as "not being 100% political", power brokers differentiated themselves from what they often perceived as a corrupt elite and, in addition, wanted to be seen as potential candidates for arenas other than the state apparatus. All in all, they have successfully interwoven the spheres of state bureaucracy, government, political parties, the municipality and civil society to legitimise their power and authority. Thus, they were often simultaneously involved in different but interlinked socio-political and economic fields of activity. They may therefore be described in line with Englund, in his work on politicians in Malawi, as "chameleons" (Englund, 2002), who successfully played multiple roles as civil servants, politicians and NGO activists. The different roles are, as Eilenberg frames it regarding Indonesian leaders, "mixed in a complex dance, with elites wearing several hats at once" (Eilenberg, 2012: 6). The metaphor of a dance performed by numerous dancers wearing – probably depending on the rhythm – a number of hats, nicely illustrates the power brokers' manoeuvring in the local political terrain. In addition, one may assume that it is not only so-called state-actors and government institutions "make the state" and wield authority, but a variety of groups and actors: "Mayors, district chief executives, district commissioners, magistrates, chiefs, 'strong-men', and professional associations, societies, parties, home town and youth associations, churches, revolutionary defense committees, development projects, and so forth – all take an active interest in local politics and the shaping of governance, and in defining and enforcing collectively-binding decisions and rules" (Lund, 2007: 4). The various actors dancing on the political stage in Guéckédou included "official parts of local state administration and 'leftovers' from previous political regimes such as families of first-comers, colonial chief's descendants, socialist-inspired neighborhood committees and elected members of town councils" (Schroven, 2010a: 120). Thus, ideologies and the people in governing institutions did not just disappear with the change of government (Schroven, 2010a: 120).

---

26 Cf. Derlugian's interesting contribution on the topic of bureaucrats who have successfully navigated the political transition from socialism to post-socialism in the Caucasus (Derluguian, 2005).

In the course of my research, and while talking to many different female and male office holders and political actors, I found that these power brokers particularly stressed that it was not their personal desire or aspiration to take a leadership role; rather it was the will of the community, of their parents or elders that finally brought them to that office or position.[27] It would seem that admitting to harbouring ambitions for such a task would be morally reprehensible and would have been unusual within the community. This assumption proved true, as it was very difficult to find people willing to talk about their political aspirations or objectives. Instead, my interlocutors preferred to tell stories of "political awakening and nomination" through others. In addition, they did not talk about "networking" or relations to other Big Men. Instead, they wanted to portray themselves as rather lonely actors who, thanks to God and the community, had obtained a leadership position and political authority. Thus, while describing these actors as being part of the "Big Men networks" (Utas, 2012a) that form and shape the political terrain in the Guéckédou borderland, I do not mean to infer that the actors themselves describe their intentions and practices as those of networkers. Hence, I argue that from an analytical perspective that one may describe these actors as creating a network. In their own discourses, however, these actors do not describe themselves as being part of, or as looking to be integrated into, local power configurations. Instead, they perceive and discursively represent themselves as independent actors, who came to power through the will of the people alone. Nevertheless, by drawing on the biographies of local power brokers I argue that avenues similar to continuously making and negotiating the local state and political terrain do exist. These always require the power brokers' personal assessment of the national political situation, then its appropriation and local reimplementation. Moreover, the local power broker network seems to be quite persistent in the Guéckédou borderland and can be described as living organism; if you change its environment it will mutate in order to survive (Utas, 2012b: 20).

But how about the younger generation yearning to make a place for themselves in the Second Republic? How does this new generation interact with the various power brokers and in which public buildings do they enter – what kind of arenas do they shape? As a point of departure, the next chapter concentrates on answering the question of what it actually means to be young and to grow older in the Guéckédou borderland.

---

27 For further information on women and political participation in Guinea, see for example, the recent publications of Ammann (2018; 2017; 2016a; 2016b).

V. Meandering
Being young and growing up

> "Moi, je rêve d'avoir un mari que j'aime.
> Mais je ne veux pas être la co-épouse de quelqu'un, non [...]
> et un enfant, je veux vraiment devenir maman bientôt",
> "oui, moi aussi. Mais d'abord je veux un boulot et mon propre salaire!",
> "ehhh toi, tu es un rêveur!",
> evening talk with two female friends.[1]

When I first met Fatoumatou in 2009, she was looking for a husband and a job. When I met her again in January 2012, she had made no progress in either area but she was not complaining. On the contrary, she was in a very good mood. Her father's former brother in arms, Alpha Condé, had recently been elected president of Guinea. Surely a good omen. And more importantly, Alpha Condé should remember Fatoumatou, too. Didn't she use to sit on his knee as a baby? She really should try to visit him in Conakry; he would definitely remember her. But what should she ask for once she was in his office? Fatoumatou had three clear wishes: a husband, a job and a house. But what would be the first priority should she only have one wish fulfilled, she asked herself. At length, she decided that first and foremost she would like a job. With the money she would earn, she would sooner or later be able to buy a house of her own. As for a husband, she dreamt up the following plan: she wanted a child and she would probably fare better without a husband. Getting pregnant is easy, she said. But finding a good husband? Almost impossible, even with the president's help. So she decided to cross the wish for a husband off the list. Instead, she explained that she would simply get pregnant in 2013 at the latest and therefore start a family without a husband. Before that, she

---

1 The conversation can be translated as follows: "I dream of having a husband that I love. But I do not want to be the second wife of somebody, no [...] and I wish to become a mother soon", "yes, me too, but before that I would like to have a nice job with my own salary", "oh! you're a dreamer!"

would have to meet with Alpha Condé as soon as possible so that she had a job and could feed and house the child, Insha'Allah.

Fatoumatou was one of my best friends in Guinea and we also tried to stay in contact after my return to Switzerland. It was via phone calls and text messages that I learnt in 2014 that she found a stable job with an international NGO and, in 2015, that she gave birth to a healthy child. However, she never met Alpha Condé and also had no husband or official boyfriend but stayed on her own.

I discuss Fatoumatou's life trajectory in more detail later in this chapter, which attempts to give an account of young peoples' youth and social becoming, their agency, their sources of identity, their crucial times and key moments in life. The chapter starts with some general reflections on youth and growing up. The next couple of paragraphs then provide an introduction to the everyday life of young people in the Guéckédou borderland on the basis of a number of life trajectories. I examine topics such as intergenerational relations and "survival work", and also look at social and spatial mobility, education, marriage and religious contexts (Engeler, 2017). Finally, I propose an approach to youth that conceptualises being young and growing up in terms of meandering and socially embedded lives.

Life courses form the main basis for this chapter. The concise portraits are primarily about Albert, Boubacar and Fatoumatou. Secondly, they refer to Finta, Mariama and Amara. All of the portraits are extracted from in-depth life history interviews, as well as many informal conversations. While I was recording the portraits, I considered the important aspects and relevant turning points the interviewees themselves had highlighted. However, I am also aware of the interpretative and constructed character of the portraits and consider them ethnographic narratives informed by my own perspective and research focus.

There are several reasons for my decision to pick the examples of Albert, Boubacar, Fatoumatou and their relatives and not those of other young people I got to know. First of all, their life trajectories address most of the important issues I learnt were key to understanding youth in Guéckédou. In addition, I could make use of different kinds of data (interviews but also many informal conversations and observation notes) that I had collected during a number of field trips to write these portraits. Thus, I spent quite some time with those portrayed and got to know their everyday life beyond the strictly limited time frame of an interview. Boubacar and Fatoumatou also lived very close to my home, so we saw each other on a daily basis and also spent almost every evening together, sitting in front of one of our homes, chatting, laughing or listening to *BBC Afrique*. In the course of my field stays I also became acquainted with their friends and various members of their families, some of them beyond the urban area of Guéckédou and the broader Guéckédou borderland. That fact allowed me to track the life histories in a wide spatio-temporal map of manifold interrelations.

Finally, each of the portraits talks about both men and women from different educational, ethnic and religious backgrounds and this brings the making of gender, religious and ethnic relations into the discussion. Hence, I consciously reflect that the Guéckédou borderland is populated not only by Kissi-speaking youth but also by recent immigrants and long-established "latecomers". This is particularly visible in the urban space of Guéckédou but also true of villages and rural sites throughout the Guéckédou borderland.

Owing to the fact that youths do not constitute a homogenous category, I do not claim that either the portraits or the interpretations can be generalised to Guinean youth as a whole. After conversations with many people in the field I can nonetheless assert that some parts of the stories presented here can be taken as illustrative of the meandering lives of many young people in Guinea today.[2]

1.   Defining youth and growing up

Young people in Africa, writes Abbink, "are facing tremendous odds and do not seem to have the future in their own hands" (Abbink, 2005: 1). He further states: "The simple fact is that most of Africa's young people are no longer growing up in the relatively well-integrated societies described in rich detail by anthropologists and historians only one or two generations ago; monographs on, for example, the Nuer, the Dinka, the Murle, the Tiv, the Meru, the Kpelle, the Somal, the Acholi, the Kikuyu or the Karimojong give the impression of another world. Only faint traces of social order and cultural integrity still exist" (Abbink, 2005: 2). The dilemma, he says in concluding the paragraph, is how to write about youth in Africa "without falling back on the bleak picture of crisis, crime and violence that the available statistics and research reports seem to confirm time and again" (Abbink, 2005: 2). Thus, it would be a mistake to deny African youths' intentionality of action and agency, as has so often been the case, according to him, in Africanist discourses (Abbink, 2005: 2).

In what follows, I do not deny that young people face enormous challenges (in Africa and the entire world); however, I plead for a closer look at particular arenas, thus at youthful agency and the youth's room for manoeuvre under specific circumstances (Engeler and Steuer, 2017). I therefore follow an anthropology of youth which is "characterized by its attention to the agency of young people" and "documents not just highly visible youth cultures but the entirety of youth cultural practice" and, lastly, is "interested in how identities emerge

---

2 For those interested in biological age, the age range of the young men and women I worked with was between 18 and 34.

in new cultural formations that creatively combine elements of global capitalism, transnationalism, and local culture" (Bucholtz, 2002: 525).

As depicted in Chapter 1 of my study, I perceive "youth" to be a social construct and I therefore consider age boundaries to be loose and dependent on time, place, culture and social context. In Guéckédou, various factors came into play to determine whether somebody was still young or had already reached social adult status. These debates mentioned marriage, childbirth and economic independency, but also referred to responsibility and general demeanour. All of these factors, however, are strongly embedded in the social environment. Hence, a woman could be married with two children but still be perceived as young because she dressed and did her hair like a "young woman". A man might be considered an adult despite not yet being married because he was employed by an international NGO and therefore was accorded great respect but also great responsibility. All in all, I agree with Honwana, who states that the idea of "social adults refers to people who are recognized by their culture as able to partake in the social responsibilities of adulthood" (Honwana, 2012: 171) and, further, that being young refers instead to "a time of growth, of searching for meanings and belonging; a stage of molding characters, interests, and goals; a process of constructing and reconfiguring identities; a creative period with both risks and possibilities" (Honwana, 2012: 11). Thus, youth should be seen as a relational concept situated in the dynamic context of the entire society. Nevertheless, I agree with Mannheim and acknowledge the fact that young people do not have as many life experiences as elder people may have. Actually, this might be the reason why they are, as written in this book's prologue, considered as "courageous": "That experience goes with age is in many ways an advantage. That, on the other hand, youth lacks experience means a lightening of the ballast for the young; it facilitates their living on in a changing world. One is old primarily in so far as he comes to live within a specific, individually acquired, framework of useable past experience, so that every new experience has its form and its place largely marked out for it in advance. In youth, on the other hand, where life is new, formative forces are just coming into being, and basic attitudes in the process of development can take advantage of the moulding power of new situations. Thus a human race living on forever would have to learn to forget to compensate for the lack of new generations" (Mannheim, 1997: 296).

In the following section, I would like to analyse the way in which young people shift or rather switch between the youth and the adult worlds and concur with Johnson-Hanks and her analytical concept of "vital conjuncture". This refers to socially structured zones of possibility that emerge around specific periods of potential transformation in a life or lives. According to her, vital conjunctures are "particularly crucial durations when more than usual is in play, when the futures at stake are significant" (Johnson-Hanks, 2002: 871). In other words, vital conjunctures "are the moments when seemingly established futures are called into question and when actors are called on to manage durations of radical uncertainty" (Johnson-Hanks, 2002: 878). People chart a course (or navigate) through these conjunctures by referring to their "horizons" (Johnson-Hanks, 2002) or an imagined future. However, young people can also lose their imaginative skills and live instead from day to day, referring to an "unimagined future" (Honwana, 2012: 29).

I am aware that habitual practices in the contested and conflictive borderland of Guéckédou, which is constantly influenced by political crisis and economic hardship, have the potential to rapidly become vital conjunctures. However, for the purposes of this chapter I would like to look at uncertainties and challenges in relation to young people's life histories. I thereby argue that these stories can tell us a lot about youth agency and about what it means to be young and to grow older.

Finally, the following references to different youthful life trajectories are not just about the portrayed themselves but simultaneously give insights into related lives and perspectives. This mirrors Durham's definition of youth as social "shifter" (Durham, 2000, Durham, 2004, Durham, 2009). Thus, youth is a relational concept situated in a dynamic social landscape of power, knowledge, rights, and cultural notions of agency and personhood, constantly re-made through the socio-political practices of different members of society.

2.   Albert

Albert, part of the Kissi-speaking community, was born in the town of Guéckédou and completed most of his primary and secondary education (collège and lycée) in the city. He lived with his mother and his three sisters – two of them, Finta and Angeline, with their own children. Albert's father had lately separated from his first spouse (Albert's mother) and lived close by with his second wife, who was expected to give birth to a child soon. The relationship between the two families was not particularly good, but they managed to organise themselves, Albert told me. When asked about his childhood he explained that he was raised as a Catholic and emphasised the time when he was an altar boy (*enfant de cœur*) at the local Catholic Church. Back then, his father must have been a Sunday school teacher, but he was never very clear about that.

Always on the go

In Albert's accounts of his personal life, the Mano River War figured prominently. During the war and the related rebel attacks in 2000 and 2001, Albert and his family fled to neighbouring villages in the prefecture. There he tried to continue his schooling but finally dropped out to eventually restart when they moved back to Guéckédou a year later. He then finished secondary education and went to university in Conakry. At the time of my research, Albert was a second-year student in Conakry, but returned to Guéckédou whenever possible – during the semester breaks but also during times of low activity at the university. Once in Guéckédou, Albert was kept busy doing various small jobs to support his family, ranging from running a mobile phone repair service together with others of his age, cultivating a small field just outside the town with one of his younger brothers, to helping out some other friends with their video club. He was always on the go. I got to know Albert in 2009 while he was doing an (unpaid) internship with the local branch of an international NGO. In between these jobs, he also worked for various elders, mostly for a reward in kind. For instance, he assisted a well-respected man who was involved in a range of civil society organisations. Albert accompanied him on different missions and respectfully called him his tutor.[3] The same was true of two other male elders he visited regularly. Both of them lived in the same neighbour-hood and Albert decided to establish a small mobile phone repair and assembly shop there. Both of the elders, one of whom came from Guéckédou's founding families, the other one was a former minister, accepted and (morally) supported his initiative to build this small shop. Albert showed his gratitude by regularly dropping by the two men's houses, often running errands for them, for instance copying papers somewhere in town. In return he had access to their knowledge of what he called local traditions and local knowledge. He was very keen to learn about what he called the region's past strength and also wished to be initiated into this world.

In addition to constantly establishing and investing in intergenerational rela-tions, Albert was a member of various youth associations in both Guéckédou and Conakry, thus he had also invested in relationships with peers since his secondary school days. He regularly met up with other members of these groups and organi-sed different events and activities, most of them for community development and charity purposes. In fact, one of the youth groups he was affiliated to in Guéckédou was closely linked to the Catholic Church. In Conakry, Albert was involved in a youth group that brought together youngsters from the Guéckédou area. Albert told me that the group was intended to bring together students from Guéckédou and to organise cultural events to promote Kissi culture in Conakry. During the semester break, most of his friends who were involved in this youth group met up again in Guéckédou. Thus, the youth group served as a social meeting place both in Conakry and back home.

Family-wise, Albert had many obligations and the money he earned was very important for his mother and sisters, who also contributed to their common hou-sehold. For example, one of Albert's younger sisters, Finta, saw to the children and took care of household chores. At the time of the research she also cooked corncobs

---

3   In local French tutor corresponds to *tuteur*.

and tried to sell them at the taxi rank. In addition, she left Guéckédou from time to time to help out in a relative's field. Finta left school when she was pregnant with her daughter who was two at the time of the research. The child's father took no responsibility for the child and Finta rarely talked about him. However, she did mention several times that she was dreaming of getting married officially in the near future so as to have a husband and a household of her own. In the meantime it was often Albert who helped out with the child and, for instance, took the little girl along to a vaccination programme.

From time to time, Albert left Guéckédou to go back to university. Sometimes he seemed quite happy to leave his family behind, becoming "just" a student again. He did explain to me that life in Conakry wasn't easy, particularly since his father could not support him financially and he therefore had to cover the costs on his own. But Albert was lucky, he had found a "good old Samaritan" who offered him a room without great expectations (at least that is how he told it). He attributed this good fortune to his father's blessing when he left Guéckédou for the first time to go to Conakry. So Albert came to terms with his father, who had given him no financial support when he left, by relating his good fortune in finding affordable accommodation to his blessing. In times of uncertainty he realised that although he had no financial means of his own, he would find someone to support him.

Networking

Albert was, besides being a student, constantly working and establishing social relationships. The networks to local elders at times replaced Albert's difficult relationship with his father. Thus, by establishing alternative relationships with old men (I refer to them a junior–tutor relationships), Albert tried to circumvent or replace his father by creating his own entrance into the world of Guéckédou's initiation societies or by reinforcing his income strategies. However, I argue that by attempting to create intergenerational relationships, he was also attempting to confirm his youthful status. In Conakry, for instance, the newly established relationship with the old Samaritan compensated for the lack of a father–son affiliation. In this new relationship, Albert accepted a junior position as a strategy for having a place to stay. In this way, he was able to trust in his own future despite being from a poor family. Thus, Albert simultaneously affirmed his youthfulness through the establishment of intergenerational relationships and opened up a future in which he could, finally, grow older.

Back home in Guéckédou, this strategy was not particularly successful, as his status as a young man was often challenged and he often changed his social category and with it his relationships with his father and other family members. Sometimes he took care of his sisters' children and he decided which school they should attend, for instance. He thus acted like the male head of the family and communicated accordingly. Sometimes, however, he preferred to be a son him-self in the hopes of getting some support from his father. But this switch became increasingly difficult after his father left to set up another family. Thus, the pos-sibility of switching social categories was restricted in Guéckédou, and Albert's mother and sisters often forced him to take responsibility like an adult. In his university town, however, he was still a youngster, living as a young student under the protection of an old man.

3.   Boubacar

Boubacar, a 30-year-old Pulaar-speaking Muslim, lived in a two-roomed house next to his father's home in one of Guéckédou's urban neighbourhoods. He had a room of his own; the other bedroom was shared by two of his younger brothers. Boubacar's father was born in Fouta Djallon but migrated for economic reasons to the Guéckédou borderland and started to engage in cross-border trade. Boubacar himself was born in Guéckédou and considered it his hometown. I got to know Boubacar because he was one of my host family's best friends. He ate breakfast, lunch and dinner with us almost every day. We therefore got to know each other quite well and spent a lot of time together. We also visited his extended family in Guéckédou as well as Nongoa and certain other places in the Guéckédou border-land.

Love and other challenges

When talking about his past, Boubacar emphasised how much he had loved going to school. Because of his father's health condition, however, he was soon forced to contribute to his family's livelihood and abandoned secondary education. He then started to work as a teacher at a private nursery school (*Ecole Franco-Arabe*) and started to associate with an Islamic circle established by young Muslim men. During one of our talks, Boubacar told me that around that time he fell seriously in love with a young Pulaar-speaking woman, Mariama. This was a crucial time for him and when his heart finally "got broken", he reorganised his entire life.

He got to know her at school when he was attending high school (*lycée*) and she was in middle school (*collège*). However, it took two years for their relation-ship to develop. Boubacar had already dropped out of school and was working as a teacher when he really started to take notice of Mariama. They started to meet here and there, more or less coincidentally, and got to know each other better. She then told him that she had dropped out of middle school a year previously. Her father had decided that she should leave school, primarily to help at home. Al-ready in love with the young woman, Boubacar suggested to her that he talk with her parents. He wanted to convince them that her daughter should finish middle school. At the same time he would convey his interest in Mariama and present his wish to marry her once she finished school. And so he met her family. They finally agreed that Mariama could go back to school. Boubacar got all the paperwork done, and Mariama attended classes again. However, Boubacar later realised that her parents had not agreed to his wish to marry Mariama. Soon after Mariama went back to school, her father decided to marry her off to a man living in Dakar. Mariama tried to oppose her parents, claiming that she would rather marry Boubacar. Finally she came to see him, he told me, and suggested they elope together. Boubacar, however, decided differently. Although he was bitterly disappointed in Mariama's family and felt cheated, he accepted her parents' decision. In addition, he dissociated himself from Mariama and asked her to do the same. He explained to me that he wanted to avoid rumours about a dishonourable relationship before marriage that might ruin both their reputations. Thus Boubacar decided to turn his back on Mariama, who soon after married and left Guéckédou for Senegal. He explained his decision to distance himself from Mariama with strong references to common practice within his ethnic group and religious community. Thus he felt obliged to accept and follow the norms and values of his social milieu. For him, this meant that he accepted the decisions of his parents and of the elders of his broader ethnic kin. Previously he had decided differently and fought against Mariama's parents' decision to take her out of school. Thus, back then, he had challenged the practice of taking young women out of school at around the age of fourteen. At the time, he had argued that nowadays young women should also be allowed to finish school and learn to read and write. And he had been successful: Mariama continued her schooling. But he could not imagine confronting his community with a love affair before to an official marriage – which would probably force him to leave his town and his family.

Boubacar explained that the reasons it was not possible for him to marry his beloved girlfriend were related to his economic situation, which was not good enough for Mariama's parents, who considered him to be "too young". As a schoolteacher, he only had a small salary. After he broke up with Mariama, he decided to completely change his income strategy by setting up in cross-border trade. As a result of his language skills (he learnt Krio from some Sierra Leonean friends who fled from the civil war and lived for a time in the Guéckédou borderland) and his ethnic community, he was considered capable of buying merchandise in Sierra Leone and soon earned the trust of some local economic players. At the time of the research, I witnessed some of Boubacar's first business trips; he was about to become part of a transnational business network, trading palm oil, kola nuts, coffee and other merchandise throughout the border regions of Sierra Leone, Liberia and Guinea. In addition, he had agreed to marry a young Peul woman from his neighbourhood, whom his sister had introduced him to. He had therefore started visiting the family and had saved up as much as possible for the marriage ceremony, which was due to take place in about a year's time; when the girl finished high school, he proudly explained to me.

Becoming somebody

After a difficult time related to his unhappy love story, Boubacar changed his income strategy, redefining his identity and future prospects. Instead of being a schoolteacher who worked in the neighbourhood, he became somebody who travelled abroad, did business in different countries and was embedded in a network of traders. Although this new economic activity provided only an irregular salary and economic success was dependent on various circumstances, it did provide some social advantages.

Within this network, Boubacar enjoyed new career prospects and an alternative future began to take shape. He finally accepted the woman put forward by his family and had already started to prepare for the marriage. In addition, as described above, he had recently become part of a transnational trading network with strong links to his ethnic group and religious community. He had thus found not only an alternative income strategy but also a place in society. Marriage to an appropriate woman was the next step toward becoming a respected man. To be a respectable, you need to be married, as Boubacar explained to me several times, always making strong references to his ethnic community: "In our community, if you are not married, you're a nobody. You're not considered a responsible person."[4] Obviously, he had decided not to disagree with his community but to follow their advice and had accepted the suggestion that he should marry a young woman from the neighbourhood.

All in all, Boubacar complied with the paths laid out by his ethnic and religious community and saw marriage as key to becoming a respected person. The success of a "love story", which should in terms of his worldview end in marriage, thus depends on economic status and independence. Boubacar therefore tried to establish himself in the potentially profitable and relatively flexible cross-border trading network, which nevertheless remained dependent on economic and political stability. At the same time, he maintained strong links with his ethnic community

---

4 *"Ici, chez nous, si tu es pas marié tu es pas quelqu'un. On te prend pas comme une personne responsable"*, 01.10.2010, conversation with Boubacar. The expression "ici, chez nous", complete with an explanation of how social relations or specific situations were handled or interpreted, was generally only used by members of the Peul ethnic community. They used it not only to distance themselves from other ethnic groups, but occasionally also to mark the difference to my own social background. I perceived the different members of the Peul ethnic community in my circle of friends and acquaintances as living very close to each other, and so I decided to translate the expression quoted above by "in our community".

and extended family. This social safety net was important to his youthful identity and growing up, and Boubacar perceived trade and the mobility that came with it to be key for marriage and social becoming – probably like many generations before him.

4. Fatoumatou

At the time of the research, Fatoumatou was 33 years old and lived with relatives very close to my home. We used to see each other on a daily basis and became friends over the course of my field trips.

Detouring

Fatoumatou was not originally from Guéckédou but came from a village in Haute Guinée. She was the daughter of a Peul mother, who was the third wife of a Malinké man. As a young girl, Fatoumatou was sent to live with relatives and grew up in Conakry, where she attended school and finished her education. Soon after, she married Amara. Fatoumatou explained me that she was very happy during that time, as she had a home and a husband to take care of. She was certain that her final wish – to become pregnant – would soon come true. Shortly after the wedding, however, Amara started to restrict her movements for religious reasons. He claimed that as a devout married Muslim woman, she should change her dress by covering her arms and legs and avoiding trousers and any kind of decorated outfit. In addition, she should not go to the market on her own and should return home immediately after shopping. Fatoumatou tolerated these restrictions for several months, hoping that she would soon become a mother and thus a respected wife. However, her dreams were not fulfilled and after a turbulent time of mistrust and domestic abuse, Fatoumatou decided to leave Amara and went back home to her father. For some months, she stayed in her native village back in Haute Guinée and her father allowed her to divorce Amara. Thus, her father made her "young" again; Fatoumatou was once more a "young", single woman.

   Soon after, Fatoumatou decided to leave the village to go to Kissidougou, a town not far from Guéckédou. In Kissidougou, she stayed with her brother and his family and looked for a job. After a while she had the good fortune to obtain temporary employment with an NGO, of which there were many during the war and in the post-war period. She enjoyed her time in Kissidougou and made lots of new friends. Finally, she fell in love with one of them. Their relationship had been going on for some months when Fatoumatou realised that she was pregnant. Fatoumatou told me that she was again very happy during that time, as she imagined marrying soon and having her own family. These dreams did not come true, however, as she found out that her lover was already married and was not willing to leave his family in Conakry – she was heart-broken, she told me. In addition, her brother heard about her pregnancy and was furious. He even threatened to banish her from the family. During these turbulent and emotionally difficult times, Fatoumatou lost her longed-for unborn baby. Thus, her attempt post-divorce to re-establish herself as a modern young woman with her own job and as someone free to take a boyfriend and maintain a sexual relationship outside marriage finally failed. She lost her unborn child, her boyfriend and her brother's support.

Subsequently, an invitation from another relative to come to Guéckédou came at just the right time and Fatoumatou decided to move again. Soon after, she started work as a receptionist at a local hotel. There, she established a close friendship with the other young women employed as chambermaids or in the hotel bar and restaurant. They not only spent their working hours together but also started to support each other beyond the hotel and, for instance, launched a small tontine, a savings association. In addition, Fatoumatou joined a local youth group and thus became integrated in local socio-political activities.

During the numerous conversations I had with Fatoumatou, I learnt that she was very afraid of no longer being able to find an suitable and still unmarried man around the same age. She saw her age and job as a handicap to realising her dream of starting a family. By "age" she meant her biological age and was afraid that she would soon lose her fertility. Her work situation was not really to her liking because the job had a poor reputation; for many Guineans, working in a hotel is equivalent to working as a prostitute. To compensate for this, Fatoumatou represented herself to me and other people in town as a very devout young woman. Fatoumatou rarely missed ritual prayers and claimed that her Muslim friends did not either. To broaden the scope for finding a husband she started to use the Internet. As she had free access to the World Wide Web in the hotel, she quickly learnt how to navigate the different dating platforms and created several accounts to reach different men, also beyond Guinean territory. Here too she portrayed herself as a devout Muslim and clearly stated her wish for love, marriage and a family.

Dead ends and ways out

Fatoumatou fought uncertainty by among other things chatting to and emailing various men. In "real life", however, she preferred to avoid the image of a woman who regularly switched relationships and boyfriends. Thus, the proactive search for a husband could only take place in a space that was out of reach of most of the town's habitants. In other words, Fatoumatou's room for manoeuvre was restricted by her social environment. However, her courage, creativity and cleverness allowed her to open new spaces for action. Nevertheless, her dreams for the future did not change: she was looking for love, marriage and children so as to become a respectable Muslim woman and wife.

Fatoumatou's case accordingly emphasises further aspects of how to manage growing up. She perceived her first marriage as unsustainable, especially as she had been terrorised by her husband and her wish to become pregnant had been unfulfilled. She left and moved back home to her father; he made her "young" again. A love affair and pregnancy outside a socially recognised relationship, however, complicated her social becoming after the divorce – mainly because her boyfriend did not marry her. Hence, Fatoumatou reformulated her sexual identity and her sexual practices after the divorce, but she still maintained that marriage would be her life goal. After separating from her boyfriend and losing her unborn baby she again changed towns and started life yet again in different surroundings. Here, she attempted to combine her modern lifestyle with more conservative ideas of gender relations. Living as a young woman in a small town restricted her room for manoeuvre, as the social control of unmarried women is still very strict in Guinea and she therefore expanded her search for love and for a new husband into social spaces that were not accessible for most people in town. In addition, religion became less a tool of restriction and more a means of reinforcing her image as an devout young woman, despite working in a hotel. This strategy also informed the way she represented herself on the Internet; despite the use of new technology, she sought marriage with the sole objective of becoming a respected woman in society. Echoing Johnson-Hanks' observations about Cameroon, love and romance mediated by the Internet is a recent phenomenon, but its practice is grounded in old structures of gender, honour and marriage (Johnson-Hanks, 2007: 656). The same was true of her spatial mobility. Such mobility was probably not possible in former times, but in contemporary Guinea women too are quite mobile. Thus, like young men, young women start to manage uncertainties and social mobility through spatial mobility – although usually to places where they have relatives.

5.   Meandering lives

Albert's, Boubacar's and Fatoumatou's youthful practices in the context of their life courses can be seen as related to an attempt to grow up relationally – not primarily in years but in social status. Aging, or social becoming is neither a linear nor a continuous process, however. All examples – in addition to writing about Albert, Boubacar and Fatoumatou, I also include Finta, Mariama and Amara – refer to what I would like to call "meandering lives".

The manoeuvring or managing of vital conjunctures related to failed relationships confirms the importance of marriage and the founding of a family as a so-

cial institution, particularly in the Muslim community but also in other contexts.[5]
Most youngsters I talked to actually dreamt of having an official wedding ceremony, thus becoming accepted by their communities as a married man or woman.
However, a look at gender relations also shows that gender roles are changing.
Boubacar, for instance, was trying to become a breadwinner for his future family,
as was expected of him by both his own and his future wife's family. According
to Roth, who worked on gender relations in Muslim milieus in Burkina Faso, this
indicates a more contemporary and urban way of organising the division of labour
within marriage (Roth, 1997). In former times and in more rural sites, Roth describes how both marriage partners contributed to the income of the family (Roth,
1997: 198). Nowadays, in the urban environment, the husband is often the only
breadwinner. Moreover, these husbands often try to control their wives' mobility.
Roth relates these practices to the young men's difficulties in fulfilling their role
as breadwinner and to the modified labour division between men and women in
urban settings. Women are claiming more and more room for manoeuvre, often
beyond the household and/or market, and this challenges the relationship between wife and husband. This again leads to various negotiations between marriage partners on how to live life as a couple and how to organise their work life and
income strategies (Roth, 1997: 206).

Lastly, reaching adult status means much more than just getting married and
having children. Childbirth outside an official marriage is quite common and can
also complicate a young woman's social becoming, as Finta's example suggests. In
addition, many young men cannot afford the marriage ceremonies and the expen-
se of a family, and thus may also be seen as trapped in "unmarried youthfulness".
Nevertheless, I also got to know forms of living together without being officially
married. Bintu and Benjamin, two other young people I met during my field trips,
lived with Benjamin's mother and sister in one household without being officially,
religiously or traditionally married. Each of the family members contributed to
the income and an outsider would probably have thought that Bintu was just another of Benjamin's sisters. The couple shared one room and also had a common
child, who was raised by Bintu, Benjamin's mother and his sister. Interestingly,
this way of dealing with the problem of unmarried youthfulness – cohabitation
without expensive marriage costs – was not really discussed in public and was
much more common among the Christian community. In addition, as mentioned

---

5 For further background information on marriage in Guinea, among those addressing the question of traditional marriage vs. civil marriage, cf. Koundouno-N'Diaye and Sona (2008). In general, only a few scientific contributions deal with the topic of conjugal relations in the Guinean
context.

in Finta's context, Bintu dreamed of getting married officially some time in the future.[6]

Marcelline was one of the women I met who finally got married after years of cohabitation and having given birth to two children. I got to know her as a socially well-accepted woman who had already reached adult status. I only realised that she was not married when she started to talk about the planned wedding.[7] After the Christian marriage ceremony, Marcelline proudly showed me pictures of the event and talked as if she were newly enamoured of her now husband. I realised that only a married couple had "pictures" to share and that the idea of living together was indeed very much shaped by images of marriage. At this juncture, the Christian minorities agreed with the practices and ideas of the Muslim majorities, who were generally not open to cohabitation, as I learnt from various interview partners. To conclude my argument: some young men and women I met practised alternative forms of living together but preferred to communicate only the ideal image of a marriage ceremony. Thus, the alternative is not (yet) socially accepted and lacks "pictures" to share and talk about. Nevertheless, the alternative refers to a lived reality. Thus, rather than being trapped in youthfulness or an "unimagined future" (Honwana, 2012: 29), life goes on and, as I argue, one can also grow older by following fairly meandering life trajectories.

A further common characteristic among young people in Guéckédou is the importance of religion for their social lives. Religious practices and belief systems are deeply enmeshed in their social and ethnic communities, serve as important sources of youthful identities and can also be considered extremely formative for youthful agency. I will return to this topic in Chapter IX.

Young people also greatly appreciate education while they are young. They refer to two forms of knowledge: the one they can obtain through official schools and universities and the local knowledge transmitted by their community elders. Unlike in former times when the transfer of knowledge was regulated by the secret societies, at least within the Kissi community, modern Kissi youths have to find other ways to learn what they consider "traditional knowledge". The rites of passages of former times are no longer the most important institutions for crea-

---

6 Surprisingly, I met Bintu again in 2012 in Conakry, where she had resumed her education. She had left her child and boyfriend in Guéckédou – obviously, she had changed her dreams for the future. I was very surprised as I had talked to Bintu many times but she had never mentioned her plans to go back to school.

7 Bauer describes a similar example of a couple in Ferkessédougou, Côte d'Ivoire, who had a common household with six children but had not had a civil or a church wedding (Bauer, 2005: 493f). However, the woman could convince her husband to get married officially and thus promote their social belonging to the milieu of better-off civil servants. Hence, marriage may also confirm socioeconomic status or reputation within a couple's specific milieu and is not just about reaching adult status.

ting adult men or women and consequently indicating a clear border between the generations. However, some youngsters actively look for this border when establishing new forms of tutor–junior relationships. They thus consciously try to stay young, as they cannot imagine their future as adults, mostly because of their economic situation. Spatial mobility and the changing of sites, as described, can also be used to stay young and is not necessarily linearly related to social becoming. However, spatial mobility is also strongly related to growing up – the literature often refers to young men going abroad to look for adventure and to become men (cf. for instance Semadeni and Suter [2004]). As the example of Fatoumatou shows, young women are also becoming more and more mobile for that purpose. However, Fatoumatou's mobility sometimes appeared to be more of an escape route, whereas Boubacar's cross-border migration is probably linked to a more planned trajectory.

Both the young men and women discussed here were almost constantly occupied by their attempts to earn a living. As youngsters they would accept being junior to some local bigwig or local elder, as this created an important social network that was often but not exclusively intergenerational in nature. Thus they tried to link up with some economically established actors to build their own economic foundations for future activities. However, as the example showed, establishing relations with elders may also be related to the remaking of generational borders in order to, finally, stay young for a bit longer. Fathers may deliberately reject these relations as it means responsibility for their children. Youngsters, however, may look to them to manage economic uncertainties. Albert accordingly navigated between economic independence and interdependence, as most of his income went to support not only himself but also his family. Constantly looking for the next job, he was one of the many youngsters "hustling" for work, as Munive describes the economic activities of young people outside formal employment and jobs (Munive, 2010a: 335).[8] These economic activities are often unrelated to achieving social status and are simply survival strategies for young men and women and their families; Utas appropriately talks about "survival work" (Utas, 2012c: 4).

In the Guéckédou borderland, most Kissi youths also engage in agriculture such as gardening or rice farming. This finding is therefore in contrast to other youth studies that claim that young people prefer to move to urban areas rather than become farmers, thereby breaking with the traditions of their older relatives (Eguavoen, 2010). The young people I met also felt connected to the local economic attitudes of their parents (cf. Fanthorpe and Maconachie (2010) for similar observations in Sierra Leone). Hence, being young does not automatically mean neglecting the (economic) pathways of one's parents. Albert was a student in a distant

---

8   The IMF country report for Guinea states that in 2007 more than two-thirds of the working population were "independent workers" and not working for a formal company (IMF, 2011).

Guinean coastal region but still came back during the rice harvest. He perceived agriculture and "part-time" farming as being self-evident. Although he lived close to promising economic areas such as Conakry, he loved coming home and working in a more familiar setting.

Besides intergenerational relations, most of the young men and women I met in and around Guéckédou were also involved in establishing relationships with peers, generally through various youth organisations which they called youth associations. These important arenas will be explored in further chapters; however, at this point I would like to stress their significance not only for a better understanding of being young and growing up but for grasping youthful agency vis-à-vis the youth–state nexus. Within these arenas, young people not only organise huge parts of their everyday life but also build up a voice vis-à-vis and in relation to the local everyday state (Engeler, 2016).

In summary, being young and growing up may be conceptualised as an amalgam of different social relations, continuously built and rebuilt in various arenas and in relation to different times and spaces. Youthful life histories are not about a clearly defined passage from youth to the adult world but can be best described as meandering lives. This meandering is never complete and young people continuously grow older, at times waiting, at times pushing, for vital conjunctures. Honwana and others describe the period of suspension between childhood and adulthood as "waithood" and talk about "youth in waithood" (Honwana, 2012, Masquelier, 2005): "It represents a prolonged adolescence or an involuntary delay in reaching adulthood, in which young people are unable to find employment, get married, and establish their own families" (Honwana, 2012: 4). Vigh talks about youth in similar terms and describes being young as a "social moratorium" (Vigh, 2006b: 37, also addressed in Utas (2009) and Boersch-Supan, [2012]). However, I met many rather "restless youth" (Gavin, 2007) who were not simply waiting but were actively looking to change and manage the uncertainties of their life course – at times also by purposely staying or re-becoming young. Thus, youths are probably "in waithood" but are nevertheless dynamic and are using their creativity to invent forms of being and interacting with society (Honwana, 2012: 4). In other words, instead of simply waiting, the young people I met were constantly on the move. Interestingly, although always on the go, most of the time they stayed on socially acceptable terrain: Both young men and young women actively negotiated and reformulated their economic activities, identities and sexual practices amid socio-political changes, but their ways of managing life course uncertainties and envisaging the future were reconfigured in close relation to their social community in order not to alienate themselves from the social and religious context of their origins and families. This mirrors in part what Paulme wrote in the 1960s when she spoke – in a rather romanticised style by present-day standards – of the strong affinities of the young to their Kissi community: *"Plus nombreux chaque année, les jeunes gens émigrent, poussés par un besoin croissant d'argent [...] Les émigrés restent très attachés à leur famille et à leur village ; ils en parlent avec nostalgie et songent toujours au retour, quelle que soit la supériorité des conditions matérielles à l'étranger. Jusqu'ici, très peu de Kissi ont été perdus pour leur communauté d'origine. Rentrés au village, ils reprennent leur mode de vie traditionnel : lorsqu'avec l'argent ont disparu les vêtements et les quelques objets acquis en ville, les souvenirs du monde extérieur s'effacent très vite [...] Les Kissi, en un mot, ont conservé la culture matérielle et l'organisation sociale léguées par leurs pères"* (Paulme, 1960: 76). The next chapter describes the background to the Mano River War and takes a closer look at how young people mobilised to defend their homeland between 2000 and 2001. This time was particularly significant for the Guéckédou borderland and, as I learnt not least through many youth life histories, gave rise to specific arenas which are important for understanding youthful agency vis-à-vis ongoing state formation processes.

VI. Dangerous times
In defence of the homeland

> "Guéckédou is located on the edge of Guinea's so-cal-
> led "Parrot's Beak", a diamond-rich thumb of ter-
> ritory jutting into troubled Sierra Leone. The Par-
> rot's Beak today shelters 140,000 of Guinea's total
> population of some 450,000 Liberian and Sierra
> Leonean refugees. But the proliferation of arms and
> fighters in the tri-state region where Guinea, Sierra
> Leone and Liberia meet has made the Parrot's Beak
> a very dangerous place"
> UNHCR official who visited Guéckédou in
> March 2001, quoted in Del Mundo (2001: 1).

War does not stop at national frontiers or at socio-cultural boundaries and, hence, through the circulation of arms, diamonds, militant groups and refugees, the
Guéckédou borderland became part of the Mano River War in the 1990s. Around
the turn of the century the tensions increased significantly. Between 2000 and
2001, members of both the Liberian and Sierra Leonean rebel movements started
to attack the Guéckédou borderland and the town of Guéckédou in particular. During that time, a youthful vigilante group, the *Jeunes Volontaires*, formed out of a
multilayered web of local relations to defend their homeland.

While conducting my research in Guéckédou, the aftermath of war was still
clearly visible. Many ruined houses were riddled with bullet holes and some wre-
cked tanks close to the national border testified to the fact that the borderland,
also called the "Parrot's Beak", was a contested and still "dangerous place" (Del
Mundo, 2001: 1). Besides visible effects, the conflict was also reproduced in local people's discourses and imprinted on their memories. When talking about the
rebel attacks, all of my interview partners labelled the time as "during the war"
(*pendant la guerre*) and discursively positioned themselves and the entire Guéckédou borderland in a former war zone. The urban space of Guéckédou is to this day
associated with the war and the rebel attacks. It lost most of its appeal, people
explained, and the weekly market, previously known as the largest in the entire

Guinée Forestière, never fully recovered.[1] When crossing bridges, scrubby fields or street corners, my conversation partners often spontaneously remembered escape routes, refugee camps or dead bodies. I also heard many confused stories of flight and return, of loss and recovery. Some of my interlocutors reported having seen masked and heavily armed rebels coming from Liberia and Sierra Leone. Others again spoke mainly about the dead bodies of brutally killed people that they had seen in Guéckédou's main street near the town centre and the marketplace. Often I gained the impression that these war stories took on a life of their own, constantly combining the things they had heard – for instance from refugees arriving from distant battlefields – with their own experiences. This is probably quite typical of a war-affected area where rumours are constantly intertwining with the reality of risk and the constant feelings of fear. All in all, I consider the war and its related dynamics as crucial moments for understanding local youth and state–society relations in general. Placing the violent youth project of the *Jeunes Volontaires* within the context of the Mano River War helps to further situate and understand the youth–state nexus in the Guéckédou borderland and, to some extent, other war-affected countries. For other Guinean regions, however, the following analysis might not be as important, as people living in Fouta Djallon or in Haute Guinée do not see themselves as living in a former war zone.[2] Thus, it is important to contextualise the following paragraphs as being specific to the Guéckédou borderland and to certain other regions along the Sierra Leonean and Liberian borders.

This chapter drew on a range of data sources. I conducted interviews and had more informal conversations with diverse actors and discussed what they labelled as the wartime with them. This included talking with young people, local elders and various other actors who had witnessed the events. I also talked to former members of the *Jeunes Volontaires*, listened to their memories and tried to understand their perspectives. These conversations included life history interviews and resulted in different portraits of these former fighters. These narratives are also used in the following chapter.

All of the former fighters I met were men, although people also mentioned a few female fighters. Additionally, this chapter deals with a topic I could only grasp

---

1 This downgrading of Guéckédou was also confirmed by Christian Højbjerg, who has known the city for a long time and who supported the image of a former war town that was still suffering severely from the rebel attacks, an insecure border town (personal communication, 26.09.2012).

2 While visiting different other parts of Guinea, for instance Fouta Djallon or Haute Guinée, I became very aware of the Guéckédou borderland's regional particularities. Only people who lived in one of the regions that were attacked talked like my neighbours and friends about the wartime. In addition, war-affected towns have a completely different imagery, which includes bullets holes as well as NGO signs mentioning cross-border peace-building and reconciliation projects.

empirically in retrospect and, like the gender aspect, the reader should consider this in the following paragraphs.

1.   The Mano River War

Many West African countries may be described as having experienced civil war or violent conflict in the past few of years. The destructive civil wars during the 1990s, known as the Mano River War, are particularly well known and were named after the river that forms the border between Sierra Leone and Liberia (Hoffman, 2011a; 2007).[3] Other approaches also refer to these conflicts as a new type of "forest war" across a region stretching from Zaire to the forested regions of Liberia and Sierra Leone and extending into the Guéckédou borderland (Koning, 2007, Richards, 1996; 1997). This approach indicates that the Mano River War was also about natural resources, and "insurgence movements like those in Liberia and Sierra Leone emerged in areas that contained spatially concentrated, high-value resources such as diamonds and gold" (Koning, 2007: 37). The forest itself can also be read as a resource contested by states and rebel movements (Richards, 1996).

The Guinean border regions were involved in the Mano River War from the start. Accordingly, some authors perceive Sierra Leone, Liberia and Guinea as one single conflict zone "without borders" (Marchal, 2002: 7), "orchestrated especially through the entrepreneurial abilities and ambitions of Charles Taylor" (Sawyer, 2004: 437). Taylor did indeed imagine his state building project of a "Greater Liberia" as including the Guéckédou and Kissidougou prefectures.[4] In addition, the conflict zone shares some ethno-linguistic, socio-political, ecological and economic traits, something that has been often been highlighted in the literature published in the last decade (Chauveau and Richards, 2008, Richards and Vlassenroot, 2002). One recurring general characteristic of the entire West African conflict zone is the mobilisation of civilian recruits, most of them youths. Actually, many of the scientific contributions focus on these crowds of youths – mostly male – who were caught up in the different battles as both victims and perpetrators.[5] The phenomenon of so-called child soldiers has been broadly discussed, often in relation to

---

3   The Mano River Union, consisting of Guinea, Sierra Leone and Liberia, was established in 1973. The idea was to form a customs and economic union between the member states. The Mano River subregion includes the Parrot's Beak area of Guinea, Liberia's Lofa County, and the Kano and Kailahun districts of Sierra Leone.

4   Personal communication with Mike McGovern, 26.09.2012.

5   To name just some of the influential works by different scientists: (Richards, 1996; 1997; 2005b; 2005a, Utas, 2005, Vigh, 2006a, Persson, 2012, Hoffman, 2011b, Peters, 2011).

discussions of power, powerlessness and agency.[6] Purely economic explanations for violent youthful rebellions fuelled the "greed vs. grievance" debate, explaining youthful participation in war solely as a reaction to economic hardship and related social immobility. This debate was largely initiated by Collier and Hoeffler and has been much discussed ever since (Collier and Hoeffler, 2002).[7] Many authors based their analysis in terms of a general crisis involving both African youths and so-called failed African states.[8] The formation of various rebel movements, civil militias and other armed units active in the blurred reality of in-/security providers is often perceived as a serious threat to future development. Accordingly, the media, international development actors and the academia often define young violent actors as being similar to unruly, unorganised mobs of young men (critically reflected in [Persson, 2012: 104]). Often, it is only the gun that provides any kind of new meaning for these youthful individuals (Bøås and Dunn, 2007). In the debate, generational relations are described as fragile and social cohesion as steadily disintegrating. Richards writes: "When enfeebled regimes lost their grip over remote countryside a long deferred revolt of the rural under-classes welled up, led by intransigent youth" (Richards, 2005a: 588). Thus, the Mano River War reminded scholars that weak states and young combatants and hired guns were part of the youth landscape across West Africa. Many authors argue that a generation defined by its political and economic marginalisation forms a discontented group ripe for political manipulation and recruitment by (violent) rebels; these young people seek to bring about socio-political change by violent means.[9] From this perspective, the use of violence can be read as a strategy used by young people to foster socio-political change and to turn "society's power structure upside down" (Utas, 2005: 141). Thus, the marginalised youths active within different rebel groups are often allowed "to carve out a domain of alternative careers and self-assertion in line with traditional cultural notions as well as new social values acquired in the setting of struggle" (Abbink, 2005: 14). Many of these rebellions are understood to be directed against the older generation, the political elite and the central state. Some of the engaged young people thus became new political actors, building up *"une nouvelle génération politique, qui, si elle ne rompt pas fondamentale-*

---

6 The distinction between children and youths participating in war is often blurred. However, some publications explicitly deal with child soldiers as both victims and perpetrators in the context of different African conflict zones, cf. Honwana (2006), Honwana and De Boeck (2005), Shepler (2010a), Murphy (2003), Denov (2010), or Boyden and Berry (2004).

7 Many articles could be cited, cf. Korf and Engeler (2007), Peters and Richards (2007), Reno (2007), Korf (2006), Peters (2010), Sawyer (2004).

8 For an insightful overview and critical discussion on the "failed state" debate, cf. Hagmann and Hoehne (2009).

9 Cf. Peters and Richards (1998), Peters (2011), Richards (1995; 1996; 1997), Archibald and Richards (2002), Richards and Vlassenroot (2002).

ment avec les pratiques antérieurs, est porteuse d'autres référents et d'une nouveau style politique" (Banégas and Marshall-Fratani, 2003: 7). Konate adds, speaking of the context of Côte d'Ivoire, *"entrer en rébellion, c'est prendre le parti de la violence pour faire entendre sa voix"* (Konate, 2003: 69). In this way, young people may finally even take over and/or replace the state through the rebellious projects. This perspective is often also related to the secret society and initiation argument. According to many authors, the Mano River War disrupted cycles of initiation offered by secret societies and "participation in combat – initiation into the militia – becomes the passages into manhood" (Hoffman, 2003: 303). In Sierra Leone, Hoffman writes, the general perception is that "only initiation, even into an organization the purpose of which is the exercise of violence, transforms the child into its fully human state" (Hoffman, 2003: 301).

To summarise, then, many of these contributions perceive the rebellious youth projects within the West African conflict zone and beyond as something new, as something that aims at a new political formation "beyond" the state; young people enter the political space as, for instance, "saboteurs" (Durham, 2000: 113). However, many authors also wonder whether these young rebellious saboteurs will actually be able to play a key role within the future political landscape (Cruise O'Brien, 1996: 62). Vigh, who has done research among young combatants in the context of the civil war in Guinea-Bissau, states that young people who joined and negotiated the war to become important political leaders and respected adults, reverted to being "children" – i.e. political "nobodies" – again after the conflict. Vigh calls this process a "generational re-categorization" (Vigh, 2006a: 221). Exceptions to this "re-categorization" apply mostly to young women: according to Coulter, the civil war in Sierra Leone opened up new spaces and provided women with new influence in post-war political life (Coulter, 2005: 2).

All in all, many authors understand young people engaged in the West African conflict zone to be bearers of alternative political ideas beyond the often weak and fragile nation-states. These political ideas are often directed at the ruling elite and/or at the older generation. Violence is thereby not only a means to foster socio-political change but also a way of forcing social mobility and social becoming. These youthful rebellious projects seem to have had varying success depending on the national context. In the case of Guinea-Bissau, for instance, social mobility finally rebounded.

2.   Refugees, arms, combatants, attacks

By the late 1990s, Guinea can be said to have been "surrounded by civil wars in Sierra Leone, Liberia, Guinea-Bissau and, later, Côte d'Ivoire" (Arieff, 2009: 338). Many of the jungle camps of the RUF (Revolutionary United Front) – the main rebel movement in Sierra Leone – were actually based in the Kailahun District bordering Guéckédou prefecture (Peters, 2011: 68).[10] This resulted in, among other things, the influx of thousands of refugees from Liberia and Sierra Leone into Guinean territory between 1990 and 2005 (Arieff, 2009: 338).[11] Thus, Guinée Forestière became home to large exile communities. This also gave rise to resource scarcity and environmental damage such as deforestation related to change in land use (Black and Sessay, 1997: 588f).

Yet Guinea was not only a host country but also an active participant in the Mano River War, for instance in Sierra Leone. According to the International Crisis Group, the Guinean state supplied weapons and soldiers to the ECOMOG peacekeeping contingent (ICG, 2005: 18). In particular, the Guinean state assisted rebel movements opposed to Charles Taylor, who was said to be Conté's regional nemesis (Arieff, 2009: 339). Guinée Forestière became an important hub for refugees, arms, diamonds and combatants and also hosted various armed groups from neighbouring countries, for instance the anti-Taylor rebel groups ULIMO (United Liberation Movement for Democracy) and later LURD (Liberians United for Reconciliation and Democracy) (Arieff, 2009: 340, Chambers, 2004: 143). Chambers even describes some Guinean border towns as "LURD zones" that can no longer be considered to be under the supremacy of the Guinean state (Chambers, 2004: 145). Højbjerg writes that LURD fighters – based in, among other places, Macenta – were of both Liberian and Guinean origin and often recruited from the local Mandingo communities (Højbjerg, 2010: 278). The local population, however, often feared the Guinean government soldiers positioned in the border region more than the rebels, as the former were said to be badly trained and psychologically unstable and to commit unpredictable acts of violence (Højbjerg, 2010: 278). Fairhead adds that the ULIMO/LURD combatants were based in the borderland refugee camps and therefore even benefited from the support of international humanitarian aid agencies, especially between 1996 and 2002 (Fairhead, 2010: 78).[12]

---

10 Several in-depth ethnographies concentrate on the RUF, cf. for instance the insightful contributions of Peters (2011) or Denov (2010) or the articles by Abdullah (1998), Marriage (2007) and Richards (2005b).

11 For a recent reflection on the Mano River War refugees in Guinea as catalysts of debate and critique, cf. (McGovern, 2015).

12 In this very instructive contribution, Fairhead describes political alliances and struggles in a Guinean border town and focuses especially on the effects of locating a refugee camp without any consideration of local socio-historical power relations (Fairhead, 2010). He thereby accentuates how the discourses and practices of nineteenth-century political and economic conflicts still shape the conflicts of the twentieth century (Fairhead, 2010: 75).

Gerdes describes similar conditions when discussing the phenomenon of "militarized refugee camps and settlements" in Guinée Forestière (Gerdes, 2006).[13]

It is within this context of twilight refugee camps and regional alliances with anti-Taylor rebel movements that pro-Taylor combatants finally attacked Guéckédou and other Forestière border towns several times between 2000 and 2001. In other words, the hosting of foreign rebels was a factor in a series of armed attacks on Guinean towns lasting about a year (Arieff, 2009: 340). The invaders entered the country from Liberia and Sierra Leone but several reports indicated that people known to the local population as refugees also guided the invading forces (Gerdes, 2006: 86). During that time, the Guéckédou borderland became one of the primary sites of violent clashes in the Mano River War. Furthermore, the attacks must be interpreted as a serious threat to the Guinean nation-state (McGovern, 2002: 89) and represented "the most significant destabilizing spillover from conflicts in neighboring countries during Conté's rule" (Arieff, 2009: 342). According to the International Crisis Group, the rebel offensive sought to capture the forest region (ICG, 2002) with the final aim of "toppling the Guinean government" (Arieff, 2009: 342). This reflects my earlier comment that Charles Taylor conceived of "Greater Liberia" as including Guéckédou and Kissidougou prefectures.

The time around the rebel attacks must have been a challenging experience for the local communities living in Guéckédou. The attacks created a new climate of anxiety, and many people fled into the interior, both Guineans and refugees from Sierra Leone and Liberia based in the region. Chambers even declares a *"déstabilisation progressive de la région Forestière"* that was strongly related to ethnic tensions between the *"peuples forestiers"* and the *"peuples d'origine mandingue"* (Chambers, 2004: 144). The formation of violent non-state actors such as the *Jeunes Volontaires* was, according to him, a further indication of a destabilised region with a profusion of security providers (Chambers, 2004: 144).

3.   A youthful self-defence movement: *Jeunes Volontaires*

Who were these *Jeunes Volontaires* attempting to resist the invading rebels? According to different sources, around 9000 youngsters between 13 and 25 years old, the majority of them male, became part of the *Jeunes Volontaires* self-defen-

---

13 The militarisation of the refugee camps became a matter of concern for the various humanitarian organisations after the rebel attacks, not least because of an increase in negative sentiment among the local population towards the refugees. Prior to 2001, most refugee settlements in Guinea were less than 50 km away from the national border. The UN Refugee Agency (UNHCR) subsequently decided to relocate the refugees up-country to escape the blurred borderland with its many armed factions.

ce movement, which was active in Guinée Forestière and also in the Forécariah prefecture bordering coastal Sierra Leone. About 3000 young men are mentioned in Guinée Forestière, most of them based in the border towns of N'Zérékoré, Macenta and Guéckédou (Chambers, 2004, Wrons-Passmann, 2006). Other sources, however, contain estimates of around 5000 youths in Guéckédou prefecture alone (Ouéndéno, 2007). During the rebel attacks of 2000 and 2001, these young vigilantes actively participated in the defence of their hometowns. Thus, while most of the residents left Guéckédou to seek refuge in up-country villages, these young men initiated group vigilante activities and stayed in town.

Defending the homeland

The *Jeunes Volontaires* organised roadblocks and nightly patrols to protect their family property and to patrol the war-affected borders. They therefore protected and defended national territory, whereas representatives of the Guinean state apparatus (e.g. the local prefect) left the area at least temporarily. During that time, the local youngsters organised themselves into various small units stationed around different crossroads and observation posts to protect the residents' belongings and – probably much more importantly – to remain in what they perceived as their homeland. Thus, these young vigilantes controlled public space in the war-affected border area.

Interviews and more informal conversations with Seydou, a former member of the *Jeunes Volontaires*, made clear that they started to organise themselves as young vigilantes because they felt the need to act. "After the first attacks we were obliged to protect and to react. That's how we got organised and finally took up arms."[14] They also explained that many of the rebels were very young too, so they felt especially concerned as young people. It was their obligation to fight and to protect their families and property during this dangerous and insecure time of war. They did not use any ethnic arguments, and I got the impression that individuals of various ethnic backgrounds had joined forces. However, I couldn't find any data for the different ethnic backgrounds of the *Jeunes Volontaires*, and my own examples only represented a small number of people compared to those who were active during the conflict. This makes it difficult to argue persuasively for some cross-ethnic unity within violent youth figurations of the kind Peters observed in Sierra Leone (Peters, 2007). In the case of Guéckédou, I guess that the majority of the youngsters were actually from a Kissi background, as they also represent the majority of the town's residents. However, I also met former fighters representing other Forestière ethnic groups or from a Malinké background. In addition, all of

---

14 *"Après les premiers attaques on était obligé de agir, de réagir. Comme ça on a finalement organisé et pris les armes"*, 14.12.2009, interview with Seydou, a former member of the *Jeunes Volontaires*.

the residents of Guéckédou with whom I talked and who had witnessed the war were very proud of them and spoke respectfully about the *Jeunes Volontaires* engagement, whether they were Peul, Kissi or from another ethnic community.

While talking with many different people who witnessed the war, I learnt that the *Jeunes Volontaires* was also a nexus of complex relationships closely related to local politics and the national army. Thus, various other actors became involved in recruiting, training and finally demobilising these young vigilantes. One of the crucial actors was the then lady mayor, who said herself that she had recruited the *Jeunes Volontaires* "by asking for the young and brave residents of the town to help".[15] She therefore asked the state army based in the Guéckédou borderland to collaborate with and train the young informal fighters. In the words of Seydou, "the youths from the town went to see the authorities close to the mayor to express their will to fight side by side with their brothers from the state army".[16] Wrons-Passmann adds that the elderly *chef de quartiers* also pushed youths to back up the town's defence (Wrons-Passmann, 2006: 8). In addition, the young volunteers were given protection and strength from the local council of the elders and from local elders' medicines "to become bullet-proof", as Moïce, another former *Jeunes Volontaires* told me. My interlocutors associated such medicine with initiation ceremonies and secret societies. A commonly held notion among the young was that rebel attacks would not have been possible in former times, when initiation-based Poro politics protected the area. Accordingly, they wished to be like they imagined the former times – a powerful community with strong medicines and customs that protected the *pays Kissi* from all its enemies. In one of my conversations with Moïce, he related this dream of regained traditional strength to Kissi traditions of social hierarchy: "In Kissi tradition, the arguments which support one or the other party within a conflict tend to follow the rules of social hierarchy. Thus, no matter the conflict, the child should never oppose his father or his mother or any representatives of his parents."[17] Of course, this strong commitment to gerontocracy might not correspond to reality, but in the context of the rebel attacks young people thought that this kind of social convention would protect

---

15 "*J'ai recruté les Jeunes Volontaires entre les braves jeunes de la région. Après ça, j'ai demandé à l'armée de les former*", 11.08.2010, interview with Madame le Maire, cf. Chapter IV.

16 "*Les jeunes de la ville se sont réunis et ils sont partis voir les autorités autour de Madame le Maire, exprimant leurs désir de se battre à côté de leurs frères militaires*", 13.10.2010, explications by Seydou, a former member of the *Jeunes Volontaires*.

17 "*Dans la tradition Kissi, la méthode de raisonnement qui consiste de donner raison à l'une des parties en conflits se fait selon le type de lien qui existe entre des différentes parties opposées par le conflit. C'est à dire celui ci est fait tout en considérant l'hiérarchie sociale. Par exemple, quelque soit le conflit, l'enfant ne doit jamais avoir raison sur son papa ou sur sa maman ou bien sur l'égal de se parents*", 25.09.2009, communication with Moïce, former *Jeunes Volontaires*, who also explained much about local conflict resolution and social hierarchies to me.

them. They harked back to the old institutions and the corresponding strength that flowed from the secret societies.[18]

In addition, the *Jeunes Volontaires* learnt from ex-servicemen, the so-called *anciens combattants*, who had been active in colonial times. One of these quite famous old men, Bongoui – a crossroads is named after him so many people know both the man and the place – proudly explained to me that "those who know war"[19] were also involved in the town's defence. He explained that he himself encouraged 85 *Jeunes Volontaires* and also supported the local authorities such as the major, whose father, he added, was an *ancien combattant* too. He lost eight of his young fighters in the conflict, he admitted, but all in all he was proud of his advice.

In short, the *Jeunes Volontaires* may be simultaneously described as a youth initiative, as a socially embedded movement partially promoted and claimed by local elders and authorities, and as a youth group strongly linked to the state military. Intergenerational cooperation was crucial. Thus one may describe the young vigilante group as characterised by specific constellations and social relations, rather than by frictions between different actors, generations or institutions.

Through the different narratives it became clear that there were various forms of links to the state army during the conflict. As mentioned above, the *Jeunes Volontaires* were connected to the state army and in part trained by them. This relationship appears to have been very loose at the very beginning of the rebel attacks, when the young vigilantes were mainly armed with local *fusils de chasse* and more or less self-organised. It was only after a certain length of time that the *Jeunes Volontaires* became more and more integrated into various army units and fulfilled various official tasks within them (Wrons-Passmann, 2006: 4). One may conclude that army and state officials left after the first rebel attacks but returned soon after to gradually regain their original purview – also vis-à-vis the youthful vigilantes. Finally, the Guinean air force "re-conquered" the Guéckédou border region and bombed the town to expel the attacking rebels from Guinean territory. The Guinean state thus finally reacted and mobilised its air force to extricate Guéckédou from insecurity and rebel influences. "The former commercial hub of Guéckédou was particularly affected by the fighting: rebel forces laid siege to the town, after which it was bombed by the Guinean air force to 'liberate it'" (Arieff, 2009: 344). As Arieff's inspiring paper describes, Lansana Conté's government finally managed to protect the central structures of the state from these destabili-

---

18 On the renaissance of initiation rituals and secret societies after Touré's death, cf. Højbjerg (2007). In this book, Højbjerg hints at the important fact that the different actors do not necessarily have the same script while asking for reinforcing secret societies (Højbjerg, 2007: 198).

19 *"Ceux qui connaissent la guerre ont bien aidé a défendre la ville pendant les attaques des rebelles"*, 25.08.2010, communication with Bongoui, an *ancien combattant*, a former soldier who fought for the French during colonial times in various wars in Indochina, Algeria, etc.

sing events, thereby contributing to "state strength" instead of "state decay" in the Guéckédou borderland and beyond (Arieff, 2009: 333).

A strengthened state and unfulfilled dreams

What remained after the rebel attacks was a heavily damaged city, a "ghost town" as most witnesses called Guéckédou. Various sources thereby referred to the government's and army's promises (unfulfilled, as it later transpired) to at least integrate the courageous *Jeunes Volontaires* into the official army after they had helped to get rid of the rebels. During several conversations with former members of the *Jeunes Volontaires* it became very clear that most of them did indeed expect to become regular soldiers at some stage or other. However, these dreams were never realised for most volunteers as the Guinean state refused to recruit the young fighters into the official army. This state reaction had consequences for Guéckédou. Disappointed and dissatisfied, some of the young vigilantes took part in local riots to demonstrate their frustration about not being admitted into the army. Thus the social role of the *Jeunes Volontaires* changed once again, as they staged protests to draw the nation's attention to their concerns. As they were still armed, they frightened the local communities, but most inhabitants viewed this period of revolt as justified since it was not directed at the local community but toward the "distant state" and its cheap promises. Hence, although the Guinean army finally got rid of the rebels and also resolved issues of insecurity and state weakness in Guéckédou, the narratives of various Guéckédou residents highlight the role of the *Jeunes Volontaires* in defending the town and fighting the rebels.

This revolt lasted only for a very short time and soon after the rebel attacks the young vigilantes became disorganised. Most of the ex-*Jeunes Volontaires* adapted to the more or less stable setting. In the aftermath of the violent clashes, many international development actors returned to the border region and started to focus on the "potentially violent youth" in Guéckédou. In collaboration with the local state, the community authorities and local civil society organisations, they launched a range of outreach projects and programmes for the former violent young actors. These will be discussed in more detail in Chapter VIII.

4.   Local heroes

Many interpreters ascribe young male violence and intergenerational tensions entirely to the demographic bulge in African countries: "This youthfulness of the African continent is generally perceived as an exclusively problematic phenomenon, and it must be acknowledged that many of the conflicts that exist in Africa, particularly the violent ones, are inter-generational" (Bierschenk and Spies, 2010: 7).

In the context of the Mano River War, young men were considered violent and dangerous segments of the population and were often seen as the main cause of conflicts. The case of the *Jeunes Volontaires* can be interpreted differently. This violent youth project can be read as an initiative that coordinated attempts to defend their homeland with different local authorities and generations. By doing this the young vigilantes created an arena and defined their own space in relation to the state, a process Utas and Jörgel call "military navigation", meaning strategically organised social navigation related to different actors such as politicians or members of various security forces in a wider militarised landscape (Utas and Jörgel, 2008: 490). During these processes, some of the *Jeunes Volontaires* became local heroes – unlike the prefect, for instance, who left the area when the situation became critical. Nevertheless, young people's engagement in violent conflict is not necessarily a revolt against the older generation, but also a conservative action on behalf of the existing local community. Thus, contrary to other regional settings, the violent youth project of the *Jeunes Volontaires* drew on what they perceived to be local traditions and values, instead of turning them upside down or replacing them with alternative initiation rituals in their youth group.[20]

Finally, the *Jeunes Volontaires* did not, as one might conclude, usurp or undermine the security provision and the effectiveness of the security function of the state, although in part they emerged as a self-help response to increasing insecurity and also rioted against the state in the aftermath of the attacks. We therefore have to be wary of perceiving vigilante groups, civil militias or violent juvenile movements merely as a subversive or emancipatory force. I argue instead that rather than perceiving violent juvenile movements as directed against somebody/something, it is crucial to understand to whom they might be related. The example of the *Jeunes Volontaires* demonstrates that this can include a broad set of actors. In addition, we have to consider the specific tempo-spatial dynamics and trajectories of such arenas: as with other armed groups or social movements, their structure might change only to reappear in slightly different forms (Schlichte, 2009).

During this process, the besieged and fragile Guinean state finally regained its strength and the Conté regime profited extensively from the conflicts in the neighbouring countries, "even as these conflicts spawned armed attacks on Guinean soil" (Arieff, 2009: 344). Arieff relates this to, among other things, the successful manipulation of neighbourhood instability, which allowed the central

---

20 Förster describes a similar phenomenon in Northern Côte d'Ivoire and elucidates that self-defence groups may be based on mutual solidarity (Förster, 2009). Their organisational model was quite similar "like the age sets of the poro who had defended the Senufo villages a hundred years ago" (Förster, 2009: 335).

state to draw political and economic benefits. On a local scale, the state also managed to delegate the "dirty jobs" to local youths only to return to the region with a revived state apparatus, "co-sponsored" by international aid, since the US, for instance, provided strong support for the Guinean army during that time (Arieff, 2009, Arieff and Cook, 2010). This hints at the complex relations between the diverse local and national power brokers. In the words of François, a local elder: "The Guinean army finally liberated Guéckédou, but this was only possible with the assistance of the *Jeunes Volontaires* and the elected authorities."[21] By elected authorities he meant the major and her aides. The local representative of the state, the prefect, does not figure prominently in the war stories. However, the prefect as the central state representative managed to regain strength with the help of the state army and the central state apparatus. This was also symbolised by the new prefectural building I described in Chapter IV. Finally, the local state apparatus in Guéckédou manoeuvred the difficult situation in the aftermaths of the rebel attacks quite successfully and thus had a handle on potentially dissatisfied and mutinous youths.

---

21 "*Guéckédou* était *libéré grâce à l'armée, mais seulement à cause de l'assistance des Jeunes Volontaires et des élus*", 18.08.2010, communication with François, a respected local old man who also stayed in town during the attacks. In fact, many people sent me to him for information regarding the *Jeunes Volontaires* and the rebel attacks.

VII. War-peace continuum
On the move

"Je suis initiateur, j'ai une vision et je reste toujours en mouvement",
a statement of Seydou, a former member of the Jeunes Volontaires.[1]

During the fieldwork, I generally took motorbike taxis to get around quickly in Guéckédou town and out into the surrounding area. It was usually quite easy to find one on the next street corner or at one of the small crossroads. Sometimes, only the yellowish motorbike would be in view while the taxi driver sat in a nearby pavement café taking a strong coffee or simply leant against the wall of a shed to avoid the sun or the rain. Over time I learnt to distinguish the motorbike taxi driver from the other young men hanging around the crossroads.[2] During the dry season, they generally wore a warm coat to protect themselves from the cold air while driving and a cap and, ideally, sunglasses, to prevent the dust from irritating their eyes. Usually, their entire body would be covered in a fine layer of red soil – at least when there was enough work to do. When busy, the taxi drivers barely found time to dust themselves off, particularly on market days. They also drove quite long distances between the different villages and the town, loaded with various commodities and purchases. On such days, they would spend almost the entire time on the road and it could be difficult to find one for just a short ride inside the town. During the rainy season the taxi drivers' equipment frequently included a piece of towelling, which they carried around their necks or wrists to dry the motorbike saddle after heavy showers. They managed the rain quite well by pursuing "stop-and-go" tactics: they drove during pauses in the rain and ran for cover during intense showers. The motorbikes, however, were often left out in the rain and the towel proved very useful for drying the seat.

---

1 The statement can be translated as follows: "I am an initiator with a vision and I constantly remain in motion or on the move."

2 In other Guinean towns the drivers had yellow waistcoats to avoid being confused with official drivers.

At the beginning of my time in Guéckédou I did not know that motorbike taxis did not exist before the war. Thus, this transportation system only came to the city after the rebel attacks and was, more generally, also related to the demobilisation and disarming of the region. This chapter focuses on that time and takes a closer look at what happened with the members of the *Jeunes Volontaires* who mobilised to defend their homeland and later demonstrated because they felt betrayed. How did they manage the war–peace continuum, and what about their relations with local power brokers such as the mayor?

In particular as a result of the Mano River War, the conflict-ridden Guéckédou borderland became a minor hub of humanitarian and development aid projects carried out by both national and international NGOs. These new actors, who entered the political terrain at the end of the 1990s, also launched various youth projects in the aftermath of the attacks and therefore opened up new arenas relevant for young people. These organisations play an important role in understanding the complex youth–state nexus in the Guéckédou borderland, in particular after the violent conflicts. Accordingly, this chapter looks at the non-violent youth groups related to agriculture or to the motorbike taxi business in Guéckédou, which some of the former *Jeunes Volontaires* organised in the form of the *Union des Transporteurs Taxi Moto*. Finally, the life stories of three different young men encapsulate different ways of navigating the Guéckédou borderland.

There is a huge body of literature on young people managing the war–peace continuum in the context of the Mano River War, the entire West African conflict zone and other conflict regions in and beyond Africa. The debate has been informed in particular by examples from Sierra Leone and Liberia, along with more recent contributions from Guinea-Bissau and Côte d'Ivoire. In the following sections I have no intention of including all of this literature in my own reflections but, as in the previous chapter, I do refer to some of them.

The data used for the following descriptions date back to the conversations I had with former members of the *Jeunes Volontaires*; as already mentioned, all of them were male. For the purposes of this chapter I also talked to many other actors, for instance representatives of international development agencies, whose expertise turned out to be a huge and valuable source of information. Other important informants worked for national NGOs involved in peace-building and youth development projects. During these conversations I was often faced with the problem of being seen as a potential donor – or at least as a person who could establish contact with potential donors – rather than as a mere researcher interested in everyday life in post-war Guéckédou. I kept explaining my role and over the years many of these people accepted that I was "only an anthropologist". In the course of this process, some actors from national NGOs also distanced themselves from me. Their reactions at least taught me that the local civil society organisations were very much focused on international donors. There were very few donors when I carried out my research, as many of them had reduced their engagement in recent years.[3] Thus, my positive Western appraisal of the development towards peace and stability in the Mano River Area was sometimes perceived as negative by my local interlocutors, as donors and international NGOs had predominantly left the region at the time of the research. Accordingly statements such as "development projects are not so good, we prefer humanitarian aid" confused me at the beginning of my research period; however, I soon understood that around the time of the Mano River War, when the masses of refugees called for a major humanitarian aid effort, many Guineans got jobs or profited in other ways from the "humanitarian business". Development projects with their discourses about sustainability and capacity building only "fed a few".

As indicated, I also used data I collected in the context of the motorbike union and trade unions in general in this chapter. The data collection process revealed that this arena was – at least in Guéckédou at the time of my research – not so easy to access (cf. Chapter IV). As the nationwide strikes in 2006 and 2007 showed, some of the Guinean trade unions are, at least nationally, amongst the most powerful political actors and opinion leaders. Their position under the CNDD military regime was not particularly clear and also changed over the course of Moussa Dadis Camara's presidency. Probably as a result, local members of some trade unions clearly felt uncomfortable about my asking questions, even though these questions were only related to their way of organising. So as not to complicate the situation I stopped my regular visits to them in their official offices. However, with the young members of the motorbike taxi union, I was able to visit their union office and talk to them without facing similar problems. Nevertheless I perceive them as important arenas in which in particular young men negotiate their own and their societies future trajectories.

1. Cultivating and breeding peace: *coopératives des jeunes*

In the aftermath of the war in the Guéckédou borderland, the young vigilantes – and potentially violent youths in general – became a target group for diverse peace-building projects by international humanitarian and development agencies. These projects included demobilisation and various training and schooling activities for the young ex-militia members and some other members of society.

The title of this subchapter refers to a book chapter on RUF ex-combatants' involvement in post-war agricultural projects in Sierra Leone ("cultivating peace") (Peters, 2011: 6). However, I am not arguing that one can equate the *Jeunes Volontaires* with the RUF, as the latter is a huge rebel movement and the former is,

---

3 Some of them came to an end after the establishment of the military regime in 2009.

in comparison, a rather small vigilante group organised to protect the local communities from rebel movements such as the RUF. Nevertheless, it seemed that the
post-conflict projects Peters observed in the Kenema district of Sierra Leone bear
some similarities to those I came across in the Guéckédou prefecture. Unlike Peters, however, I did not observe that the cooperatives were collectivised above and
beyond the norms of village labour cooperation or that their farming followed an
agenda they had previously launched as *Jeunes Volontaires* (Peters, 2011: 197).

One of the demobilisation projects in Guéckédou, DEMO Cooperative (*coopérative DEMO*), was launched and supported by the Guinean state, UNICEF and GTZ
(now GIZ) in 2002 and was set up for 350 former *Jeunes Volontaires* from Guéckè-
dou and Kissidougou prefectures. The objective was to demobilise and train these
young people in order to facilitate their reintegration into society (Wrons-Passmann, 2006: 3). The training included courses in computers, sewing, mechanics,
agriculture, and many more. According to Wrons-Passmann, most of the participants of the programme felt this professional training to be very valuable. But
he also mentions many negative aspects related to such projects, among other
things the non-transparent selection of participants, the relatively short period
of training, and the lack of employment possibilities after the project had ended
(Wrons-Passmann, 2006: 13). At the time of research, most of the post-war humanitarian or development aid projects were coming to an end or had already been
closed down. The aim of this chapter is therefore not to describe or evaluate these
projects but rather to look at their aftermath. It should be mentioned that I did not
deliberately look for these projects but was guided towards them by local informants and friends. This is how it came about that I got to know a group of young
people who called themselves the DEMO Cooperative. They had a small agouti
farm in Guéckédou and were thus engaged in small-scale animal breeding and
farming. When I visited their farm I found a properly maintained place with many
different cages filled with the young and mother animals. The people in charge
were visibly proud of the farm and their work and eager to show me around. One
of them explained that "they had benefited a lot from the agriculture and breeding projects launched in the aftermath of the war."[4] I suspect that this statement
was also meant as some sort of compliment to the international donors that had
sponsored the farm and whom they related to me with my white skin, despite the
fact that I had introduced myself differently. When I asked whether they hadn't
already known how to farm before the war, they said yes but those projects had
given them the initial motivation to launch their own business.

After a time I learnt about a more recently established youth group named
CAPJOAD (*Coopérative agropastoral des Jeunes démobilisés pour le développement de*

---

4   *"On a profité beaucoup des projets agriculture et* élevage", 14.12.2009, comment by one of the members of the Cooperative DEMO during the visit to their farm.

Guéckédou), which was also involved in animal breeding and farming. This group was made up of former members of the DEMO Cooperative who had left because of personal disputes. Building on their experience with the DEMO Cooperative, they decided to launch their own group and to continue their farming activities. The five members of CAPJOAD explained that it was a way to stay united, instead of every man for himself. CAPJOAD continued to work with national and international NGOs but also occasionally received funding through follow-up peace-building projects in the region. The political circumstances and the closure of most of the post-war projects in the area forced the members of this youth group to organise themselves more or less on their own. Agriculture seemed to be an activity to which many young men were attached, even beyond the group's activities. When I visited one of the CAPJOAD members at home, I learnt that he not only bred animals as part of the group but also on a more individual basis. Around his home he had various small animals such as hares, chickens and ducks, and he explained to me in detail about his plans to breed pigs as well. He also cultivated sweet potatoes on the outskirts of town. He had obtained the right to plant a small garden from a local politician who possessed large areas of land in and around the town of Guéckédou. Thus, even though the young man had no land of his own he had managed to obtain access to some through a local big man who "possessed" the land and not through customary law or through registration with an officially recognised state institution (cf. Chapter IV and V). Along with youth groups organised for agriculture I also met a group of former members of the DEMO Cooperative (and former *Jeunes Volontaires*), who had entrepreneurial ideas but instead of agriculture were trying to establish a small construction company. I got the impression that the business was not really flourishing, but they were indefatigable in their attempts to attract new business.

The aim of this chapter is not to go into further detail but to briefly describe the development and shape of these different youth groupings. I thereby argue that post-war youth groups, which were often initiated by NGO peace-building or demobilisation programmes, probably often look like mere patronage systems to possible donors. However, they are also peer networks with their very own dynamic. Sometimes they simply disappear after the development agencies leave the region but occasionally they do persist and/or turn into something different. The rural setting of the Guéckédou borderland seemed to be a breeding ground for youth cooperatives engaged in farming and small animal breeding.[5] In the words of a young man living in Guéckédou town, "I am also an agriculturalist, like my

---

5 The Condé government made a push in 2012 to revive agriculture and agro cooperatives. Future research will show the impact this will have on local youth initiatives and agriculture.

father and my mother. The soil is very important to us. I very much like working in the fields."[6]

2.   Still at the crossroads: *Union Taxi Moto*

Besides "returning to the fields", some of the ex-fighters and former *Jeunes Volontaires* also organised "on the streets": Motorbike taxis, I learnt from my local interlocutors, did not exist in Guéckédou before the war. Back then there were some taxicabs but generally people had to organise themselves without the help of a well-established urban transport system. It was the taxi drivers' youth initiative that finally brought the solution. Some of them were former members of the *Jeunes Volontaires*, others simply young people tired of not having much work in the post-war setting. Thus, after the turbulent and war-affected times at the turn of the century these young men started up a motorbike taxi business. Finally, they also organised and formalised the taxi drivers by creating a membership-based trade union called *Union des Transporteurs Taxi Moto Guéckédou* (UTTMG), hence motorbike taxi union, in 2005. At the time of my research, the key members of the union were busy distributing officially recognised licence plates and organising registration processes for the many drivers. From time to time, they also mediated between taxi drivers and their customers in cases of dispute and disagreement.

The general perception of the motorbike taxi union and the business was very positive. Some of my neighbours even went so far as to claim that before some of these youngsters had become taxi drivers the town had experienced far more crime such as robberies and thefts. Now, the former thieves, often ex-*Jeunes Volontaires*, had their own businesses and were thus busy and no longer needed to steal. And their service was, after all, very much appreciated.

The motorbike taxi union sometimes took an important intermediary position not only between customers and drivers but also vis-à-vis the local police and gendarmerie. Like other unions and associations, the motorbike union was especially concerned with the professional or employment interests of their members. As Little has described, the motorbike taxi union's main purpose was to look after the interests of its drivers (Little, 1965b: 57). Little lists the union in the context of various other professional unions and associations such as carpenters, shoemakers or traders in West Africa (Little, 1965b: 56). The leading members of the motorbike union in Guéckédou, however, also perceived themselves as a "youth organization

6 *"Moi, je suis aussi un agriculture, comme le père, comme la mère. La terre est très importante pour nous. Moi, j'aime travailler au champ"*, 25.09.2009, communication with a young graduate who was attempting to generate income from, among other things, gardening on the urban periphery.

and social movement",[7] as they were all young men looking out for and supporting each other, even beyond their work as taxi drivers. In fact, I learnt that the union included nearly all the drivers in town or approximately 150 members,[8] thus creating a very large youth network. In conclusion, one may describe this youth grouping as a new and innovative means of fostering economic progress. Interestingly, research in post-war Sierra Leone also mentions the development of motorbike unions and associations started by former combatants in 2000 (Bürge, 2011a, Bürge and Peters, 2010, Peters, 2007). As in Guinea, there were no motorbike taxis before the war. This indicates that the idea of launching such an organisation spread among young people and also crossed national boundaries – very much like former violent young actors. One of the Sierra Leonean towns in which the motorbike taxi business is now well established is, according to Peters, Koidu in eastern Sierra Leone, which is actually geographically very close to the Guéckédou borderland. Many sources in fact say that the Chinese motorbikes themselves are mainly imported (or smuggled) from Guinea (Peters, 2007: 16).[9] Hence, it was not only ideas but also the motorbikes themselves that travelled between the different towns and along related trade routes.

Although conditions in post-war Sierra Leone and post-war Guinea differ – also because different violent actors participated on very different scales – there are some similarities when one looks at the youth groups involved in the motorbike taxi business. I find it particularly interesting that these groups negotiate their business and their way of organising themselves through the classic instruments of trade unionism. Based on the examples from Sierra Leone, Peters argues that these "former fighters are laying the foundations for a new, post-war modality of solidarity based on craft unionism" (Peters, 2007: 20). In the case of Guinea, trade unions have a long history and have proved to be important political actors not just since the recent political transformation processes in 2006 and 2007 (on the particularities of the Guinean trade unions vis-à-vis other African unions, cf. [Berg and Butler, 1970]). The members of the motorbike taxi union in Guéckédou denied, however, that they had any connections to this national Guinean union movement. Nevertheless, I learnt that they were at least linked to the local branch of the trade union for long-distance drivers, the *Union et Syndicat des transporteurs routiers de Guéckédou*, whose members organise long-distance taxi traffic. After a

---

7 *"Nous sommes une organisation de jeunes, un mouvement social"*, 19.11.2009, statement taken from a group discussion with various members of the motorbike taxi union at their office in Guéckédou.

8 Various members of the motorbike taxi union mentioned this number of members on request. I suspect that this number varies and should be taken only as a rough estimate. This nevertheless represents a relatively large network.

9 In fact, many personal conversations with both Guineans and researchers working in neighbouring countries confirmed that the motorbikes were said to "come from Guinea".

number of visits to the office of this large union, I gained the impression that these trade unionists were in general very well connected among themselves and also nationally. But they did not like to be related to the more political union movement based in Conakry. As one of the motorbike taxi drivers said, "We just want to earn a living, we're not into politics."[10] Hence, they thought of these Conakry unions as being political and did not want to be linked to them. In the case of the long-distance drivers' union, I also got the feeling that they were afraid of being seen to be in contact with these political actors and very firmly denied any relations. After all, unions seem to be politically controversial, with the potential to seriously affect the local political landscape.

Finally, one may state that some of the former *Jeunes Volontaires* had successfully navigated a path through the post-war socioeconomic landscape by becoming organised in the motorbike taxi union. In part, they thus remained the "masters of the crossroads", to refer to Bürge's insightful article on motorbike riders in post-war Makeni in Sierra Leone (Bürge, 2011b). By driving around the town and its surroundings, by occupying specific crossroads and street corners, these former young militias also maintained public spaces as important negotiating arenas, "embedded in social relations between contending groups and characterized by spatio-temporal dynamics and a certain informality" (Hagmann and Péclard, 2010: 551). Thus, as during wartime, these youngsters were still occupying the crossroads, demonstrating their presence and fighting the territory. As Bürge writes, crossroads are places where people meet and where the invisible worlds condense and interfere with humans and their destinies (Bürge, 2011a). By distributing officially recognised plates and organising registration processes for their drivers, I furthermore argue that the members of the motorbike union in Guéckédou also attached themselves to the local state apparatus (e.g. the state administration and also the police). Thus they managed to hold the line: as during wartime, young people were still the masters of the crossroads and therefore continuously part of state formation processes – although the prefect came back after the conflict and the state apparatus refused to officially accept or include the former young vigilantes in the state army.

---

10 *"Nous, on veux juste gagner notre pain de vie. On est pas dans la politique"*, 19.11.2009, communication with a taxi driver member of the motorbike taxi union.

3.   Three young men's life trajectories

In the following paragraphs I depict the life courses of three young men, all of them former *Jeunes Volontaires*. I do not claim that these examples are representative, the idea is rather to indicate that they had very different, meandering life trajectories.

Still a soldier

At the time of research, Mamady was 30 years old and worked as a night watchman for a private household.[11] As this household was very close to my own, we often shared tea in the evening and would sit together in front of one house or another. While we talked about our lives – sometimes just the two of us, sometimes with other neighbours – I gradually found out about some of Mamady's past. After reaching a certain age, he had never stayed in the same town for very long he often explained. His wandering was strongly correlated to developments within the war-affected region and the course of the Mano River conflicts. Mamady had crossed different battlefields – both his personal ones and the ones related to the civil war. His life trajectory had thereby taken many loops – not only geographically but also regarding his personal social becoming.

The challenges started when Mamady turned 16. Around that time, he made his girlfriend pregnant and nine months later became the father of a baby girl. After family disputes and economic difficulties, he left Guéckédou in 1996 and went to Sierra Leone for a few years. He never told me what he did while staying in the bordering country, but he explained that he returned from Sierra Leone to Guéckédou in 1999 and soon after became part of the *Jeunes Volontaires*. Like many others, he dreamed of becoming a regular soldier in the Guinean army, not least because of his commitment to defending the nation against foreign rebels.

However, this dream did not come true and at the same time his plan to marry his former girlfriend did not succeed either: her father refused to allow the marriage, claiming that Mamady had lost his way whilst in Sierra Leone and accused him of being violent and a drug addict. The relationship broke down and the young woman left town to marry another man. Disappointed and confronted with serious financial problems, in early 2004 Mamady decided to leave Guéckédou and go to Conakry. There he worked on several building sites and got to know another girl. She fell pregnant as well and Mamady became father to a baby girl for a second time. Soon after that, however, he broke off with the woman and

---

11 I gathered Mamady's life history over many different conversations. As we were neighbours I talked to him nearly every day while I was in Guéckédou, and I thus have many records and transcripts from 2009 to 2010.

left Conakry and his daughter for Kissidougou. He had a distant relative who was a high-ranking military man based in Kissidougou, and Mamady hoped that his cousin could help him to become part of the army too. Arriving in Kissidougou, he fell in love with another woman and became a father for a third time, this time to a boy. However, the child was seriously ill and only survived for a few months. After the baby's death, the young couple's relationship became difficult. Subsequently, the recruitment did not materialise and Mamady's financial difficulties became quite serious.

Finally, a better-off relative of his girlfriend got him the job as a night watchman in Guéckédou. Mamady decided to take this opportunity and started working in Guéckédou in early 2009. The salary he earned, however, was always split into two parts: one part for his girlfriend in Kissidougou, the other for himself. Mamady was very dissatisfied with the situation as he was breaking up with his girlfriend and his half of the pay hardly allowed him to survive. However, he did not have another job opportunity and thus continued to work as night watchman. During the daytime he exercised a lot and still dreamed of someday becoming a regular soldier. He believed that the omens were favourable: Guinea had a military regime, so he thought that the national army would soon need a lot of new soldiers. He also communicated his wish to become a regular soldier through everyday habits such as saluting instead of greeting civilians normally. This was how he continuously tried to maintain, strengthen and demonstrate his identity as a modern warrior who was ready to take up arms and fight.

An initiator on the move

Seydou was also a member of the *Jeunes Volontaires* in Guéckédou[12] and was 32 years old at the time of the research. Unlike Mamady, Seydou had never left the region but remained in Guéckédou and stayed in touch with his former comrades-in-arms. He and some of his friends became especially involved in various youth group activities, most of them funded by international NGOs. Thus, Seydou successfully entered the world of the various community development projects launched by international development agencies. He figured as a prominent representative of the "ex-*Jeunes Volontaires*", who were now organised into new groups, and he was well accepted by the local community. Seydou once also featured as the president of the DEMO Cooperative. At the time of research, Seydou was busy founding another youth group and at the same time trying to establish a small construction company.

---

12 I got to know Seydou back in 2008 on a brief visit to Guéckédou in the context of my preliminary field trip. Thus, the first more formal interviews were conducted in 2008. In 2009 and 2010, the conversations took on a more informal character and I visited Seydou several times at his home.

Seydou described himself as an "initiator with a vision" who constantly tried "to be in motion", because "if you're not in motion, if you just sit around and have too much time, you will start to engage in politics, in violence. You will try to get something, even by violent means."[13] This was an indirect reference to his own past. He was part of the *Jeunes Volontaires* who had rioted when they realised that they had not been accepted as regular soldiers by the state. Seydou always emphasised that "they shot but did not kill anybody" during this uprising.[14] I accordingly got the impression that he regretted this short period when former *Jeunes Volontaires* used violent means for personal purposes.

During my research, Seydou started a family and had recently become the father of twins. He was especially concerned about the fragile political situation and hoped for stability, which he considered necessary for the economic growth of both his own business ideas and the nation as a whole. When asked about his dreams for the future, he mentioned the well-being of his children first and foremost and less his own personal fortunes. Unlike Mamady, who still dreamt of becoming a soldier again, Seydou now had another perspective. He was benefiting from the post-war setting by forging links to different humanitarian – and later development – aid programmes and projects.

Although at the time of my research Seydou was struggling financially, he still perceived himself as being "on the move". His dreams for the future took shape as part of his social becoming, however, so he seemed to have arrived in the adult world. Mamady by contrast refused to accept that he could not become a professional soldier and somehow kept going round in circles. He was still acting like a soldier but remained trapped in an imaginary reality. Although he was growing up, and therefore becoming more and more unattractive as a recruit for the national army, he remained young in social terms. All of his attempts to create a family had ended in serious problems with his own and the women's relatives. His children did not become his "true descendants", so to speak, but remained with the women's families. In addition, he was trapped in economic obligations and dependencies, and had no idea how he should overcome this situation and become a soldier.

---

13 *"Je suis initiateur, j'ai une vision et je reste toujours en mouvement. Si tu t'assoies, si tu as trop de temps, tu vas te mettre dans la politique, dans la violence – tu va chercher à avoir quelque chose, soit d'une façon violente"*, 01.10.2009, communication with Seydou, former member of the *Jeunes Volontaires* and member of diverse youth groups.

14 *"On a tiré mais pas tué"*, 19.01.2008, communication with Seydou, a former member of the *Jeunes Volontaires*.

A driver of the everyday

Different again was Moïce's situation. He was also a former *Jeunes Volontaires*[15] and, like Mamady and Seydou, he had joined the civil defence force in 2000 and now found himself struggling for money in post-conflict Guéckédou. Unlike the other two examples, however, Moïce explained to me that he had never thought of joining the army. Instead, he got the chance to become a motorbike taxi driver and was a founding member of the previously mentioned motorbike taxi union UTTMG (*Union des Transporteurs Taxi Moto Guéckédou*). He also took part in a few "post-conflict" training courses provided by local NGOs and sponsored by international aid agencies. For instance, he became involved in some agricultural training. However, at the time of research he was working mainly as a taxi driver. As a well-liked driver he earned a small but more or less stable income and managed his own household with his girlfriend and recently born child. All in all, he did not talk much about his war experiences but preferred to talk about his present-day activities as a taxi driver, his dreams of having his very own motorbike and his wish to raise at least two children. He was not particularly interested in the activities of the diverse youth groups but preferred watching soccer games in his free time. As he was the owner of a small generator and a TV, his home frequently turned into a small cinema that hosted many of his neighbours.

Born into one of Guéckédou's founding families, Moïce was well accepted in his neighbourhood and also supported by his extended family; one of his uncles was the owner of the motorbike he drove. I also found out that he helped out in the family's fields from time to time, growing extra vegetables that provided relief from some of the daily expenses. Moïce seemed to manage his everyday life quite well.

Generally, the three different life trajectories hint at many features of being young men in a contested borderland. While some of the former *Jeunes Volontaires* had reached adulthood in the meantime, others were struggling to overcome the past and remain fairly trapped in a more youthful way of life. The community did not trust every former fighter, and those who continued to flaunt their identity as modern warriors had particular trouble navigating this environment. Others, however, have profited from every opportunity that has come their way in the donor-sponsored post-war period and continuously build on their youthful creativity to generate an income and to actively shape their own and their children's future.

---

15   I got to know Moïce while I was looking for motorbike taxis in Guéckédou. He soon became one of my favourite drivers and I used to travel with him a lot. Only later, when I became interested in the motorbike taxi union, did I find out that during the war he had been part of the *Jeunes Volontaires*.

4.   Managing the war-peace continuum

In the context of the West African conflict zone, youths have often become syno-
nymous with ex-combatants (Munive, 2010c). Both the state and the international
community especially point at the youth bulge as a cause of conflict and this is
critically reflected by McGovern: "To say that most combatants in a conflict are
young men is a banality, and to assert that where there are more young men there
will be more violence is contradicted by many cases where youth bulge demographics do not result in mass violence of warfare" (McGovern, 2011: 201). However,
according to many interpretations, the "youth bulge" becomes a "youth crisis" and
has to be addressed, otherwise violent clashes could well be the outcome. As a
strategy, various state projects – often sponsored by international development
agencies – try to involve youths in work, mostly for security reasons and to rebuild
the state peacefully (Munive, 2010c: 200). However, through different demobilising programmes, the state and international aid agencies were also "making
combatants" as non-fighting youths tried to benefit from the donors' programmes
as well (Munive, 2010b; 2010c).

As this chapter has described, being a former young warrior was a challenge.
The example of Mamady shows how he was stigmatised by his community and
remained "young" as a former member of a vigilante or rebel group. Nevertheless, he continued to dream of becoming a soldier, of regaining strength and ac-
ceptance as an armed man – probably referring to what Bøås explains as the gun
providing new meaning for the youthful self (Bøås and Dunn, 2007). However,
some *Jeunes Volontaires* had managed to enter new arenas and thus were still at the
crossroads and on the move. That indicates that the war–peace continuum was
managed in very different ways. Peace-building and demobilisation programmes
by humanitarian and development aid agencies may be described as influential effects that imprinted specific discourses and aims on many post-war youth
groups. Start-up financing for farming activities fell on fertile ground, although
I never heard of any initiative based on the computer skills that youths had learnt during these projects. In general, I would like to end this chapter with the
statement that managing the war–peace continuum and "being young in a (former) war zone" is challenging but it also opens up opportunities for new arenas of
youthful socio-political projects and various forms of participation.

VIII. Entrepreneurial spirit
Associational life

> "D'abord, c'est toi. Il faut avoir une source
> d'inspiration",
> extract from a discussion with two members
> of a youth association.[1]

Besides cooperatives or unions I encountered many young people who were organised into what they labelled as "youth associations".[2] Most of these youth associations had been launched in the past few years. However, I also got the impression
that the landscape of youth associations was constantly under construction; thus
some associations disappeared while I was on site during fieldwork, others newly
emerged. I even had the impression that some of the associations (re-)appeared
simply because I asked after them. Moreover, most young people were not just
members of one or the other association but very often juggled different mem-
berships at the same time. Many of them were students or recent graduates and
through their associative commitment became involved in community development projects – mostly under the auspices of some local or international NGOs;
thus, like the youth groups described in relation to agriculture or unionism, youth
associations in the war-affected Guéckédou borderland received a boost from
international actors and related funding possibilities. Accordingly, the wartime
and subsequent socio-political transitions must be seen as formative for youth
associations as well. However, this chapter is not only devoted to this relatedness
but notably hints at the fact that youths' practices quickly adopt, transform and
reappear in manifold projects related to different institutions, actors, or ideas.
Moreover, what seems "new" at first sight might actually be closely related to past
practices and, conversely, apparently old approaches may include quite new ideas
and political thinking. I was made aware of that while following a couple of youth

---

1 The statement says that everything starts with your own motivation and inspiration.

2 Elements of this chapter appeared in 'Being young in the Guinée Forestière. Members of youth
   associations as political entrepreneurs.' *Stichproben. Wiener Zeitschrift für kritische Afrikastudien*
   vol. 16, issue 30 (2016): 63-86.

associations active in Guéckédou town. Most of the members sooner or later had the intention to register their association at the DPJ – the prefectural youth department that had its office within the walls of the Maison des Jeunes. Thus, present-day youths met at that very same place in which, during the First Republic, revolutionary youth groups had met, which stimulated my reflections on youth associations. Moreover, researching their encounters with the DPJ, hence researching the interactions between youthful clients and "the state at work" (Bierschenk, 2010), provided me with further insights to grasp the youth–state nexus in the Guéckédou borderland. Finally, I argue that we can describe young members of associations as political entrepreneurs, as they combine political participation with income-generating entrepreneurial ideas (also elaborated in Engeler [2016]).

This chapter is broadly informed by data I collected in the context of diverse youth associations and related actors and institutions. To gain further insight into youth–state relations I also collected data in and around the Maison des Jeunes in Guéckédou town centre. Thus, I carried out interviews with the various civil servants working for the DPJ and also visited the mayor's offices and other institutions based in the building. In addition, I not only went there by appointment but also dropped by on an almost daily basis. Thus, I also had many fairly informal discussions about public service delivery, the management of the Maison des Jeunes and registration processes for youth associations. However, it took me some time to realise that the public service was not merely fuzzy and dysfunctional but actually followed particular political imaginations and mindsets that are informed by both present-day politics and past state building efforts.

1.   Youth associations

During my research, several youth associations were active in urban Guéckédou and I ended up following six of them. These included the Association des Jeunes de Tékoulo (AJT), founded in Tékoulo, a sub-prefecture of Guéckédou, but which was also active in Guéckédou, the Associations des Jeunes Artistes de Guéckédou (AJAG), the Jeunes Patriots[3], the Club des Enfants, the Club des Jeunes and, finally, the Guides des Jeunes de Guéckédou (GJG). All six associations were, as I have said, based in Guéckédou town, but some of them maintained relations with rural areas. In addition, their activities can all be subsumed under "community development". Thus they engaged, or at least planned to engage, in cleaning and fixing roads, campaigning for health education and good governance, and promoting vulnerable

---

3   They did not relate themselves to the Ivorian movement of the Jeunes Patriotes described by Koné (2011).

children and youth in schooling issues. Their fields of activities also included the organisation of entertainment like concerts or dancing parties.

In order to focus on some of the important aspects of young people who organise and meet in youth associations, in the following section I write about the *Association des Jeunes the Guéckédou*, abbreviated to AJG. Thus, I anonymise the context by creating a fictive group and name. However, the example feeds on data I collected in the context of the six associations I followed at the time of research.

Firstly I take a short look at the scientific reception of youth associations.

Groups of people with a common purpose

Associations – generally understood as groups of people with a common purpose or interest – occur in various African countries and were present during pre-colonial and colonial times. Scientists are interested in social change implemented by the colonial authorities, especially contextualised associations (not only, but also youth associations) in West Africa with regard to urbanisation processes, migration from rural to urban centres, educational reforms, and the division of labour. Wallerstein for instance argued in the 1970s that these processes resulted in the growth of "a new form of social organization, the voluntary association, which is different in function and structure from the associations found in tribal societies" (Wallerstein, 1970: 319). In his analysis, these associations should help people to orient and organise themselves in the new urban centres of colonial Africa. Wallerstein explained associations by comparing them to the pre-colonial associative groupings, which were merely functional divisions of the different communities and whose members did not in principle choose to join. Instead, they were assigned a certain social role in a specific association (Wallerstein, 1970: 318). Accordingly, he named the new social organisations of the colonial period *voluntary* associations, as membership is attained due to personal choice and not by force (Wallerstein, 1970: 319, for a similar comment, cf. Little [1965b: 2]). Another author who discusses associations in the context of colonial West Africa is Meillassoux. Associations, he writes, offered townspeople in the growing urban centres – in his case Bamako – a context in which traditional village values, based on family ties and seniority, could be reconciled with the Western emphasis on money and education (Meillassoux, 1968: 77). Little described very similar processes in the context of rural–urban relations and the role of associations in the newly established cities of colonial West Africa (Little, 1965b). Little pointed especially to the importance of interactions between the actors within these social groupings and also described the emergence of such associations as a reaction to social change and transformation in the context of urbanisation processes in colonial Africa (Little, 1965b). He further claimed that voluntary associations can act as political pressure groups and actors of social change and, as Little emphasised, serve as an

important means for young people "to include achieved as well as ascribed forms
of status" (Little, 1965b: 117).

More recent elaborations on colonial youth associations, these too in the context of colonial Guinea, are discussed in the rich readers edited by D'Almeida-Topor and co-authors (D'Almeida-Topor et al., 1992a, D'Almeida-Topor et al., 1992b).
Goerg, who writes on the Guinean context, thereby states that the colonial state
sponsored youth associations but often also supervised their activities and even
controlled their members (Goerg, 1992: 23). Hence, the colonial authorities were
well aware of the political power of these groups, which Meillassoux describes as
excellent recruitment pools for the newly established political parties (Meillassoux, 1968: 69). Also in Guinea, the struggle for independence built on the various
associations, and organised young people were an important driving force in these political transformation processes (Schmidt, 2005, Goerg, 1989).

All in all, the socio-political transformation processes on the ground led to
different scientific emphases. Older contributions by social scientists, which addressed colonial times and their related social change, primarily discussed issues
of urbanisation and migration. Newer perspectives, influenced by independence
movements and the like, concentrated on the political power of associations, most
often in the context of the newly established political parties and state institutions. More recent publications on youth associations in African studies still tackle
topics like urbanity, migration and/or politics. Utas, for instance, describes such
youth associations in the context of urban youth in Sierra Leone and calls them
"social clubs" (Utas, 2012c). He includes associations of car washers as well as mo-
ney-saving associations. In addition, he points out that what matters is not so
much the differentiation among different sub-groups but that these social clubs
are more than anything else forms of social security arrangements that fill the
voids in the Sierra Leonean state. "If you get ill, the social club will assist you, and
if you get arrested by the police [...] they will do the same thing" (Utas, 2012c: 3).
Most authors also agree that membership of such social clubs or youth associations can generally be described as highly political (Honwana, 2012, Lentz, 1995;
1999). Lentz argues that youth associations in Ghana offer an important forum for
political participation and discussion (Lentz, 1995). In addition, she hints at the
important aspect of regional identities when she writes that being a member or
being able to join an association is often linked to a particular territory or ethnic
affiliation (Lentz, 1995: 395).

An example: *Association des Jeunes de Guéckédou*

The AJG was founded in 2008 and had 30 members. I participated several times
in their weekly reunions, which were usually held at the office of a local NGO that
allowed them to use their premises on Saturdays, and I thus got to know fifteen

active members, most of them male. In fact, only three of the active members were female and none of them held a leading position. However, the president of the group, Richard, complained a great deal about this. Almost all of the AJG members were born in the Guéckédou borderland, meaning either in the town of Guéckédou or in villages of the sub-prefectures, and were of Kissi origin. Most of the followers attended higher education institutions. Some of them were students and a few were recent graduates. Therefore, most of them had studied in distant towns but came back during semester breaks or when they had finished university. In Guéckédou they were (re-)united with their friends of about the same age and often described themselves as all being "intellectuals" – because of their education – and "sons and daughters of Guéckédou" – because of their regional affiliation. Moreover, they described themselves as youths and identified with this social status not least as a political strategy.

Of those who had already finished university, only two were able to find employment, one with an NGO branch and one in the state administration. All the others, including the students, organised themselves without any regular source of income. Thus, in addition to their studies and their commitments to youth associations they were busy with different collateral activities: the young men for instance worked as motorbike taxi drivers or were involved in small businesses such as DVD rental stores and worked seasonally in the local rice fields. The young women tried to obtain a traineeship at one of the local branches of national or international NGOs, financial institutions or the state administration and, depending on their family situation, kept house and worked in the fields and gardens on the urban periphery.

All in all both young men and women can be described as highly creative improvisers busy with various – ideally income-generating – activities. Jones (2010) and Jeffrey and Dyson (2013) appropriately describe this as "zigzag capitalism": "Young people feel they have to constantly move about, hustle and find novel lines of approach to get things done" (Jeffrey and Dyson, 2013: R2).[4]

Asked about what inspired them to form an association, two of the founding members, Richard and Charles, told me: "First, it is about you. You need to have a source of inspiration. If your idea is good, your friends will support and follow you."[5] Interestingly, another member, Alphonse, stressed outside influences like information from an NGO as their motivation for finally creating a youth association: "You know, we once got a journal distributed by the NGO Plan. The journal

---

4 For recent overviews on the growing body of literature regarding youth employment in the South, in particular in sub-Saharan Africa, cf. Gough et al., (2013), Langevang and Gough (2012) or the recent issue of the Africa Development Series, cf. Filmer and Fox (2014).

5 „D'abord, c'est toi. Il faut avoir une source d'inspiration. Si ton idée, c'est bon, les amis vont te supporter, ils vont te suivre", 01.12.2009, communication with two members of a youth association.

is called *Planète Jeunes*. It portrayed a youth association in Senegal. So we thought, we want to have a youth association too."[6] The members of the AJG finally stated two good reasons for being part of a youth association. Firstly, they explained that by launching and being part of a youth association they created an additional working environment for themselves; secondly, they saw their work within the association as making a contribution to the country's development. They linked both arguments to the state, as most of them saw the state as the main employer and as an important development actor. But as the state could not fulfil both expectations, they got together to foster development and at the same time created jobs – and ideally an income – for themselves. Anne told me accordingly: "After finishing university you should look for employment, you should make a traineeship. As we know, the state is the largest employer. The state hires a lot of people. However, our country has problems hiring everybody at state level. But as young people, you cannot sit back and do nothing. You have to get together with others, you have to affiliate and unite with others, you have to create an association that helps the state in its process for development."[7] On another occasion, Charles told me: "You know, we the young, we are the motor of this country's progress and development."[8]

2.   Participating in development and creating local networks

The diverse activities usually initiated by youth associations – also by the AJG – broadly followed a specific idea of "development". The activities were for instance related to the education of "underprivileged" or "vulnerable" parts of society, including young children from rural areas and illiterate mothers. Other projects especially addressed "peace-building", "reproductive health" and "good governance". The organisation and implementation of small-scale events around these topics were usually co-financed by external funds. One example was a play for local school children performed by the AJG. The play indirectly informed the children

---

6   *"Tu sais, un jour, Plan nous a donné un journal, 'Planète Jeunes'. Là, on a parlé d'une association de jeunes au Sénégal. Donc, nous, on pensait que nous aussi on veux avoir une association"*, 05.12.2009, communication with a member of a youth association.

7   *"Après avoir terminé les études, tu dois chercher de l'emploi, tu dois faire des stages. Nous savons que l'Etat, l'Etat c'est le plus grand employeur. Il emploie beaucoup de personnes, l'Etat. Mais dans notre pays, il y a des difficultés au niveau de l'Etat pour employer tout le monde. Alors nous en tant que jeunes, on peut pas rester bras croisés. Il faut qu'on soit ensemble, qu'on se réunit pour mettre en place une association qui va aider l'Etat dans son processus de développement"*, 14.09.2010, communication with a member of a youth association.

8   *"Tu sais, nous, les jeunes, nous sommes le moteur du progrès et du développement dans ce pays"*, 06.09.2010, communication with a member of a youth association.

about the dangers of unprotected sexual intercourse and was organised on World AIDS Day. The event, which took place at the community hall in the *Maison des Jeunes*, was supported and financed by a branch of MSF. In fact, many of the youth associations regularly applied for such external funding. Accordingly, their project ideas and their language fell into line with these organisations' discourses on "good governance" or "reproductive health". In other words, the youth associations' discourses, planned activities and projects were closely related to the language, ideas and imagery of NGOs and international donors. This was not only visible in the youth associations' projects but also in their way of representing themselves. Most of them tried to project images of their group, either through flyers, signboards or handwritten posters in their homes or on printed t-shirts. Thus, like the local branches of NGOs or international development agencies, which often displayed their names on their headquarters and offices, cars and clothing, the youth groups tried to become visible in the public space of Guéckédou through specific activities and also with logos, group names and emblems.

Green very fittingly labels such groups "development agents in waiting", as they occupy a position close to development relations (Green, 2012: 310). Thus, most of these youth groups' everyday practices were oriented to preparing to be included in development.

However, the AJG's activities and planned events often spoke an additional, more "local" language. On the one hand, many of the associations never gained access to donor funds and relied first and foremost on their own financial means. On the other hand, the fact that the associations did not just take part in a sponsored event but also participated as youth representatives in a prefectural day to support peace-building gave these youth associations a popular platform. I thereby argue that by planning and participating in such events, these young people gradually built up a network of diverse actors. It is not only international donors that are important here but also actors and institutions with local roots with whom the members of the youth association could connect to. Although usually claiming being "apolitical" (which for most youth associations meant having no relations to political parties) such events gave them a chance to actively participate in various discussions on a specific topic as well as to become part of local networks of decision-makers. I therefore claim that the reason they met was very often far less important than the opportunity it gave them to meet and connect with local institutions and power brokers. Seen in the light of this interpretation, the fact that many project schedules and planned activities of youth associations peter out also makes sense. Hence, the planning phase of youth associations, with regular meetings, already connect young people to each other – sometimes also beyond their ethnic group – as well as to other local institutions and actors. In other words, the launching of a youth association with regular meetings already creates important networks and connections without necessarily having many concrete results.

The launching of a cultural week can also be read as an attempt to foster local culture and folklore. Thus, in the context of a fading military regime and upcoming presidential elections, the reorientation towards what they considered their local values and traditions seemed to be important to the youth associations. In view of the fact that most members of the youth associations were from a Kissi background, one may state that these associations provided a somewhat exclusive form of participation, although people from other ethnic backgrounds were in theory welcome.

3. Interacting with the state at work

At the time of the research, the head of the DPJ's spacious office was equipped with wooden tables and chairs and decorated with large posters, one of them showing a portrait of Capitain Moussa Dadis Camara, the then president of Guinea with the caption "Candidate of the People" (*Candidat du People*). The man sitting at the table, Jean-Paul Maoumou, was a civil servant of about 50, who was born in the Guéckédou borderland. He started his public service career in 1993 when Lansana Conté was still in office. However, he clearly remembered Sékou Touré's socialist state and was a JRDA member when he was young. He described the JRDA as very close to the one-party state: "The JRDA was a political organism, it was itself the state."[9] He thus discursively positioned himself as having been very close to the state even as a teenager. In addition, he may be described as being part of the historical and political generation of most of the local power brokers, as I described in previous chapters. His more recent period of service, however, started in Yomou prefecture and later continued in N'Zérékoré prefecture before he was appointed director of the DPJ in Guéckédou in 2009. He emphasised that he had always lived in the forest region but only recently had started working for the DPJ in Guéckédou.

When asked about his efforts on behalf of the local youth and his duties as head of the DPJ, he repeatedly used the French expression *encadrement/encadrer*, which can be translated as guiding, but also as framing and embedding. "On behalf of my department I am busy guiding and framing young people's socio-political activities, because you have to care for the young, you have to frame them so that they can think in the right way."[10] Hence, he perceived the ideas of guiding

9 *"Cette JRDA, c'était un organisme politique, c'était elle-même l'Etat"*, 20.09.2010, interview with Mr Moumou, the head of the DPJ. He was often simply referred to as "DPJ", as the local people used to call him.

10 *"Au nom de mon département je m'occupe de l'encadrement de jeunes et de leurs activités socio-*étatiques. *Parce qu'ils faut s'occuper des jeunes, il faut les mettre dans un cadre qui puisse les permettre de réfléchir dans le bon sens"*, 21.09.2009, interview with the head of the DPJ).

and "framing" youths and their diverse activities as the DPJ's key task and main service. By "socio-political activities" he was mainly referring to the local youth associations in town and demonstrated that he perceived the department's main responsibility to be formalising, registering and supervising the different youth groups. By formalising and registering he meant legalising the youth association, which was finally done through their recognition and authorisation by the prefect. By supervising he referred to the need to check the groups' internal structure and to see whether they were democratically organised, meaning that they were based on by-laws that stipulated regular elections and the division of tasks. He conceptualised these guiding processes also as a chance for youth associations to come into contact with international donors, who sometimes came to the DPJ to ask for local youth initiatives that they might support.

The head of the DPJ was very aware that he himself could not offer much in terms of funding for youth initiatives. He explained away this low level of service provision for young people mainly by referring to the difficult political situation and the lack of financial means. He perceived this situation as very difficult: "It is not easy; we still do not know what kind of opportunities we can offer when young people visit us."[11]

The head of the DPJ also argued for the need to revise and re-establish the national youth policies introduced in the 1990s: "This new youth policy should guide the young, should guide and assist them towards a better, peaceful future."[12] To substantiate this idea he recalled attending a workshop organised by international agencies such as UNDP and UNICEF in 2008, where he learnt about the importance of youth-centred peace-building activities. Accordingly, he imagined the *Maison des Jeunes* as a future facility to care for youths, fostering peaceful dialogue between the generations and within society: "Once the *Maison des Jeunes* becomes a drop-in centre for youth, they will learn a lot, including democratic living, for instance through joining an association. Thus, through the *Maison des Jeunes* we can inform young people, we can orient them and, finally, we can mobilise them and introduce them into socioeconomic and professional life."[13]

---

11 *"C'est pas facile, jusqu'à présent nous savons pas [les fonctionnaires travaillant pour le DPJ], quelle est l'opportunité qu'on peut les offrir s'ils [les jeunes] viennent vers nous"*, 20.09.2010, interview with the head of the DPJ.

12 *" [...] je pense qu'il faut mettre en place une politique de la jeunesse qui encadre les jeunes, qui les oriente, qui les intègre dans la vie socio-économique et politique"*, 20.09.2010, interview with the head of the AJC.

13 *"La maison des jeunes en temps que center d'accueil des jeunes doit permettre à ces jeunes là d'apprendre beaucoup des choses, d'apprendre la vie démocratique, par exemple dans une association. Ça doit permettre de les informer, ça doit permettre de les orienter, et ça doit permettre de les mobiliser, de les instruire dans les domaines socio-économique et professionnel"*, 20.09.2010, interview with the head of the DPJ.

Youthful clients

The DPJ and its affiliated institutions inside and outside the *Maison des Jeunes* provided few public services and were generally perceived as being part of a vast and mazy state bureaucracy with little output. Accordingly, young people could think of very few, if any, services delivered by the DPJ. "It exists only in name,"[14] one youngster put it in a nutshell. Young people referred to possible corruption and unnecessary time-wasting when visiting branch offices such as the DPJ. Furthermore, most of the youths I talked to displayed a general mistrust of civil servants, attributing this to the advanced age of the civil servants and their long terms of service. Some of my young interlocutors also explained that the civil servants' way of communicating was difficult to understand and generally misleading, which recalls Weber's concept of the office secret (Weber, 2006: 64). However, some of the youth groups did nevertheless register and worked together with state institutions. Thus, some of the youth associations presented themselves and their group to the DPJ and actively entered this negotiating arena. When they were asked why, they argued that the head of the DPJ might possibly communicate with or pass on their contacts to international donors. In the words of Charles, vice-president of the AJG: "The DPJ registers youth groups. Thus, if you have created a youth association, you should go there and register because a donor can come asking for a particular service. The DPJ will check and contact us and the donor comes to visit us. This is the reason why we also registered with the DPJ. We work together."[15]

Various statements by different youth group members further showed that they had also registered with other prefectural offices, for example the DPM (*Département Préfectoral pour la Réalisations des Microprojets*), the department responsible for local micro-projects, again with the aim of gaining access to possible donors. Thus, the different official associations established partnerships with the state bureaucracy through registration processes in order to have access not merely to state resources but rather to potential non-state/international sponsors. They did not really care which state institution they went through for this registration process.

---

14 *"Ça existe que par le nom"*, 07.09.2010, note from a group discussion with Albert and Anne on the service delivery of the state.

15 *"Avec la jeunesse, ils [les fonctionnaires travaillant pour le DPJ] enregistrent les associations. Donc, si vous créez une association, allez-y, enregistrez, parce qu'un bailleur peut venir pour dire que j'ai besoin de faire telle ou telle activité, ils font voir quelle est l'association qui fait cette activité. Directement on nous oriente, et le bailleur vient voir cette organisation. C'est pourquoi nous aussi, nous sommes enregistrés au niveau de la DPJ. Nous travaillons ensemble, nous travaillons ensemble"*, 14.09.2010, communication with a member of a youth group (CJG).

Framing, guiding, registering youth

Generally speaking, then, the DPJ can be said to have performed poorly and shown fairly low productivity. In more general terms, its service provision to youth and youth associations can be described as technical and ideological support to help them with their own organisation and internal structure, at least on paper. The practices of registering also recall Scott's explanation that state simplifications such as maps, censuses and statistics are "in order for officials to be able to comprehend aspects of the ensemble, that complex reality must be reduced to schematic categories" (Scott, 2006: 259). However, the overall idea of this practice is to guide, further educate and advise young people. The DPJ's conception and practice in guiding and registering local youth associations thus refers to a particular idea and image of the state, its duties and its responsibilities. Registration and guiding processes recall the idea of incorporating young people into Sékou Touré's one-party state, among other things to control their activities and their "revolutionary" potential. So, youth-oriented politics and the blurring of the state, the political party and the state administration of the socialist state are not only noticeable in the name and premises of the *Maison des Jeunes/ex-permanence*, but also steadily influence ideas about public services for youth. Hence, socialist ideology lives on in ideas about service provision and providing guidance to youth, as well as informing the everyday routine practice of civil servants. I therefore perceive post-socialism as an important frame for analysing contemporary processes and transformations, also in regard to public services and state bureaucracies, since "socialist ideology can endure and continuously shape the post-socialist present" (Pitcher and Askew, 2006: 180). Thus, a closer look at history helps us to understand the initially fuzzy logic of public service (Olivier De Sardan, 2005: 55). Public service is not just dysfunctional or patrimonial but follows imaginations and mindsets informed by past state building efforts. However, the contemporary setting also interweaves old and new idioms, discourses and ideas, as public servants are also strongly informed by development discourses and practices. This creates distinctive images of the state that become entwined with everyday service delivery by the local state.

Finally, the contemporary youth landscape, with its diverse changing associations, often poses a challenge to long-term civil servants. They use registration to try and keep track of youth groups and their relations with international donors. However, youths have various strategies for gaining access to international donors and relating to local political actors. The registration processes offered by the DPJ are just one of several practices.

4.   Young political entrepreneurs

In a recent publication, Honwana concludes that "[y]oung people are involved in a myriad of associations and activist groups and deeply engaged with the issues that matter to them" and, more importantly, she claims that this engagement is "often on the margins of formal political structures and ideologies" (Honwana, 2012: xiii). She concludes that youth practices in relation to associations can be described as new ways of doing politics: "Young people are refusing to take part in 'politics as usual' and are not joining or creating political parties. In spite of this, they are not apolitical. They are building new ways of 'doing' politics by engaging in more flexible associations and social movements within civil society" (Honwana, 2012: 162). By taking this perspective, she complies with other recent debates that situate youthful associational life merely as part of civil society organisations. One example is the previously mentioned contribution from Utas (2012c) but others argue along quite similar lines: Bratton perceives associations as civil society groups and situates them beyond formal political parties and "beyond the state" (Bratton, 1989: 411). Diouf, too, argues that youth associations can be seen as situated in opposition to the state, as they often challenge state institutions (Diouf, 2003: 8).

I would argue that young people active in youth associations such as the AJG do not only get together to meet as youngsters; they also create a complex network of relations with various actors, including the state as an institution (Engeler, 2016). They thereby also participate actively in negotiation processes about the allocation of resources by the state and/or international donors. Thus, they do not simply wait to be included in development but can also be seen as active entrepreneurs, taking advantage to provide for their own needs. In addition, youth association members don't just represent "entrepreneurs" but also have ideas and ideals as civil society or social movements. Finally, I agree with Lentz, who says that discussions of "new social movements" (which see youth associations as merely civil society groups) analyse them as forging new collective identities, whereas the "resource mobilization" paradigm (which stresses the economic aspects of youth associations) stresses the instrumental character of group formations and the role of entrepreneurs (Lentz, 1995). Both approaches are "capable of stimulating analysis of the youth associations, so long as one avoids the rationalist bias of one paradigm and the insufficient consideration given to strategic action by the other" (Lentz, 1995: 424). All in all, youth associations are important arenas for political participation and entrepreneurship. The members of the AJG did indeed, at least temporarily, become *political* entrepreneurs, linking development projects with the local state and the economic landscape. Hüsken argues that such political entrepreneurs may also act beyond the world of development and organise the entire process of interlacing with, as well as the appropriation of, the state (Hüsken, 2010: 178).

IX. Distant horizons
Belief and innovative development

> *"Dieu confia à un certain nombre d'individus la mission d'assurer la communication*
> *entre le monde visible et le monde invisible. Ce furent les aînés et les devins"*
> (Iffono, 2008: 11).[1]

Previous chapters have shown that youth associations cluster around state institutions, which they saw as gatekeepers to international donors but also to the internal secrets of the state. At the same time, they realised that many donors had left the former war zone and that much of the state's secrets were just an empty shell. So what else was there to look for? Some youth initiatives like the motorbike union or some agricultural cooperatives simply restarted "cultivating peace" while also trying to gain an income. I argue that we can label these youthful practices that combine economic with socio-political practices as political entrepreneurship.

In this final chapter before the conclusion, I would like to address youth practices intended to manage everyday life as well as to imagine or, indeed, trust in a social future by engaging in religious movements. The first section introduces the characteristics of the religious terrain in Guéckédou before giving some insights into two youth groups that attach themselves to the Catholic Church. The members of these youth groups made a community and, indeed, became part of an imagined community to use Anderson's famous saying (Anderson, 1991 [2nd edition]). This community did not, however, in the first instance strengthen a local or national identity but especially encouraged an international frame of reference, which will be discussed in the final section.

This chapter is largely based on data gathered in the context of youth groups linked to the Catholic Church. But I also started to look at the religious terrain

---

1 In this publication, Iffono collects various myths and legends of the Kissi-speaking people. The quoted statement says that God entrusted a couple of people with a mission to enable communication between the visible and the invisible world. These people are the elders and the diviners.

through life history interviews, in which the importance of both Islam and Christianity turned out to be very important for the meandering life trajectories of youth. I concentrated on Catholic youth groups not least because I myself was identified as a Christian/Catholic person. The youngsters therefore welcomed me into their community. The Pentecostal and other related religious groups were on the other hand far more difficult to access, since they felt persecuted to a degree.[2] This was also true of the Wahhabis, who were difficult to access with my research approach. However, I found the more common forms of Islam very open and quickly became integrated in everyday Muslim life, not least because I lived especially close to a Muslim family. Thus, by accepting their values and attitudes and their feasts over many months of living together I could at least scratch the surface of what it meant to be part of a religious community like the Muslim one, which united people far beyond the local, "visible" group of people.

1.   The local religious terrain

Guinea can be described as an Islamic nation; according to some scholars even one of the most Islamised nation-states of West Africa (Camara, 2007). Camara accordingly argues that "no study of this country's past and present can be fully comprehensive without giving Islam its due consideration" (Camara, 2007: 169). He backs this up by explaining the central role of Islam in the delicate balance of state building and globalisation.[3]

Most Guinean Muslims are members of either the Qadiriyya or the Tijaniyya brotherhood (Devey, 2009: 61). The former was the dominant Muslim Sufi order or brotherhood in West Africa in the nineteenth century and remains important among the Muslim elite in Touba, the Fouta Djallon and Kankan (O'Toole and Baker, 2005: 167). The latter was founded in the late 18th century in North Africa and is also quite a popular and active form of Islam in Guinea (Smid, 2008, O'Toole and Baker, 2005: 193). However, some Muslims also follow the Wahhabi Muslim movement, founded in the eighteenth century in Arabia. These Muslims live simple lives, heeding what they see as the strict rule of early followers of the Prophet

---

2   Some of the members of Pentecostal churches even expressed serious concerns about talking to me because they considered me and my research topic as "too dangerous". Thus they were afraid that my research would attract some sort of state surveillance and preferred not to be seen with me because they would come under surveillance too. Of course I accepted this decision and did not bother them with my visits and/or questions anymore.

3   On Muslim imagining the state in Africa, in particular in West Africa, cf. Cruise O'Brien (2003). In regard to Guinea, especially the contribution of Smid provides crucial insights by discussing Muslim women's agency in the Fouta Djallon (Smid, 2010). Bayat insightfully describes youth, Islam and socio-political change in the context of the Middle East (Bayat, 2010).

Muhammad and avoiding the changes and compromises of later Islamic teaching (O'Toole and Baker, 2005: 208). Women accordingly completely cover their faces, bodies, hands and feet.

The Guéckédou borderland is influenced by many different religious groups or sub-groups related not only to Islam or to Wahhabism but also to Catholicism, Baptism or Pentecostalism. This religious diversity must be seen as generic for the entire Guinée Forestière and officially regained strength in the early 1990s, when the post-revolutionary state of Lansana Conté declared people's freedom of religion (Højbjerg, 2007: 6). However, the roots of the religious diversity are, as described in Chapter II, also entangled with early population movements, in part due to waves of Islamisation. The spread of Christianity was strongly related to French and British attempts to colonise the contested borderland through, among other things, the establishment of Christian missions. State iconoclasm and religious suppression characterised the post-independence era and turned out to be particularly relevant to Forestière communities. During that time the Forestières' religious practices, seen as outside the officially tolerated Islam, came under serious attack. All in all, Guinée Forestière and by implication the Guéckédou borderland as well must be seen as having a very complex religious terrain that combines and in part intermingles various facets of animistic, Islamic and Christian beliefs and institutions.[4] Fascinatingly, the past and present shape of this religious terrain says much about changing generational relations and state oppression, as well as about contemporary youthful agency and creativity. Contrary to the view of Honwana (2012: 119), who perceives young people engaged in religious organisations to be mere followers rather than bearers of creative and independent youth action, I prefer to adopt a more open mindset. Previous chapters have already indicated that young people are very often followers and creative inventors or initiators, sometimes even both at the same time. Thus, religious institutions can be just as important arenas as any other kind of social space. As Jones writes when explaining his research focus in Uganda: "I look at religious and customary institutions and show how important these are as sites of innovation. In Oledai people invest time, energy and money into churches, burial societies and clan institutions. These institutions provide new mechanisms of social organization and household insurance. They open up spaces where questions over land and property are negotiated, or where new social identities are formed [...] There is an important point to make here about the significance of religion in processes of social change" (Jones, 2009: 10).

Moreover, while political imaginations are expressed by what we at first sight consider "creative" or "innovative", references to past institutions or religious va-

---

4 A similar religious terrain might be found among the Baga of coastal Guinea, cf. Sarro (2009).

lue systems have implications for the present and future shape of socio-political imaginations and state–society relations.

To understand the local religious terrain it is very important not to think of the Guéckédou borderland as a religious playground or as visibly overcrowded with immensely popular churches and religious institutions. On the contrary, compared to other West African regions, Guéckédou does not bear many visible signs of its religious diversity. Besides the many mosques and the large Catholic Church, one seldom finds any other clearly marked buildings or community halls indicating the presence of the Pentecostal or born-again movements prevalent in other African towns (e.g. Ghana, cf. Lauterbach [2010]). Conversations with various religious authorities led me to the conclusion that this lack of symbols in part reflected the actual number of members in the different religious communities, as well as the fact that non-Islamic religious movements, with the exception of the Catholic Church, still find it difficult to establish themselves on Guinean territory.[5] In the following sections I introduce the reader to two youth groups related to the Catholic Church. I decided to concentrate on these because many of the young people I talked were very attached to Christianity and the Catholic Church in particular. With this focus I account for a characteristic of the Guéckédou borderland and not about lived realities in other parts of Guinea. In other words, while youth branches of the *Communauté de Sant'Egidio* or the *Scouts* also exist in Conakry and other towns, the religious terrain in Guéckédou may be more fertile, mainly due to the region's specific past.

2.   Community building: *Communauté de Sant'Egidio*

The *Communauté de Sant'Egidio* refers to an international Christian movement that is officially recognised by the Catholic Church. It was founded between 1968 and 1986 in Rome with the intention of praying for and assisting the poor in general (Mercier, 2010). The movement – sometimes also labelled a spiritual movement – spread to various countries and also engages in peace-building activities (Anouilh, 2005).

In the following section I describe a meeting of the youth branch of the *Communauté de Sant'Egidio* in Guéckédou. The gathering took place in a small annex in the grounds of the Catholic Church situated in the centre of the town. Thus, the intention of the following paragraphs is not to review the organisation throughout Guinea but rather to focus on the local context of the young people engaged in this religious movement. The following narrative therefore describes a particular

---

5 However, I could not find any numbers or official statistics that would back up this judgement.

event and includes some of the members' voices and perspectives I noted on various occasions, as well as throughout the entire research process.

Creating meaning of life

On a very warm late Wednesday afternoon, more than 50 young men and women were attending a meeting of the *Communauté de Sant'Egidio*. The young men and women clustered together on the wooden benches of the small annex close to the Catholic Church. I was visiting the group together with my research assistant and we were asked to take a seat alongside the others. I ended up sitting close to three young men who seemed rather quiet. I later found out that they were attending the meeting for the first time. I estimated their age at around fifteen. However, not far from my bench a group of two young women and three men were having a lively discussion. They were approximately 25 years old and I later learnt that one of them, Jacqueline, was in charge of the charity event at the local prison, the other girl, Stephanie, led the choir, and Augustin and Roger were engaged in some schooling activities organised by the *Communauté de Sant'Egidio*. The last one, Benjamin, was the group's leader and was coordinating the meeting. The remaining youths in the room were mostly pupils at the town's secondary schools, Benjamin told me. The group comprised approximately two-thirds males and one-third females. However, Benjamin said that the *Communauté de Sant'Egidio* in Guéckédou, which was founded in 2001, has more than 500 members overall. The international movement of the *Communauté de Sant' Egidio*, he proudly reported, consisted of millions of people. In addition, he emphasised that the movement had been founded by a young man in Rome and that this founder was "under twenty years old" and considered "prayer, solidarity with the poor, ecumenism, and dialogue as key to everything, including reconciliation in times of conflict".[6] The local group in Guéckédou, Benjamin explained, followed these principles.

After twenty minutes' wait (some of my neighbours had already nodded off, but nobody complained about how hot it was in the little annex), Benjamin finally launched the event with a short welcome address. He then handed over to Stephanie, who exhorted the entire group to start singing. For the next hour the community sang one song after another, always accompanied by two young men playing djembe drums. The songs were all in French and the lyrics were Christian in content. The entire group was very enthusiastic and everyone tried to join in with the choir; no one seemed sleepy anymore. Surprisingly, most of them knew

---

6 "*La Communauté de Sant'Egidio, est née à Rome en 1968 à l'initiative d'un jeune de moins de vingt ans. Les aspects les plus importants* étaient: *la prière, la solidarité avec les pauvres, l'oecuménisme, le dialogue, aussi comme méthode pour la réconciliation dans les conflits*", 30.10.2009, communication with the leader of the *Communauté Sant' Egidio*.

the songs by heart and only a few had a hymnbook with the words to the songs. Moreover, there was no sheet music in the hymnbook. How was I to sing? Finally, I just tried to follow the rhythm and sway of the group, and it worked quite well. It was actually a very interesting experience, and I could physically feel the power of music, which really did unite us as a group.

After the communal singing, Benjamin gave a speech addressing different aspects of communal life. Among other things he spoke about how the attendants could help each other as well as other people who were not part of the *Communauté de Sant'Egidio* to foster community spirit. He suggested helping the poorer people in the neighbourhood and supporting children in their everyday lives. These practices, he emphasised, were "about giving meaning to our lives".[7] In addition, he stressed that everybody was always welcome to the group, whatever their ethnic or religious background. "We are all friends."[8]

Benjamin then started to address the group's activities and local projects. One of the important issues was offering encouragement to local prisoners. This segued into a short discussion between Benjamin and Jacqueline about how they should organise the next service for prisoners. Finally, they decided on which of the coming Sundays they would again prepare some food and announced a time when those interested in helping should meet to prepare the meal and afterwards go to the prison. Besides offering a meal, they also agreed that they would clean the yard and then pray with the captives.

Benjamin completed his speech by reminding the group that the *Communauté de Sant'Egidio* was an international movement and that those in Rome knew all about the group and their activities in Guéckédou: "Rome does know what we are doing here."[9] He then welcomed all the newcomers who were asked to quickly introduce themselves. After each introduction the entire community applauded and the atmosphere was quite celebratory.

After almost two hours, Benjamin ended the group meeting with the announcement that one of the group's members had died. He suggested that after the meeting they should go and visit the family to offer their condolences. Various youngsters in the group agreed to this and started to collect some money for the mourning family. Finally, the youths began to leave the small, slightly stuffy room. Once outside, small groups of two or three people, usually of the same sex, walked home together. Another group of around 15 people, including Benjamin, Stepha-

---

7   *"Tout ça, c'est pour donner du sens à la vie"*, 04.11.2012, notes from the speech given by the young leader of *Communautéde Sant'Egidio.*

8   *"Nous sommes tous des amis"*, 04.11.2012, notes from the speech given by the young leader of the *Communauté Sant' Egidio.*

9   *"Rome nous connaît, eux ils savent qu'on se réunit le mercredi, qu'on fait beaucoup d'activités"*, 04.11.2009, notes from the speech given by the young leader of the *Communauté de Sant'Egidio.*

nie and Jacqueline, went to see the family of the friend they had lost just a few days before.

Far-reaching horizons

In times of risk and insecurity, not only did young people mobilise in defence of their homeland or founded youth associations to participate in politics and business in the aftermath of the rebel attacks, they also formed groups purely to foster communal life. Thus, discourses of solidarity, reconciliation and ecumenism satisfied young people's needs to feel secure and, probably even more importantly, to feel part of a community again. Jacqueline, for instance, was born in Freetown but, as a Kissi, she had relatives in the Guéckédou borderland. During the civil war, the rebels killed her father and she fled to Guinea with her mother and three younger brothers. After two weeks they reached some villages in the Guéckédou prefecture, where they stayed with a relative and where Jacqueline's mother later died. Now an orphan, she finally came to Guéckédou town to stay with an uncle of her father's. She had attended the Catholic Church on a regular basis back in Freetown and continued to do so while in Guinea. She was one of the first members of the *Communauté de Sant'Egidio* in Guéckédou and was still a very active member of the group at the time of this research. This example of a life trajectory and the context of turbulent war in the Guéckédou borderland in general shows that some of the young people who became part of the *Communauté de Sant'Egidio* were simply trying to reinforce their sense of community after times of conflict and dislocation. But whom could they trust? The Catholic movement of the *Communauté de Sant'Egidio*, which promoted peace and solidarity, was one of the places where they felt safe again.

Besides the prospect of enjoying community life through singing and praying, another important attraction was the global movement behind the *Communauté de Sant'Egidio*. As Benjamin stressed during his speech, the outside world knew about the activities of the youths in Guéckédou. This discourse not only united people locally but also made them part of a larger, international community. Thus, the rhetorical strategy allowed young people to imagine their own future beyond the local frame of reference. These young people thereby located themselves in a wide-reaching social space and produced a new setting for their own agency and creativity. This was visible, for instance, in new forms of spatial mobility. In one of the first conversations I had with Stephanie she told me that she has been in Yamoussoukro, the Ivorian capital, for a huge gathering of the *Communauté de Sant'Egidio*. It was the first time she had actually left the Guéckédou borderland and she was very proud of having been one of those who could visit the place. She experienced a great meeting, she said, and made lots of new friends spread all over West Africa. Benjamin told me a similar story when we met again in 2012. In the meantime he had been lucky enough to visit Rome and attend an international meeting on behalf of the *Communauté de Sant'Egidio*. He told me about the journey in great detail and I got the impression that he felt more than ever part of an international community. Rome indeed knew him! Thus as leading members of the local youth branch of an internationally active Christian movement, Stephanie and Benjamin got the chance to visit different places and one of them was even able to go to Europe – for most young people from Guéckédou this was an unbelievable dream come true. I learnt in 2012 that Stephanie and Benjamin were engaged and that they were planning to get married soon. With hindsight I understood that the meetings of the *Communauté de Sant'Egidio* not only fostered community but also provided a space for young men and women to meet and get to know each other. This could, as in the case of Stephanie and Benjamin, even lead to marriage.

Singing and praying

Like other youth groups the young members of the *Communauté de Sant'Egidio* were involved in local development. Through their charity project at the town's prison they tried to support the poor and excluded, as well as actively participating in projects for social change. However, unlike youth associations they did not tend to focus on funding from NGOs and international donors but, as I heard from Benjamin, simply collected a small amount of money among themselves to buy the ingredients for the inmates' meals. All in all, most of my interlocutors from the *Communauté de Sant'Egidio* stressed the communal singing and praying as their main motivation for attending the meetings. When I asked about their reasons for supporting the prisoners, I was told that this was some sort of "normal" social engagement, nothing out of the ordinary. Nobody perceived that as part of an income strategy, though. The establishment of a local network beyond the church, which provided the meeting place and allowed their gatherings, was not so important. Instead, they stressed their connection to the international movement, as I have noted previously.

3.   Manoeuvring between innovation, conservatism and patriotism: *Scouts*

Another youth group whose members met regularly on the grounds of the Catholic Church were the *Scouts*. They usually met on Saturday afternoon but also had camps and other activities in addition to these regular meetings. Those extraordinary activities were especially related to Christian holy days such as Christmas. In general, the *Scouts* may be compared to the *Communauté de Sant'Egidio*, but analysis showed some additional aspects I would like to address here. I do not give the reader a very broad description of the *Scouts* here; I simply add some aspects I have not yet mentioned.

Not the state but patriotic

Maurice, one of the leading members of the *Scout* group in Guéckédou, explained to me that the *Scout* movement had gained ground in Guinea after 1984. He saw this as being strongly related to the missionaries who came back to the country because of the change of regime and the increased political transparency. In the context of Guéckédou, Maurice and other members of the *Scouts* mentioned a sister who had come over from Madagascar and promoted the establishment of the local *Scout* group: "The scout group in Guéckédou was created by a sister from Madagascar".[10]

What was especially interesting about Maurice's further explanation of the formation and running of the *Scouts* was his constant efforts to distinguish it from the former pioneer movement. As both groups were organised along age lines, wore a uniform and had similar activities, Maurice felt obliged to clearly differentiate between what he labelled as "political pioneers" and the "Catholic Scouts" of today. In addition, he stressed more than once that "[t]he pioneers are related to the prefecture, the *Scouts* to the Church".[11] According to him, the former pioneers were still active but had changed their name to *Association des Scouts* (ASG). The Catholic *Scouts*, however, were united under an umbrella organisation called *Association des Scouts Catholiques de la Guinée*, shortened to ASCG. "The catholic youth group," he explained, "has the church and the fatherland for their terrain, the non-Catholic Scouts have only the fatherland".[12] Thus, he emphasised the fact that as religious *Scouts*, they followed Catholic traditions and beliefs. In addition, he described the youth group as being apolitical but nevertheless patriotic. "The *Scouts* serve God, the Church, and the fatherland,"[13] he underlined. Accordingly, the *Scouts* not only helped with various church events and activities, but also cleaned roads and carried out other work for the local community when necessary.

To sum up, Maurice discursively differentiated himself and the *Scouts* from the past by distancing the group from the socialist pioneers as well as creating

---

10 "*C'était une religieuse qui est venue du Madagascar pour créer une groupe de Scouts à Guéckédou*", 04.12.2009, conversation with a member of the Scouts.

11 "*Le pionnier c'est au niveau préfectoral, le scoutisme c'est au niveau de l'église*", 04.12.2009, conversation with a scout leader.

12 "*Le groupe des jeunes catholiques se trouve dans le milieu de l'église et de la patrie, les autres n'ont que la patrie*", 04.12.2009, conversation with a scout leader.

13 "*Les scouts servent Dieu, l'Eglise, et la patrie*", 04.12.2009, conversation with a scout leader.

a founding myth that accentuated the outside influences. To liberate himself from the political past (and probably the presence) of his own country, he therefore preferred to be part of a group that he perceived as having been introduced and led by outsiders. Nevertheless, Maurice and the other members of the group also stressed their patriotism and their service to the local community, although they preferred to relate these activities and their entire group to the international Scout movement and to the local Catholic Church, rather than to the state administration or other local authorities.

Not conservative but innovative

In the course of my investigation I learnt that the *Scouts'* relationship to the local Catholic authorities was not without its tensions. Through talking to some members I found out that many of them were in favour of a Catholic *Scout* movement that included both young men and women; "as they knew it from France", Maurice explained. The local Catholic authorities, however, were against this idea despite the fact that it had already been partially implemented on the ground. Instead, they promoted the formation of a separate young women's group, the *Guides*. While visiting some of the female members of the *Guides* I learned from Bernadette that they were very disappointed in the organisation and finally returned to the *Scouts'* meetings, which were still open to them. This reinforced the conflict between the *Scouts* and the church.

When I met Maurice for one of the last times during my research in Guéckédou, he reported that the church authorities had called them rebels and that the members of the *Scouts* were very disappointed. He, on the contrary, referred to some national agreements and said, "they do not need the Church anymore."[14]

This conflict between the *Scouts* and the local Catholic Church, together with the *Scouts'* attempt to differentiate themselves from both past and contemporary, more "state-oriented" youth groups, illustrates that youthful group activities are still hotly contested. Young people try to make their own point, for instance regarding gender equality and organisational structure. The same is true of the political affinities they try to circumvent without betraying what they perceive as one of the key motivations and obligations – service to their local communities and their fatherland. However, this manoeuvring within the local terrain may be described as very challenging and not all the youth groups managed to stick together through such complicated times.

---

14 *"On n'a plus besoin de l'Eglise"*, 14.01.2012, conversation with the Scout leader.

4.   Developing without development

Both the members of the *Communauté de Sant'Egidio* and the *Scouts* imagined themselves in relation to an international socio-religious space. And indeed, these religious youth groups did not occur in isolation but were arenas embedded in a network ranging from Côte d'Ivoire to Rome and to Madagascar. Surprisingly, some of the group members had experienced this international dimension for themselves and for instance had attended a meeting in Rome. Thus, the imagined community became real and also changed the young actors' agency in the local arena. These youths became door-openers for the other members, and the local group meetings benefited greatly from the experiences of the few who had actually experienced this international dimension and visited other places. This spatial mobility is related to social mobility and is mirrored in the young man's or woman's position within the group. Lauterbach describes the career paths of young men intending to become Pentecostal pastors in Ghana as "an attractive career path for many young people as it offers opportunities of ascending religious and social hierarchies in a situation where the more conventional modes of achieving success, through education and employment as civil servant, are decreasing" (Lauterbach, 2010: 259). Thus these youngsters boosted both their spatial and their social mobility. Although the young leaders of the *Communauté de Sant'Egidio* and the *Scouts* did not intend to become pastors, they were nevertheless similarly innovative and entrepreneurial in the sense that they created spaces "where they can build up status and where this status is socially recognized" (Lauterbach, 2010: 259). As in the case of Lauterbach, the young members of the *Communauté de Sant'Egidio* and the *Scouts* might be seen as dependent of certain senior actors in order to progress. However, as the dispute between the *Scouts* and the Catholic Church indicates, they were trying to free themselves from such constraints, among other things by innovatively claiming gender mainstreaming.

The two religious groups I describe in this chapter also emphasised their founding myths, which were characterised by the engagement of outsiders. Hence, these arenas allowed them to differentiate themselves from the local present and past political terrain. However, the young men and women also differentiated themselves from local and international NGOs, instead stressing religion as a vehicle for social change. Jones writes appropriately: "Aside from studying religious and customary institutions as sites of innovation and transformation, I make a broader point about the importance of ideological and religious concerns in explaining the way poorer people organize. Developments [...] took hold because they meant something, a point that gets lost in the economistic and institutional approach to development that has gained currency in recent years" (Jones, 2009: 10).

Elsewhere he explains that the connection to "something 'outside themselves'",
which is also outside development projects, is very important for social change
related to religious movements (Jones, 2009: 163). This reading also fits the case
studies described in this chapter and adds an important aspect to the overall discussion on young people engaged in various arenas to, not least, shape state–society relations in the Guéckédou borderland.

To summarise, the young people who formed part of the *Communauté de
Sant'Egidio* or the *Scouts* probably followed the "dreams of others" and thus emu-
lated internationally organised religious movements and their agendas. However,
in implementing that strategy they nevertheless created arenas for contestation
and negotiation within their local communities. And these arenas, as others have
described in previous chapters, hold potential for the long-term rearrangement
of societal relations. Thus, by imagining being part of an international community or by dreaming of gender awareness, young people shape common ways of
thinking. Moreover, Diouf explains that by aligning themselves to such religious
groups, young people select and confirm their own past and their own "founding
fathers" – they refuse to become embedded in the memory of the state (Diouf,
2003: 9). Hence, through young people's attachment to these movements they produce their own local memory and reconstruct the past for the sake of a socially
significant elaboration of the present (Diouf, 2003: 9). Accordingly, Catholic youth
groups in the Guéckédou borderland relate the colonial past to the present and
circumvent the socialist state building project, which oppressed non-state youth
groups and religious freedom. These youngsters nevertheless perceive themselves
as being patriotic, which creates an interesting dialectic of social mobilisation and
nationalist commitment.

Unlike many other youth groups in the post-war period, the young people of
the *Communauté de Sant'Egidio* and the *Scouts* did not primarily count on international development brokers or related national NGOs. Instead, they stressed
Christian values and a sense of community as being very important. Thus, the organisational form and the religious value system of these religious youth groups
are, above all, a response to the feelings of vulnerability and national isolation in
the post-war period and did not need to be an entrepreneurial undertaking.

Importantly, many of the young people I talked to were member of various
youth groups, associations or unions at the same time. Accordingly, these young
men and women simultaneously manoeuvred and invented different arenas in
which to grow older and to creatively shape the local political terrain by at once
relating to local political actors, national and/or international NGOs and international religious movements.

X. Concluding remarks

> *"Il y a l'espoir, quand même [...] surtout avec la période politique-là",*
> extract from a discussion with Albert following the presidential elections in 2010.[1]

Looking at youth and the state from an anthropological perspective had several advantages. One of these was that the close-up analysis of the local setting brought greater nuance to the bigger picture of understanding young people and their agency vis-à-vis ongoing state formation processes in Guinea. Inescapably, these findings, which are based on an ethnographic approach, are suffused with and framed by my own fieldwork experiences. Thus, my perceptions and sensations guided me through the field and led me to focus on certain aspects. While my view was restricted by my own lens, the information I received was also filtered by the impression people made on me. This final chapter bears this in mind and brings the main findings of this study together.

From a purely geographical point of view, the Guéckédou borderland is at the edge of Guinean national territory. Hence, the region may be described as on the margins of the state and somewhat peripheral for state formation processes. However, a more detailed perspective clarifies that the Guéckédou borderland has often been and still is very central to state making and political transformation processes in Guinea. Thus, rather than describing it as marginal or peripheral, I suggest that the conception of the region as a dynamic space in which to study both youth and the state presents an insightful endeavour.

Ethnographically, this study has its origins in the Kissi-speaking community, which has its home in the ever-changing borderland in and around the town of Guéckédou. The different touchstones of local people's self-perceptions became obvious when they described tales of Kissi origins as well as Guéckédou's founding myth. "Who is the crocodile that is only dangerous for non-autochthons", I

---

1 Albert was very positive about future political developments after the presidential elections in 2010 and said: "There is hope, after all [...] especially with the political period we are facing right now".

asked. Having talked about early population movements and uncommon names for rivers and mountains, Albert actually had no answer to this. The fact that the area belongs to the transnational *pays Kissi* and at the same time to the Guinean nation-state further highlight the borderland's complex territorial and identity issues. Hence, the region may be described as a crossroads, where ethnic and national references to local identities are in a constant state of flux. Thus, secret societies are often described as important, not just for managing intergenerational relations but also for regional integration. However, it is difficult to say to what extent they still play a role in present-day Guéckédou, mainly because Guinea's First Republic, which was established after 1958, had a huge impact on the local social fabric and seriously changed local power configurations. Therefore, the making of the revolutionary state in Guinea left its mark on Guinée Forestière and influenced people living in the Guéckédou borderland.

The socialist state building efforts were particularly targeted at the country's youth, who were meant to constitute the independent nation's new citizens. In other words, the revolutionary youth movement was instructed to get the independent state to work. Moreover, socialist state iconoclasm attacked local ways of managing intergenerational relations through secret societies and gerontocracy, not least in order to reorganise and exercise control over the country's peripheries and local power institutions. In a nutshell, the socialist postcolonial state proclaimed authority over both the political and the religious and cultural development of its citizens, especially its young Forestières, not least to suppress potential opposition among them. Today's tales about that time still deplore this serious state assault on local communities. However, the first-hand witnesses I talked to also considered their youth, at least in retrospect, to have been an active time during which they were able to participate in a range of activities. Thus, they stressed that membership and engagement in the JRDA or the pioneer movement allowed them to participate politically and gave them access to various jobs and political bureaus. One may therefore describe the socialist state's efforts to "make youth" as being simultaneously related to "youth making the state". Nevertheless, the "embodied state" of long hikes and parades that formed part of these elders' narratives also reminds us of the physical and psychological force of the socialist state. All in all, the youth–state nexus during socialist times can be described as one-sided mechanisms of control and influence to invent, organise and frame youth and its potential oppositional energy. The state with its educational projects became the ultimate patriarchal authority; there was little to negotiate between youth and the state. At the same time, however, young people built the heart of Revolutionary Guinea and were considered its new citizens, forming the bedrock of the newly born nation-state and social utopia. Thus, one may describe the youth–state nexus in Revolutionary Guinea as complex dialectical interplay, while also allowing some space for agency in seemingly predetermined conditions. This space was not, however, intended for political opposition but rather to unify all opposing political tendencies.

The post-revolutionary state was established in 1984, when Sékou Touré finally died after 26 years in power. The regime of Lansana Conté, who established the Second Republic, promised more room and more influence for society vis-à-vis the state; the opening up of the country both in terms of the economy and religion, the decentralisation reforms and other socio-political changes should have allowed people more autonomy to organise and articulate alternative political ideas. Instead, however, the reorganising and renaming of institutions neither changed the state apparatus nor created new political ideologies. Thus, people working for the state, for instance, did not simply fade away with the regime change, as my analysis of different local power brokers in the Guéckédou borderland showed. In fact, most political actors I talked to had very similar career paths, which had started either in the JRDA or in the pioneer movement during socialist times. This political generation still occupies important posts in present-day local deconcentrated and decentralised state institutions. Moreover, they have become successfully involved in new arenas like those provided by international donors, NGOs and political parties. Accordingly, they effectively adapted to and shaped the Second Republic and, more recently, updated their discourses and fields of activities with regard to international development aid and campaigning.

At the time of research, these actors still felt quite comfortable with the state as an institutional framework, since it provided them at least with a source of income. Accordingly, they navigated the political terrain and the regime changes in 2008 and 2010, when Lansana Conté died after 24 years of rule and the CNDD military junta seized power before elections were organized. Generally speaking, they were able to restage their political subjectivities fairly successfully. At the same time they remade the local state through their practices. Thus, the state's continuity finally rests with people who constantly remake it, despite regime changes. At the same time, regime changes allowed certain actors to remake themselves while remaking the state.

But do young people simply wear appropriately printed t-shirts and silently celebrate the state in the making? What about my introductory encounters with young people who opposed the state and the old guard by successfully turning the streets into a powerful negotiating arena?

As several chapters have illustrated, the socio-political practices of the new generation in the Guéckédou borderland were first and foremost related to the Mano River War of the 1990s, the rebel attacks in the 2000s, and the subsequent political developments. Thus, the new room provided by the Second Republic to organise and articulate coincided with the war experiences of today's youths living in Guéckédou. During that time, attempts by the central state to govern the Guéckédou borderland can be described as coming in different waves. During the rebel attacks, the central state control became weak and its representative, the prefect, left the region. Young people who had strong connections to locally rooted power brokers such as the mayor and the elders filled this gap and defended their communities by establishing the *Jeunes Volontaires* vigilante group. In the aftermath of the war, however, the central state power returned and the local state was remade, partly with the help of international development aid and partly by local authorities and political actors. No notice was taken generally of the young vigilantes. Some of the former fighters, however, were able to transform their agency – not by violent riots or by entering the national army (some of them had rather unsuccessful ventures into these territories) but by organising the streets or returning to the fields. Thus, by organising themselves in motorbike taxi unions or agricultural cooperatives, young people creatively informed the post-war situation – they "cultivated" peace and were able to "hold the line".

Moreover, the Second Republic along with the impact of newly established international development projects inspired young people to form youth associations. As this study has argued, young people who launch an association do not simply navigate the political terrain but often create their very own meaningful arena in which they show their readiness to be included in development, establish their own working environment and relate to various local actors – hence, they may be described as political entrepreneurs. Importantly, the young people I talked to did not reject the state as an institution or oppose the political parties but rather interacted with these actors when trying to organise, for instance, a cultural week. The Scouts and other religious groups I encountered positioned themselves similarly. However, the religious groups in particular stressed their relationships with international movements or ideals.

Generally speaking, young people in the various groupings imagined their communities' future creatively – not by undoing the state but, as I would describe it, more in tandem with local power actors and institutions. Hence, most of the young people I talked to perceived the local state – or the people who were running it – not as a source of coercion, violence or fear but more as a potential resource. They therefore voluntarily embraced tasks one would assume to be the responsibility of the state – for instance maintaining the roads or caring for local prisoners. Unlike socialist times, post-revolutionary Guinea no longer perceives young people as the nation's "new citizens" who will get the state to work. Accordingly, those people who occupy a post within the state administration, for instance, simply try to hold on to it for as long as possible. These civil servants very often promote an image of the state that is hidden behind a veil of secrecy rather than an accessible institution intent on public service delivery or a potential workplace. Thus, through their distorting practices, they promote the perception that the state is full of secrets and inaccessible to ignorant young people. Young people are well aware of that and while driving along the streets or organising youth associations and Scout movements they do not lose sight of the state and its representatives. At the same time, they have to be much more creative than their parents' generation – they have to become political entrepreneurs, managing the political, economic and social terrain simultaneously. In other words, youthful agency is exercised simultaneously in different arenas. Up to now these arenas were embedded in largely socially accepted spaces. Things were changing, however and I discovered that come young people were using new ways of creating a self in relation to society. For example some of my interviewees had decided to pursue unusual trajectories and bravely entered unknown territory – for instance by planning and later having a child without a potential husband, as in Fatoumatou's case. In a society in which cohabitation is largely influenced by an oft-expressed intention to get married soon, willingly becoming a mother in the absence of a relationship can be read as a strong statement for female independence. Hence, a woman's pregnant body can become a personal political arena and an expression of an alternative attempt to be young and grow older socially. It also hints at a lack of possibilities to enter other arenas in which a woman like Fatoumatou would be able to discursively negotiate her future and participate in the making of her society.

Future socio-political transformation processes will further reveal how youthful agency and youths' room for manoeuvre will change in this particular region. In this book I looked at youths defending their homeland, managing the post-war setting, meeting as youth associations and, finally, imagining distant horizons. Hence I offer the perspective that (youth) agency is not simply a state of being but is related to processes of becoming. Importantly, not all meandering lives shift or move and push somewhere else. Thus, the evaluation of the past and the prospective future often eventuates in quite conservative life plans. One of the very common resources for managing vital conjunctures amid socio-political uncertainties and economic constraints was hope, which is closely linked to faith. Hence, references to Christianity or Islam and their respective communities allowed young people to hope for and trust in a better possible future. Nevertheless, hopelessness is sometimes very close to hope and so the ability to reorient or adjust to new situations – to constantly reconstruct one's horizons – does not always proceed peacefully and may occasionally bring one into conflict with other actors and/or institutions.

The methodology applied in this monograph originated in the grounded theory approach and has a strong commitment to research based on fieldwork. For my research on youth and the state in Guinea, I built on, among other things, life history interviews. However, in order to grasp "being young" and "making the state", I used a combination of methods which allowed me to obtain more sophisticated data. Hence, listening to people's memoirs formed only part of my approach. This study suggests that, in addition to understanding crucial conjunctures and grasping youth agency by both young men and women, it is just as important to include parts of youthful trajectories and everyday life situations. Thus, listening to the story of Boubacar's lost love and witnessing at the same time the preparations he was making for his marriage gave me a good understanding of how this young man gave meaning to his past alongside his intention to become a respected man in his ethnic community in the future. Similarly, only by accompanying Bintu and then seeing her again in Conakry in early 2012 was I able to grasp that she was actually intending to go back to school: a fact she never mentioned in our life history interviews and informal conversations about her future plans.

This broadened life history approach, which included sharing experiences and following people over a certain period of time, led to a more thorough understanding of the life trajectories of the young people and the other actors in their lives. In research on the state and, more importantly, on people who are doing and making the state, life history interviews very often shed light on people's perspectives and images of the state. Interestingly, during these conversations these power brokers acted like true state actors who had successfully negotiated the regime change from Sékou Touré to Lansana Conté. However, again it was only by spending time with these people and observing their lives that I could research contemporary state-making practices. Thus, witnessing the way in which these actors had managed the tumultuous political transitions from Dadis Camara, to Sékouba Konaté and Alpha Condé added further details from which I was able to obtain a more accurate understanding of the state's functioning, of regime change, political continuities and local interruptions. Sometimes, for instance, I saw these actors representing themselves as political party activists; at others they simply wore a military uniform. Hence, the biographies of the state are indeed intermingled with the meandering lives of people and vice versa, as it is only people who can finally stage the state in the local political terrain. Accordingly, I would underline the importance of fieldwork carried out in phases over a longer period of time, which has the potential to layer different kinds of experiences and information from various arenas and social spaces.

Finally, this book is a contribution to the broad body of literature that discusses youth and the state in Africa and beyond. Most importantly, this study brings these two topics together by adopting a socio-anthropological approach based on fieldwork. Hence, it brings a holistic approach to the youth–state nexus: it does not neglect being young and growing up in its various social facets, nor does it look at the state as a mere institution or only from a bird's-eye, rather impersonal, view. Contrary to other youth studies, this study has focused on literate young people living in a small town and its rural peripheries. Accordingly, this monograph complements the debates on youth in Africa by researching what it means to be young in a significantly under-researched research area. Moreover, this study has answered questions about how young people who live in this particular research area participate in, negotiate and/or shape the state in a variety of arenas.

Embedded in an ethnography of the local state, the answers contribute to understanding youth better as well as to broadening our anthropological perspective of state formation processes in Guinea.

Epilogue
Mutual dependency

> *"Hé! Kon! Kon! Kon!*
> *Oui!*
> *Kon! Kon! Kon!*
> *Hé! C'est qui encore? Bonjour Ah!*
> *Bonjour, je suis la démocratie. Est-ce que je peux*
> *avoir la place ici?*
> *Hé! Non! Non! Non! Allé! Va!"*
> lyrics of 'Démocratie', a song by the hip hop
> artist Elie Kamano who originates from
> Guéckédou.[1]

In early September 2010, I discussed the relations between youth and the state
with Albert and Anne. Albert explained: "You know, the state cannot proceed without
youth. For instance, when we elect a new president, in a democratic way, the
president, he heads the country. However, it's not by paying the civil servants that
he can solve all problems. There are the streets, for instance, in the neighbourhoods,
in the villages. It is not the state that will repair them. Accordingly, the
state and the state's way of governing people needs to please young people, who
redo the streets, who form the grassroots, who keep moving. Thus the state rule
starts with youth. So if the young like the state, they will automatically mobilise
to support it. And when young people support the state, development will automatically
start. So, you see, the state cannot work without youth. They are interdependent."[2]

---

1 The entire lyrics can be found on the homepage http://eliekamano.fr.gd/D-e2-mocratie.htm (latest access 27 January 2014). The quoted dialogue happens between "Guinea", who is personified, and "democracy", a male person who knocks at the former's door. "Democracy" introduces himself and asks if he can enter, but "Guinea" refuses and harshly sends him away.

2 *"Tu sais, c'est que l'Etat ne peut pas avancé sans la jeunesse. Parce que quoi par exemple, si on nomme un président maintenant, démocratiquement élu, le président il est à la tête. Mais ce n'est pas en payant les fonctionnaires que l'Etat va pouvoir résoudre tous les problèmes. Par exemple il y a des routes, et mêmes les routes dans les quartiers là aux villages, c'est pas l'Etat qui va le faire. Même les routes pour aller dans les champs, c'est pas l'Etat qui va le faire. Les plantations et autres, c'est pas l'Etat. Donc l'Etat, et dans là, il est là-bas*

"So," I then asked, "how would you describe the situation at the moment?" In early September the country was under the rule of the CNDD military junta.

Anne replied: "You know, as soon as we saw that the new leaders talked the same language as we do, we automatically mobilised to support the transition, the change. Because, you know, the state cannot work without youth. The state owes youth and youth owes the state – so they are mutually dependent. That's easy to understand, isn't it?"[3]

---

sa façon de gouverner doit plaire à la jeunesse qui est ici la seule [...] le base. Qui fait rouler, c'est à dire l'Etat roule à partir de la jeunesse. Parce que si la jeunesse soutiens l'Etat, ça veux dire que le développement est commencé. Automatiquement on sent le développement. Donc tu vois, l'Etat ne peut pas fonctionner sans la jeunesse. C'est une relation d'interdépendance", 07.09.2010, group discussion with Albert and Anne.

3   *"Dés qu'on a vu que les nouveaux leaders parlent la même langue comme nous, on a automatiquement commencés à mobiliser pour soutenir la transition, le changement. Donc vous voyez, l'Etat ne peut pas fonctionner sans la jeunesse. L'Etat doit à la jeunesse, et la jeunesse aussi, doit à l'Etat"*, 07.09.2010, group discussion with Albert and Anne.

Appendix I
Timeline of important events in Guinea

The following chronology (Table 1) summarises some of the key events in Guinea since 1895, thus since French West Africa was established. The chronology is based on information provided in O'Toole, arranged and supplemented according to significance and most recent events (O'Toole and Baker, 2005). The table ends in late 2013.

Table 1: Chronology, 1895–2013

Date	Event and implications
15 June 1895	French West Africa is officially established
10 March 1896	The French colony of Guinea is officially established; repression of local resistance movements
1904	Boundaries of French Guinea are established by treaties among European countries; drawing of national boundaries, segregation of ethnic groups and communities
1906	Guinea becomes part of French West Africa
4 December 1920	French West Africa reorganised
30 March 1925	Africans are elected to the colonial Conseil d'administration in Guinea
7 December 1942	French West Africa joins the Allies; Guinean soldiers fight on diverse battlefields (Indochina, Europe, etc)
4 November 1945	Yaciné Diallo and Mamba Sano from Guinea are elected to the First Constituent Assembly in Paris, which was to draft a new constitution for the Fourth French Republic
28 September 1958	Guineans reject de Gaulle's constitution
2 October 1958	Guinea becomes an independent republic with Sékou Touré as president
November 1961	Teachers' plot put down, Soviet ambassador is expelled → shaky foreign affairs, internal problems

Date	Event and implications
January 1963	The National Assembly grants extraordinary powers to Touré against alleged plotters
1968	Guinean Socialist Cultural Revolution; Demystification Campaign, destruction of local masks and rites, social/intergenerational changes
1969	The "Labé Plot", more than 1000 Guineans are arrested. Several high-ranking army officers and many members of the government are executed; ethnic frictions increase, Fulbé exodus
22 November 1970	Portuguese troops and Guinean exiles try to take Conakry, they fail
January 1971	More than 70 people are hanged in Conakry and other towns throughout the country for alleged participation in the Portuguese invasion of Guinea; increasing violence; growing Guinean diaspora in neighbouring countries
26 March 1984	Sékou Touré dies in a Cleveland (Ohio, United States) hospital while undergoing heart surgery after a major heart attack
3 April 1984	Senior army officers and a group of civilians launch a successful coup d'état against the interim government. The Comité militaire de redressement national (CMRN; Military Committee of National Rectification) is created to serve as a national leadership body; military takeover
5 April 1984	Lansana Conté is proclaimed President of the Second Republic
February 1986	The International Monetary Fund (IMF) authorises $40 million credit, the World Bank provides a $42 structural adjustment loan; political and economic opening of the country
1990	After a constitution paving the way for civilian government is adopted, the first local and regional elections are organised throughout the country; in some areas, these elections are characterised by violent clashes between ethnic factions
February 1991	The Comité transitoire de redressement national (CTRN; Transitional Committee for National Rectification) is inaugurated, chaired by Conté
23 December 1991	Constitution of the Second Republic is promulgated. It establishes powers for the executive, legislative and judicial branches of government and authorises a two-party political system
April 1992	The constitutional system of two parties is changed, and multiple political parties are legalised; multiparty system established
1993	President Conté meets with opposition leaders but refuses to participate in a government of national unity. Police fire on demonstrators demanding elections.
19 December 1993	First multiparty presidential election held since independence. Conté, candidate of the newly formed party PUP, won 51.7% of the vote; Alpha Condé of the RPG was second with 19.6% of the vote. The opposition alleged electoral fraud, especially after the Supreme Court discounted as invalid the results in two prefectures where Condé of the RPG had received a large majority of the vote.
1995	Parliamentary elections
2 February 1996	Coup attempt; military reorganisation

Date	Event and implications
1999	Protests against the retention of Alpha Condé, repression of opposition by the authorities expands.
2001	Rebel attacks in different borderlands, Guinea's entanglement with the Mano River War becomes visible. Conté organises and wins a referendum to lengthen the presidential term.
2002	Parliamentary elections
21 December 2003	Presidential elections, boycotts by opposition parties
2006	General strikes, limited to Conakry
10 January 2007	General strike in the entire country; Guinean trade unions and opposition parties call on President Conté to resign, accusing him of mismanagement; increasing pressure of the street, trade unions gain strength
12 February 2007	Conté names Eugène Camara as prime minister; continuing strikes.
26 February 2007	Conté names Lansana Kouyaté as prime minister.
23 December 2008	Death of Lansana Conté is announced.
23 December 2008	Coup d'état, Captain Moussa Dadis Camara on behalf of a group called the National Council for Democracy and Development (CNDD), dissolves the government and the institutions of the Republic.
28 September 2009	Opposition party members demonstrate in the *Stade du 28 Septembre* in Conakry, demanding that Camara step down. Although many branches of security forces are involved, the presidential guard "Red Berets", led by Abubakar "Toumba" Diakite, is responsible for the violence, firing on, knifing, bayonetting and gang-raping the fleeing civilians, killing at least 157 people and injuring at least 1200 not just in the stadium but as many flee on the streets.
October 2009	In response to the incident, the Economic Community of West African States imposes an arms embargo on Guinea. The African Union, the European Union and the United States punish Moussa Dadis Camara and forty-one other junta members. The African Union imposes a travel ban and freezes any bank accounts owned by the forty-two. The European Union does the same, the United States opts for a travel ban alone.
3 December 2009	Camara is shot/wounded by his aide-de-camp, Abubakar "Toumba" Diakite. Camara leaves the country for medical treatment in Morocco. Vice-president Sékouba Konaté travels back from Lebanon to run the country
13 January 2010	After a meeting in Ouagadougou on 13 and 14 January, Camara, Konaté and Blaise Compaoré, President of Burkina Faso, produce a formal statement of twelve principles promising to return Guinea to civilian rule within six months. It is agreed that the military will not contest the forthcoming elections, and Camara will continue his convalescence outside Guinea.
21 January 2010	The military junta appoints Jean-Marie Doré as prime minister of a six-month transition government, leading up to elections.
27 June 2010	First round of presidential elections
7 November 2010	Second round of presidential elections

Date	Event and implications
December 2010	Alpha Condé becomes President of Guinea
19 July 2011	Assassination attempt on Alpha Condé; tensions in Conakry
28 September 2013	Legislative elections are held after numerous delays and postponements

Appendix II
Key informants

The following table (Table 2) lists some of the key informants of this study. The list is sorted alphabetically according to the pseudonyms used and includes some key words regarding their background. The third column gives the date of encounter.

Importantly, the many everyday discussions and informal talks with friends and neighbours, the visits to youth group meetings and projects, the conversations in taxis and at the market, and the numerous fieldnotes do form not part of this table. However, they were very informative and extremely important for the arguments in this study, as described in Chapter 1 and in the various introductory sections of further chapters.

Table 2: Selected informants

Names as used in the text	Shorthand background	Year of interviews (m = multiple interviews)
Albert	Student in Conakry, resident of Guéckédou, member of a number of diverse youth groups (GJG, *Communauté Saint'Egidio*)	2009m, 2010m, 2012m
Alois	Municipality, in charge of youth affairs	2009m, 2010m
Alphonse	Youth group member (GJG, scout)	2009m, 2010m
Anne	Member of the GJG, student	2010m
Barry	Municipality, pharmacist	2009m, 2010m
Benjamin	Lives with Bintu in the same household, not married, one common child	2009m, 2010m, 2012
Bernadette	Youth group member (*Guides*, *Scout*)	2010m
Bintu	Student, lives with Benjamin in the same household, not married, one common child, went back to school in Conakry	2009m, 2010m, 2012m
Bongoui	Elderly, *ancien combattant*	2009m

Names as used in the text	Shorthand background	Year of interviews (m = multiple interviews)
Boubacar	Involved in cross-border trade, former teacher, soon to be married	2009m, 2010m, 2012m
Charles	Vice-president of a youth group (GJG)	2009m, 2010m, 2012
Fatoumatou	Working in a hotel, born in Haut Guinée, divorced, looking for a new husband	2009m, 2010m, 2012
Finta	Lives with her mother and brother (Albert), has two children, not married, no contact with the father of her children	2009m, 2010m, 2012
François	Elderly, knows much about local history, rebel attacks	2010m
Jacqueline	Member of a youth group (Communauté Saint'Egidio), Kissi speaking but born in Sierra Leone, came to Guéckédou as a refugee	2009m, 2010m
Kamano	Civil servant (DMR)	2010m
Kamano	Former JRDA member, ex-mayor, political party activist, NGO activist (died in early 2012)	2009m, 2010m
Keita	Prefect of Guéckédou, colonel	2008, 2009m, 2010m, 2012
Komano	Comes from Guéckédou's founding family, knows much about settlement history, farmer	2010m
Komano, B.	Elderly, member of the council of the elders, comes from Guéckédou's founding family	2010m
Léno	Municipality, mayor, former JRDA member	2010m
Madame le maire	Municipality, former mayor, civil servant (DPE)	2009m, 2010m
Mamady	Former Jeunes Volontaires, hopes to become a regular soldier	2009m, 2010m, 2012
Maoumou, Jean-Paul	Civil servant (DPJ), former JRDA member	2009m, 2010m
Marc	NGO activist, political party activist	2009m, 2010m, 2012m
Marcelline	Respected woman, mother of two children, not married but marriage in preparation	2009m, 2010m, 2012
Maurice	Youth group member (Scouts, GJG)	2009m, 2010m, 2012
Milimouno	Former JRDA member, political party activist, ex-deputy, NGO activist	2009m, 2010m
Mohammed	Graduate, political party activist	2010m
Moïce	Former Jeunes Volontaires, motorbike taxi driver, trade union member	2009m, 2010m, 2012
Moïce	NGO activist	2009m, 2010m

Names as used in the text	Shorthand background	Year of interviews (m = multiple interviews)
Oliano	Elderly, knows much about local history, Kissi origins	2009m, 2010m
Oussa	Elderly, former JRDA member, dancing instructor	2010m
Raphaël	Member of the Motorbike Taxi Union, participant at political campaigns	2009m, 2010m
Richard	President of a youth group (GJG)	2009m, 2010
Seydou	Former Jeunes Volontaires, Member of different youth groups	2008, 2009m, 2010m,
Stephanie	Member of different youth groups (*Guides, scouts, Communauté Sant'Egidio*)	2009m, 2010m
Telno	Former JRDA member, part of revolutionary theaters and ballets	2010m

Bibliography

Abbink, Jon 2005. Being young in Africa: The politics of despair and renewal. In: Abbink, Jon & Kessel, Ineke Van (eds.) *Vanguard or vandals. Youth, politics and conflict in Africa.* Leiden: Brill, 1-34.

Abbink, Jon & Van Kessel, Ineke (eds.) 2005. *Vanguard or vandals. Youth, politics and conflict in Africa*, Leiden, Boston: Brill.

Abdullah, Ibrahim 1998. Bush path to destruction. The origin and character of the Revolutionary United Front/Sierra Leone. *Journal of Modern African Studies*, 36, 203-235.

Agier, Michel 2010. Un dimanche à Kissidougou. L'huminitaire et l'Afrique du postcolonial au global. *Cahier d'études africaines*, 2-3-4, 981-1001.

Aitken, Stuart C. & Plows, Vicky 2010. Overturning assumptions about young people, border spaces and revolutions. *Children's Geographies*, 8, 327-333.

Ammann, Carole 2016a. Everyday politics. Market women and the local government in Kankan, Guinea. *Stichproben. Wiener Zeitschrift für kritische Afrikastudien*, 16, 37-62.

Ammann, Carole 2016b. „Women must not become lions": Social roles of Muslim women in Kankan, Guinea. *JENdA: A Journal of Culture and African Women Studies* 67-81.

Ammann, Carole. 2017. *Silent politics. Gender, imagination, and the state in Kankan, Guinea.* PhD, University of Basel.

Ammann, Carole 2018. Political parties and participation: Guinea. *Encyclopaedia of Women & Islamic Cultures (EWIC)*. Brill.

Ammann, Carole & Engeler, Michelle 2013. „Guinée is back?" Ein Land zwischen Wandel und Kontinuität. *Afrika Bulletin*, 152, 3.

Anderson, Benedict 1991 (2nd edition). *Imagined communities. Reflections on the origin and spread of nationalism*, London, New York, Verso.

Anderson, Clare 2011. Introduction to marginal centers. Writing life histories in the Indian Ocean world. *Journal of Social History*, 45, 335-344.

Anouilh, Pierre 2005. Sant'Egidio au Mozambique. De la charité à la fabrique de la paix. *Revue internationale et stratégique*, 3, 9-20.

Archibald, Steven & Richards, Paul 2002. Converts to Human Rights? Popular debate about war and justice in rural central Sierra Leone. *Africa*, 72, 339-367.

Arieff, Alexis 2009. Still standing: neighbourhood wars and political stability in Guinea. *Journal of Modern African Studies*, 47, 331-348.

Arieff, Alexis 2010. Guinea's new transitional government. Emerging issues for U.S. policy. Congressional Research Service.

Arieff, Alexis & Cook, Nicolas 2010. Guinea: Background and relations with the United States. Congressional Research Service.

Arieff, Alexis & McGovern, Michael 2013. "History is stubborn": talk about truth, justice, and national reconciliation in the Republic of Guinea. *Comparative Studies in Society and History*, 55, 198-225.

Atkinson, Robert 1998. *The life story interview*, Thousand Oaks, Sage Publications.

Bah, Alpha M. 1998. *Fulbe presence in Sierra Leone. A case history of twentieth-century migration and settlement among the Kissi of Koindu*, New York, Peter Lang.

Bah, Amadou Oury, Keita, Bintu & Lootvoet, Benoît 1989. Les Guinéens de l'extérieur: rentrer au pays? *Politique Africaine*, 36, 22-37.

Banégas, Richard & Marshall-Fratani, Ruth 2003. Introduction au thème. Côte d'Ivoire, un conflit régional? *Politique Africaine*, 89, 5-11.

Bangura, Ibrahim 2018. Young people and the search for inclusion and political participation in Guinea. *African Conflict and Peacebuilding Review*, 8, 54-72.

Barth, Frederik 1970 (Repr.). *Ethnic groups and boundaries. The social organization of culture difference*, Bergen, Oslo, Georg Allen and Unwin.

Bauer, Kerstin 2005. *Kleidung und Kleidungspraktiken im Norden der Côte d'Ivoire. Geschichte und Dynamiken des Wandels vom Ende des 19. Jahrhunderts bis zur Gegenwart*, Berlin, Lit Verlag.

Bayat, Asef 2010. *Life as politics. How ordinary people change the Middle East*, Standford, Standford University Press.

Bellagamba, Alice 2008. Today's elders, yesterday's youth: generations and politics in the 20th century Gambia. *In*: Alber, Erdmute, Van Der Geest, Sjaak & Whyte, Susan Reynolds (eds.) *Generations in Africa. Connections and conflicts*. Berlin: Lit Verlag, 237-265.

Berg, Elliot J. & Butler, Jeffrey 1970. Trade unions. *In*: Coleman, James Smoot & Rosberg, Carl (eds.) *Political parties and national integration in tropical Africa*. Berkley: University of California Press, 340-381.

Berliner, David 2007. When the object of transmission is not an object. A West African example (Guinea-Conakry). *RES: Anthropology and Aesthetics*, 51, 87-97.

Berliner, David 2010. The invention of Bulongic identity (Guinea-Conakry). *In*: Knörr, Jacqueline & Trajano Filho, Wilson (eds.) *The powerful presence of the past. Integration and conflict along the Upper Guinea Coast*. Leiden Brill, 253-271.

Bertaux, Daniel 1981. *Biography and society: the life history approach in the social sciences*, London, Sage Publications.

Bidou, Jean-Etienne & Toure, Julien Gbéré 2002. La population de la Guinée - dynamiques spatiales. *Les Cahiers d'Outre-Mer*, 217, 9-30.

Bierschenk, Thomas 2010. States at work in West Africa: Sedimentation, fragmentation and normative double-binds. *Arbeitspapiere Institut für Ethnologie und Afrikastudien Johannes Gutenberg Universität Mainz*, 113, 1-20.

Bierschenk, Thomas & Spies, Eva 2010. Introduction. Continuities, dislocations and transformations: 50 years of independence in Africa. *Africa Spectrum*, 3, 3-10.

Bierschenk, Thomas & Spies, Eva (eds.) 2012. *50 Jahre Unabhängigkeit in Afrika. Kontinuitäten, Brüche, Perspektiven*, Köln: Rüdiger Köppe Verlag.

Bjarnesen, Jesper 2007. On the move. Young men navigating paths towards adulthood in Gueule Tapée (Dakar). *Specialerække* 454, 1-127.

Bjarnesen, Jesper 2009. A mobile life story.Tracing hopefulness in the life and dreams of a young Ivorian migrant. *Migration Letters*, 6, 119-129.

Black, Richard & Sessay, Mohamed 1997. Forced migration, land-use change and political economy in the forest region of Guinea. *African Affairs*, 96, 587-605.

Bøås, Morten 2007. Marginalized youth. *In*: Bøås, Morten & Dunn, Kevin C. (eds.) *African guerrillas. Raging against the machine*. Boulder, London: Lynne Rienner Publishers, Inc., 39-53.

Bøås, Morten & Dunn, Kevin C. (eds.) 2007. *African guerrillas. Raging against the machine*, Boulder, London: Lynne Rienner Publishers, Inc.

Boersch-Supan, Johanna 2012. The generational contract in flux: intergenerational tensions in post-conflict Sierra Leone. *The Journal of Modern African Studies*, 50, 25-51.

Boesen, Elisabeth 2008. Introduction. Youth in Africa - creating and transforming knowledge. *Sociologus. Zeitschrift für Ethnosoziologie und Ethnopsychologie*, 58, 111-116.

Boyden, Jo & Berry, Joanna De 2004. *Children and youth on the front line. Ethnography, armed conflict and displacement*, New York, Berghahn Books.

Bratton, Michael 1989. Beyond the state. Civil society and associational life in Africa. *World Politics*, 41, 407-430.

Braungart, Richard G. & Braungart, Margaret M. 1986. Life-course and generational politics. *Annual Review of Sociology*, 12, 205-231.

Brooks, George E. 1993. *Landlords and strangers. Ecology, society, and trade in Western Africa, 1000-1630*, Boulder, San Francisco, Oxford, Westview Press.

Brygo, Julien 2006. L'Afrique "made in China". *Témoignage chrétien*, 3207, 6-8.

Bucholtz, Mary 2002. Youth and cultural practice. *Annual Review of Anthropology*, 31, 525-552.

Bürge, Michael 2011a. Mastering the crossroads. Commercial motorbike riders in Sierra Leone struggling for steering their destiny. *ECAS 2011*. Uppsala.

Bürge, Michael 2011b. Riding the narrow tracks of moral life: Commercial motorbike riders in Makeni, Sierra Leone. *Africa Today*, 58, 59-95.

Bürge, Michael & Peters, Krijn 2010. Das Beispiel der Motorrad-Taxifahrer in Sierra Leone. *In:* Kurtenbach, Sabine, Blumör, Rüdiger & Huhn, Sebastian (eds.) *Jugendliche in gewaltsamen Lebenswelten. Wege aus den Kreisläufen der Gewalt.* Baden-Baden: Nomos, 163-176.

Burgess, Thomas G. 2010. To differentiate rice from grass. Youth labor camps in Revolutionary Zanzibar. *In:* Burton, Andrew & Charton-Bigot, Hélène (eds.) *Generations past. Youth in East African history.* Athens: Ohio University Press, 221-236.

Burgess, Thomas G. 1999. Remembering youth: Generation in Revolutionary Zanzibar. *Africa Today*, 46, 29-50.

Burgess, Thomas G. 2005. Introduction to youth and citizenship in East Africa. *Africa Today*, 51, vii-xxiv.

Camara, Mohamed Saliou. 1996. *His master's voice: Mass communication and politics in Guinea under Sékou Touré (1957-1984).*

Camara, Mohamed Saliou 2007. Nation building and the politics of Islamic internationalism in Guinea: toward an understanding of Muslims' experience of globalization in Africa. *Contemporary Islam*, 1, 155-172.

Camara, Mohamed Saliou 2014. *Political history of Guinea since World War Two*, New York, Peter Lang.

Chambers, Paul 2004. Guinée. Le prix d'une stabilité à court terme. *Politique Africaine*, 94, 128-148.

Chauveau, Jean-Pierre & Richards, Paul 2008. West African insurgencies in agrarian perspective: Côte d'Ivoire and Sierra Leone compared. *Journal of Agrarian Change*, 8, 515-552.

Christensen, Maya M. 2012. Big Men business in the borderland of Sierra Leone. *In:* Utas, Mats (ed.) *African conflicts and informal power. Big Men and networks.* London: Zed Books, 60-77.

Christiansen, Catrine, Utas, Mats & Vigh, Henrik 2006. Navigating youth, generating adulthood. Introduction. *In:* Christiansen, Catrine, Utas, Mats & Vigh, Henrik (eds.) *Navigating youth, generating adulthood. Social becoming in an African context.* Uppsala: Nordiska Afrikainstitutet, 9-28.

Coleman, James Smoot & Rosberg, Carl (eds.) 1970. *Political parties and national integration in tropical Africa*, Berkley: University of California Press.

Collier, Paul & Hoeffler, Anke 2002. Greed and grievance in civil war. *CSAE WPS*, 1, 1-43.

Conrad, David C. 2010. Bold research during troubled times in Guinea: The story of the Djibril Tamsir Niane tape archive. *History in Africa*, 37, 355-378.

Coulter, Chris 2005. The post war moment: Female fighters in Sierra Leone. *Migration Studies Working Paper*, 22, 18.

Crapanzano, Vincent 1980. *Tuhami, portrait of a Moroccan*, Chicago, University of Chicago Press.

Crapanzano, Vincent 2003. *Imaginative Horizons. An essay in literary-philosophical anthropology*, University of Chicago Press.

Cruise O'Brien, Donal B. 1996. A lost generation? Youth identity and state decay in West Africa. In: Werbner, Richard & Ranger, Terence (eds.) *Postcolonial identities in Africa*. London & New Jersey: Zed Books Ltd, 55-74.

Cruise O'Brien, Donal B. 2003. *Symbolic confrontations. Muslims imagining the state in Africa*, London, Hurst.

D'Almeida-Topor, Hélène, Coquery-Vidrovitch, Catherine, Goerg, Odile & Guitart, Françoise (eds.) 1992a. *Les jeunes en Afrique. Évolution et rôle (XIXe - XXe siècles)*, Paris: L'Harmattan.

D'Almeida-Topor, Hélène, Coquery-Vidrovitch, Catherine, Goerg, Odile & Guitart, Françoise (eds.) 1992b. *Les jeunes en Afrique. La politique et la ville*, Paris: L'Harmattan.

D'Azevedo, Warren L. 1962. Some historical problems in the delineation of a central West Atlantic region. *Annals of the New York Academy of Sciences*, 96, 512-538.

D'Urzo, Sandra 2002. Programme de recherche urbaine et de développement PRUD. Rapport de mission sur l'habitat en Guinée Forestière.

Dalakoglou, Dimitris 2012. 'The road from capitalism to capitalism'. Infrastructures of (post)socialism in Albania. *Mobilities*, 1-16.

Das, Veena & Poole, Deborah (eds.) 2004. *Anthropology in the margins of the state*, Santa Fe: School of American Research Press.

De Jong, Ferdinand 2007. *Masquerades of modernity: power and secrecy in Casamance, Senegal*, Bloomington, Indiana University Press.

De Jorio, Rosa 2006. Introduction to special issue. Memory and the formation of political identities in West Africa. *Africa Today*, 52, v-ix.

Del Mundo, Fernando 2001. Guinea: Return to a ghost town. *News Stories*. UNHCR. The UN Refugee Agency.

Denov, Myriam 2010. *Child soldiers. Sierra Leone's Revolutionary United Front*, Cambridge, Cambridge University Press.

Derluguian, Georgi M. 2005. *Bourdieu's secret admirer in the Caucasus. A world-system biography*, Chicago, University of Chicago Press.

Devey, Muriel Malu Malu 2009. *La Guinée*, Paris, Karthala.

Diallo, Geraldyne Pemberton. 1990. *The philosophy of Ahmed Sékou Touré and its impact on the development of the Republic of Guinea: 1958-1971*. The City University New York.

Diouf, Mamadou 2003. Engaging postcolonial cultures. African youth and public space. *African Studies Review*, 46, 1-12.

Dobler, Gregor 2010. On the border to chaos. Identity formation on the Angolan-Namibian border, 1927-2008. *Journal of Borderland Studies*, 25, 22-35.

Du Bois, Victor David 1970. Guinea. *In:* Coleman, James Smoot & Rosberg, Carl (eds.) *Political parties and national integration in tropical Africa.* Berkley: University of California Press, 186-215.

Durham, Deborah 2000. Youth and the social imagination in Africa. Introduction to parts 1 and 2. *Anthropological Quarterly,* 73, 113-120.

Durham, Deborah 2004. Disappearing youth: Youth as a social shifter in Botswana. *American Ethnologist,* 34, 589-605.

Durham, Deborah 2009. Youth. *In:* Barnard, Alan & Spencer, Jonathan (eds.) *Encyclopedia of Social and Cultural Anthropology.* London: Routledge, 722-723.

Eberl-Elber, Ralph 1936. *Westafrikas letztes Rätsel. Erlebnisbericht über die Forschungsreise 1935 durch Sierra Leone,* Salzburg, Verlag „Das Bergland-Buch".

Eberl-Elber, Ralph 1939. Harvest and magic among the Kissi of Sierra Leone. *The Geographical Magazine,* 8, 153-166.

Eguavoen, Irgit 2010. Lawbreakers and livelihood makers: Youth-specific poverty and ambiguous livelihood strategies in Africa. *Vulnerable Children and Youth Studies,* 5, 268-273.

Eilenberg, Michael 2012. *At the edges of states. Dynamics of state formation in the Indonesian borderlands,* Leiden, KITLV Press.

Ellis, Stephen 2010. The mutual assimilation of elites. The development of secret societies in twentieth century Liberian politics. *In:* Knörr, Jacqueline & Trajano Filho, Wilson (eds.) *The powerful presence of the past. Integration and conflict along the Upper Guinea Coast.* Leiden: Brill, 185-204.

Emerson, Robert M. , Fretz, Rachel I. & Shaw, Linda L. 1995. *Writing ethnographic fieldnotes,* Chicago & London, The University of Chicago Press.

Emirbayer, Mustafa & Mische, Ann 1998. What is agency? . *American Journal of Sociology,* 103, 962-1023.

Engeler, Michelle 2008. Guinea in 2008: The unfinished revolution. *Politique Africaine,* 112, 87-98.

Engeler, Michelle 2009. Bilder von Staat. *Tsantsa,* 14, 158-171.

Engeler, Michelle 2011. Listening, experiencing, observing. Reflections on doing fieldwork. *Basel Papers on Political Transformations,* 3, 20-24.

Engeler, Michelle. 2015. *At the crossroads. Being young and the state in the making in Guéckédou, Guinea.* PhD, Basel.

Engeler, Michelle 2016. Being young in the Guinée Forestière. Members of youth associations as political entrepreneurs. *Stichproben. Wiener Zeitschrift für kritische Afrikastudien,* 16, 63-86.

Engeler, Michelle 2017. Journeys between the rural and the urban. Mobile graduates in West Africa. *A*Magazine.* Basel.

Engeler, Michelle & Steuer, Noemi 2017. Elusive futures. An introduction. *In:* Steuer, Noemi, Engeler, Michelle & Macamo, Elisio (eds.) *Dealing with elusive futures. University graduates in urban Africa.* Bielefeld: transcript Verlag, 9-25.

Englund, Harri (ed.) 2002. *A democracy of chameleons. Politics and culture in the New Malawi*, Uppsala: Nordiska Afrikainstitutet.

Evans-Pritchard, Edward Evan 1960 (reprint). *The Nuer. A description of the modes of livelihood and political institutions of a Nilotic people*, Oxford, At the Clarendon Press.

Fairhead, James 2010. Kouankan and the Guinea-Liberian border. *In:* Knörr, Jacqueline & Trajano Filho, Wilson (eds.) *The powerful presence of the past. Integration and conflict along the Upper Guinea Coast*. Leiden: Brill, 75-99.

Fairhead, James & Leach, Melissa 1994. Contested forests: Modern conservation and historical land use in Guinea's Ziama Reserve. *African Affairs*, 93, 481-512.

Fairhead, James & Leach, Melissa 1996. *Misreading African landscape. Society and ecology in a forest-savanna mosaic.*, Cambridge, University Press.

Fairhead, James & Leach, Melissa 1997. Culturing trees. Socialized knowledge in the political ecology of Kissia and Kuranko forest islands of Guinea. *In:* Seeland, Klaus (ed.) *Nature is culture. Indigenous knowledge and socio-cultural aspects of trees and forests in non-European cultures*. London: Intermediate Technology Publications Ltd, 7-18.

Fairhead, James & Leach, Melissa 2002. Practising 'biodiversity'. The articulation of international, national and local science/policy in Guinea. *IDS bulletin*, 33, 102-110.

Fanthorpe, Richard & Maconachie, Roy 2010. Beyond the "crisis of youth"? Mining, farming, and civil society in post-war Sierra Leone. *African Affairs*, 109, 251-272.

Ferme, Mariane C. 2001. *The underneath of things. Violence, history, and the everyday in Sierra Leone*, Berkeley, University of California Press.

Filmer, Deon & Fox, Louise 2014. Youth employment in sub-Saharan Africa. *Africa Development Series*. Washington DC: The World Bank Agence Française de Développement.

Förster, Till 1987. Der Poro-Bund der Senufo heute. Institutionen segmentärer Gesellschaften und entwicklungspolitische Massnahmen. *Baessler-Archiv. Beiträge zur Völkerkunde*, 35, 191-220.

Förster, Till 1990. Der poro-Bund bei den Senufo, Elfenbeinküste. *In:* Völger, Gisela & Welck, Karin V. (eds.) *Männerbande, Männerbünde. Zur Rolle des Mannes im Kulturvergleich*. Köln: Rautenstrauch-Joeset-Museum, 315-324.

Förster, Till 1997. *Zerrissene Entfaltung. Alltag, Ritual und künstlerische Ausdrucksformen im Norden der Côte d'Ivoire*, Köln, Rüdiger Köppe Verlag.

Förster, Till 2009. Limiting violence - culture and the constitution of public norms: with a case study from a stateless area. *In:* Peters, Anne, Koechlin, Lucy, Förster, Till & Zinkernagel, Gretta Fenner (eds.) *Non-state actors as standard setters*. Cambridge: Cambridge University Press, 324-347.

Förster, Till 2012. Imagining the nation. Independence ceremonies under rebel domination in Northern Côte d'Ivoire. *African Arts*, 45, 42-55.

Furlong, Andy 2012. *Youth studies. An Introduction*, Routledge.

Galperin, Alexandra 2002. Child victims of war in Africa. In: De Waal, Alex & Argenti, Nicolas (eds.) *Young Africa. Realising the rights of children and youth*. Asmara, Eritrea: Africa World Press, Inc., 105-122.

Gavin, Michelle D. 2007. Africa's restless youth. In: Lyman, Princeton N. & Dorff, Patricia (eds.) *Beyond humanitarianism. What you need to know about Africa and why it matters*. New York: Council on Foreign Relations, 69-83.

Gerdes, Felix 2006. Forced migration and armed conflict. An analytical framework and a case study of refugee-warriors in Guinea. Hamburg: Universität Hamburg.

Germain, Jacques 1984. *Peuples de la forêt de guinée*, Paris, Académie des Sciences D'Outre-Mer.

Gigon, Fernand 1959. *Guinée état-pilote*, Paris, Plon.

Goerg, Odile 1986. *Commerce et colonisation en Guinée, 1850-1913*, Paris, L'Harmattan.

Goerg, Odile 1989. Les mouvements de jeunesse en Guinée de la colonisation à la constitution de la J.R.D.A. (1890-1959). In: D'Almeida-Topor, Hélène & Goerg, Odile (eds.) *Le mouvement associatif des jeunes en Afrique noire francophone au XX3 siècle*. Paris: L'Harmattan, 19-51.

Goerg, Odile 1990. La genèse du peuplement de Conakry (Conakry's Population in the Early Days). *Cahiers d'Etudes Africaines*, 30, 73-99.

Goerg, Odile 1992. Les associations de jeunesse: réflexions sur une méthodologie, à partir de l'exemple de la Guinée coloniale. In: D'Almeida-Topor, Hélène, Coquery-Vidrovitch, Catherine, Goerg, Odile & Guitart, Françoise (eds.) *Les jeunes en Afrique. Évolution et rôle (XIXe - XXe siècles)*. Paris: L'Harmattan, 17-34.

Goerg, Odile 1998. From hill station (Freetown) to downtown Conakry (First Ward): Comparing French and British approaches to segregation in colonial cities at the beginning of the twentieth century. *Canadian Journal of African Studies / Revue Canadienne des Etudes Africaines*, 32, 1-31.

Goerg, Odile 2006a. Chieftainships between past and present. From city to suburb and back in colonial Conakry, 1890s-1950s. *Africa Today*, 52, 3-27.

Goerg, Odile 2006b. Domination coloniale, construction de "la ville" en Afrique et dénomination. *Afrique & Histoire*, 5, 15-45.

Goerg, Odile, D'Almeida-Topor, Hélène & Coquery-Vidrovitch, Catherine 1992. Avant-propos. In: D'Almeida-Topor, Hélène, Coquery-Vidrovitch, Catherine, Goerg, Odile & Guitart, Françoise (eds.) *Les Jeunes en Afrique. Évolution et rôle (XIXe - XXe siècles)*. Paris: L'Harmattan, 5-9.

Gough, Katherine V., Langevang, Thilde & Owusu, George 2013. Youth employment in a globalising world. *International Development Planning Review idpr*, 35, 91-117.

Green, Maia 2012. Anticipatory development. Mobilizing civil society in Tanzania. *Critique of Anthropology*, 32, 309-333.

Greenberg, Joseph H. 1966. *The languages of Africa*, Bloomington, Indiana University

Gupta, Akhil & Ferguson, James 1992. Beyond culture. Space, identity and the politics of difference. *Cultural Anthropology*, 7, 6-23.

Hagmann, Tobias & Hoehne, Markus V. 2009. Failures of the state failure debate: evidence from the Somali territories. *Journal of International Development*, 21, 42-57.

Hagmann, Tobias & Péclard, Didier 2010. Negotiating statehood: Dynamics of power and domination in Africa. *Development and Change*, 41, 539-562.

Heinz, Walter R. & Krüger, Helga 2001. Life course: Innovations and challenges for social research. *Current Sociology*, 49, 29-49.

Hoffman, Danny 2003. Like beasts in the bush. Synonyms of childhood and youth in Sierra Leone. *Postcolonial Studies*, 6, 295-308.

Hoffman, Danny 2007. The city as barracks: Freetown, Monrovia, and the organization of violence in postcolonial African cities. *Cultural Anthropology*, 22, 400-428.

Hoffman, Danny 2011a. Violent virtuasity: Visual labor in West Africa's Mano River War. *Anthropological Quarterly*, 84, 949-978.

Hoffman, Danny 2011b. *The war machines. Young men and violence in Sierra Leone and Liberia*, Durham (N.C.), Duke University Press.

Højbjerg, Christian 1999. Loma political culture. A phenomenology of structural form. *Africa*, 69, 535-554.

Højbjerg, Christian 2002. Inner iconoclasm. Forms of reflexivity in Loma rituals of sacrifice. *Social Anthropology*, 10, 57-75.

Højbjerg, Christian 2006. Divergent modes of address and (re)contextualization in Loma ritual prayer. *Journal of Royal Anthropological Institute*, 12, 625-641.

Højbjerg, Christian 2007. *Resisting state iconoclasm among the Loma of Guinea*, Durham, Carolina Academic Press.

Højbjerg, Christian 2010. Victims and heroes. Manding historical imagination in a conflict-ridden border region (Liberia-Guinea). *In:* Knörr, Jacqueline & Trajano Filho, Wilson (eds.) *The powerful presence of the past. Integration and conflict along the Upper Guinea Coast.* Leiden: Brill, 273-293.

Højbjerg, Christian, Knörr, Jacqueline & Murphy, William P. (eds.) 2017. *Politics and policies in Upper Guinea Coast societies: change and continuity*, New York: Palgrave Macmillan.

Honwana, Alcinda 2006. *Child soldiers in Africa*, Philadelphia, University of Pennsylvania Press.

Honwana, Alcinda 2012. *The time of youth. Work, social change, and politics in Africa*, Sterling, Kumarian Press.

Honwana, Alcinda & De Boeck, Filip 2005. *Makers and brakers. Children and youth in postcolonial Africa.*, Trenton, Africa World Press.

Humphrey, Caroline 2005. Ideology in infrastructure: architecture and Soviet imagination. *Journal of the Royal Anthropological Institute*, 11, 39-58.

Hüsken, Thomas 2010. The neo-liberal competitive order in the borderland of Egypt and Libya. *In:* Engel, Ulf & Nugent, Paul (eds.) *Respacing Africa*. Leiden, Boston: Brill, 169-205.

ICG 2002. Liberia: The key to ending regional instability. *Africa Report*

ICG 2005. Stopping Guinea's slide. *Africa Report / Rapport Afrique.*

ICG 2007. Guinea: Change or chaos. *Africa Report / Rapport Afrique.*

Iffono, Aly Gilbert 2008. *Contes et légendes kissi de Guinée, Liberia et Sierra Léone*, Paris, L'Harmattan.

Iffono, Aly Gilbert 2010. *Le peuple Kissi (Guinée, Libéria, Sierra Leone) face aux colonisations. Résistance et survie*, Paris, L'Harmattan.

Iffono, Aly Gilbert 2011. *Naître, vivre et mourir en pays kisi précolonial. Essai d'anthropologie sociale et culturelle*, Paris, L'Harmattan.

Iffono, Aly Gilbert & Kamano, Aly 1975. Histoire et civilisation du groupement des Kisia, des origines à la colonisation. . Conakry: Institut Polytechnique Gamal Abdel Nasser Conakry.

IMF 2011. Guinea: poverty reduction strategy paper. Annual progress report. *IMF country report.*

Jackson, Michael. 2006. This is what it's like. *New Zealand Listener*, July 1, 2006.

Jeffrey, Craig 2012. Geographies of children and youth II. *Progress in Human Geography*, 36, 245-253.

Jeffrey, Craig & Dyson, Jane 2013. Zigzag capitalism. Youth entrepreneurship in the contemporary global South. *Geoforum*, 49, R1-R3.

Johnson, R. W. 1970. Sekou Touré and the Guinean revolution. *African Affairs*, 69, 350-365.

Johnson-Hanks, Jennifer 2002. On the limits of life stages in ethnography. Toward a theory of vital conjunctures. *American Anthropologist*, 104, 865-880.

Johnson-Hanks, Jennifer 2007. Women on the market. Marriage, consumption, and the internet in urban Cameroon. *American Ethnologist*, 34, 642-658.

Jones, Ben 2009. *Beyond the state in rural Uganda*, Edinburgh, Edinburgh University Press.

Jones, Jeremy L. 2010. 'Nothing is straight in Zimbabwe': the rise of the kukiya-kiya economy 2000–2008. *Journal of Southern African Studies*, 36, 285-299.

Kaké, Ibrahima Baba 1987. *Sékou Touré, le héros et le tyran*, Paris, JA Presses.

Kamano, Sylvain M. & Sagna, Pascal 2010. L'histoire de la paroisse St Michel de Mongo. *In:* Felemou, Emmanuel (ed.) *Paroisse St Michel de Mongo.* Kankan Diocèse de Kankan, 56.

Kaplan, Robert D. 1994. *The coming anarchy. How scarcity, crime, overpopulation, and disease are rapidly destroying the social fabric of our planet. Atlantic Monthly,* Frebruary, 44-76.

Kaplan, Robert D. 1997. *The ends of the earth. A journey at the dawn of the 21st century,* London, Papermac.

Katzan, Julia. 1998. *soi mendan - Die Sache mit dem Wasser. Eine medizinethnologische Untersuchung zum Zusammenhang von Wasser und Krankheit aus indigener Sicht.* PhD Inaugural-Dissertation, Ruprecht-Karls-Universität Heidelberg.

Kerkvliet, Benedict J. Tria 2001. An approach for analysing state-society relations in Vietnam. *SOJOURN: Journal of Social Issues in Southeast Asia,* 16, 238-278.

Kerkvliet, Benedict J. Tria 2003. Authorities and the people: An analysis of state-society relations in Vietnam. *In:* Luong, Hy V. (ed.) *Postwar Vietnam. Dynamics of a transforming society.* Lanham: Rowman & Littlefield Publishers, Inc.

Kirschner, Andrea 2010. Jugend, Gewalt und sozialer Wandel in Afrika. *In:* Imbusch, Peter (ed.) *Jugendliche als Täter und Opfer von Gewalt.* Wiesbaden: VS Verlag für Sozialwissenschaften, 133-174.

Knörr, Jacqueline & Trajano Filho, Wilson 2010. Introduction. *The powerful presence of the past. In:* Knörr, Jacqueline & Trajano Filho, Wilson (eds.) *The powerful presence of the past. Integration and conflict along the Upper Guinea Coast.* Leiden: Brill, 1-23.

Konate, Yacouba 2003. Les enfants de la balle. De la Fesci aux Mouvements des Patriotes. *Politique Africaine,* 89, 49-70.

Koné, Gnangadjomon. 2011. *Sociogenèse et dynamique de mouvement "Jeune Patriote" en Côte d'Ivoire.* PhD.

Koning, Ruben De 2007. Greed or grievance in West Africa's forest wars? *In:* Jong, Wil De, Donovan, Deanna & Abe, Ken-Ichi (eds.) *Extreme conflict and tropical forests.* Dordrecht: Springer, 37-56.

Korf, Benedikt 2006. Functions of violence revisited. Greed, pride and grievance in Sri Lanka's civil war. *Progress in Development Studies,* 6, 109-122.

Korf, Benedikt & Engeler, Michelle 2007. Geographien der Gewalt. *Zeitschrift für Wirtschaftsgeographie,* 51, 221-237.

Koundouno, Tamba Augustin. 2009. *La place des traditions culturelles dans la résolution des conflits dans l'espace kissi de Guéckédou.* Memoire de fin d'etudes superieur MA, Superieur des Arts de Guinée (ISAG).

Koundouno-N'Diaye, Michèle Sona 2008. *Les femmes et les pratiques coutumières et religieuses du mariage en République de Guinée,* Copenhagen, The Danish Institute for Human Rights.

Langevang, Thilde & Gough, Katherine V. 2012. Diverging pathways. Young female employment and entrepreneurship in sub-Saharan Africa. *The Geographical
Journal*, 178, 242-252.

Lauterbach, Karen 2010. Becoming a pastor: Youth and social aspirations in Ghana. *Young*, 18, 259-278.

Lentz, Carola 1995. 'Unity for development'. Youth associations in north-western
Ghana. *Africa*, 65, 395-429.

Lentz, Carola 1998. The chief, the mine captain and the politician. Legitimating
power in northern Ghana. *Africa*, 68, 46-67.

Lentz, Carola 1999. Youth associations und Ethnizität in Nordghana. *Africa Spectrum*, 34, 305-320.

Lentz, Carola 2010. 'Ghana@50': Celebrating the nation - debating the nation.
*Arbeitspapiere Institut für Ethnologie und Afrikastudien Johannes Gutenberg Uni-
versität Mainz*, 120, 1-30.

Lentz, Carola & Budniok, Jan 2007. Ghana@50 - Celebrating the nation. An eye-
witness account from Accra. . *Arbeitspapiere Institut für Ethnologie und Afrikastudien Johannes Gutenberg Universität Mainz*, 83, 1-29.

Lipsky, M. 1980. *Street-level bureaucracy. Dilemmas of the individual in public service*,
New York, Russel Sage Foundation.

Little, Kenneth 1965a. The political function of the Poro, part I. *Africa*, 35, 349-365.

Little, Kenneth 1965b. *West African urbanization: A study of voluntary associations in
social change*, London, Cambridge University Press.

Little, Kenneth 1966. The political function of the Poro, part II. *Africa*, 36, 62-72.

Lonsdale, John 1992. The conquest state of Kenya, 1895-1905. In: Berman, Bruce
& Lonsdale, John (eds.) *Unhappy valley. Conflict in Kenya and Africa*. London:
James Currey, 13-44.

Lund, Christian 2007. Twilight institutions. An introduction. In: Lund, Christian
(ed.) *Twilight institutions. Public authority and local politics in Africa*. Malden:
Blackwell Publishing, 1-12.

Luttrel, Wendy 2005. "Good enough" methods for life-story analysis. In: Quinn,
Naomi (ed.) *Finding culture in talk. A collection of methods*. New York: Palgrave
Macmillan, 243-268.

Maier, Konrad. 1990. *Das Guinea Sékou Tourés. Zwischen Traditionalismus und Sow-
jetkommunismus*. PhD PhD, Friedrich-Alexander-Universität.

Maira, Sunaina & Soep, Elisabeth 2005. *Youthscapes. The popular, the national, the
global*, Philadelphia, University of Pennsylvania Press.

Mannheim, Karl 1997. *Essays on the sociology of knowledge*, London, Routledge &
Kegan Paul.

Marchal, Roland 2002. Liberia, Sierra Leone et Guinée: une guerre sans frontières? *Politique Africaine*, 88, 5-12.

Marriage, Zoë 2007. A dirty war in West Africa. The RUF and the deconstruction of Sierra Leone. *Africa Today*, 54.

Masquelier, Adeline 2005. The scorpion's sting: youth, marriage and the struggle for social maturity in Niger. *Journal of the Royal Anthropological Institute*, 11, 59-83.

Massing, Andreas 1980-81. A segmentary society between colonial frontiers: The Kissi of Liberia, Sierra Leone and Guinea 1892-1913. *Liberian Studies Journal*, 9.

Mauri, Ruth 2007. Changing political spaces, still national history. *CroNEM Conference 2007, Comparisons of new and old forms of nationalism*.

Mbembe, Joseph Achille 1985. *Les jeunes et l'ordre politique en Afrique Noire*, Paris, L'Harmattan.

McGovern, Michael 2010. The refusal to celebrate the fiftieth anniversary of the 1958 NO. *In:* Goerg, Odile, Pauthier, Céline & Diallo, Abdoulaye (eds.) *Le NON de la Guinée (1958). Entre mythe, relecture historique et résonances contemporaines.* Paris: L'Harmattan, 17-27.

McGovern, Michael 2013. *Unmasking the state. Making Guinea modern.* , Chicago, The University of Chicago Press.

McGovern, Mike 2002. Conflit régional et rhétorique de la contre-insurrection. Guinéens et réfugiés en Septembre 2000. *Politique Africaine*, 84-102.

McGovern, Mike. 2004. *Unmasking the state. Developing modern political subjectivities in 20th century Guinea.* PhD, Emory University.

McGovern, Mike 2007. Janvier 2007 - Sékou Touré est mort. *Politique Africaine*, 107, 125-145.

McGovern, Mike 2011. *Making war in Côte d'Ivoire*, London, Hurst & Company.

McGovern, Mike 2012a. Life during wartime: aspirational kinship and the management of insecurity. *Journal of the Royal Anthropological Institute*, 18, 735-752.

McGovern, Mike 2012b. Turning the clock back or breaking with the past? Charismatic temporality and elite politics in Côte d'Ivoire and the United States. *Cultural Anthropology*, 27, 239-260.

McGovern, Mike 2015. Liberty and moral ambivalence: Postsocialist transitions, refugee hosting, and bodily comportment in the Republic of Guinea. *American Ethnologist*, 42, 247-261.

Mead, Margaret 1929. *Coming of age in Samoa. A psychological study of primitive youth for Western civilisation*, London, Jonathan Cape.

Meillassoux, Claude 1968. *Urbanization of an African community. Voluntary associations in Bamako*, Seattle, London, University of Washington Press.

Mercier, Charles 2010. Les fondations de la Communauté de Sant'Egidio et de la Société de Saint-Vincent-de-Paul. *Archives de sciences sociales des religions*, 149.

Mignon, Jean-Marie 1988. Contribution à l'élaboration d'une politique de jeunesse et d'un programme de formation des cadres et des animateurs de jeunesse en République de Guinée. *Rapport technique*. Paris: Organisation des Nations Unies pour l'éducation, la science et la culture.

Mitchell, Timothy 1999. Society, economy, and the state effect. *In:* Steinmetz, George (ed.) *State/culture: state-formation after the cultural turn*. Ithaca: Cornell University Press, 76-97.

Munive, Jairo 2010a. The army of 'unemployed' young people. *Young*, 18, 321-338.

Munive, Jairo 2010b. Ex-combatants, returnees, land and conflict in Liberia. *DIIS Working Paper*, 5, 1-24.

Munive, Jairo. 2010c. *Questioning ex-combatant reintegration in Liberia. Armed mobilization, localized histories of conflict and the power of labels*. PhD, University of Copenhagen.

Murphy, William P. 1980. Secret knowledge as property and power in Kpelle society. Elders versus youth. *Africa*, 50, 193-207.

Murphy, William P. 2003. Military patrimonialism and child soldier clientalism in the Liberian and Sierra Leonean civil wars. *African Studies Review*, 46, 61-87.

Newman, David 2003. Boundaries. *In:* Agnew, John, Mitchell, Katharyne & Toal, Gerard (eds.) *A companion to political geography*. Malden: Blackwell Publishing, 123-137.

Nguyen, Phuong An 2005. Youth and the state in contemporary socialist Vietnam. *Working Paper Centre for East and South-East Asian Studies Lund University, Sweden*, 16, 1-26.

O'Toole, Thomas & Baker, Janice E. 2005. *Historical dictionary of Guinea*, Landham, Toronto, Oxford, The Scarecrow Press, Inc. .

Olivier De Sardan, Jean-Pierre 2005. *Anthropology and development. Understanding contemporary social change*, London, New York, Zed Books.

Osborn, Emily Lynn 2003. 'Circle of iron': African colonial employees and the interpretation of colonial rule in French West Africa. *The Journal of African History*, 44, 29-50.

Osborn, Emily Lynn 2011. *Our new husbands are here. Households, gender, and politics in a West African state from the slave trade to colonial rule*, Athens, Ohio University Press.

Ouéndéno, Faya Moïse 2007. Evolution de la situation de conflits dans la préfecture de Guéckédou l'an 2007. GTZ/SARPC.

Park, Yoon Jung 2010. Boundaries, borders and borderland constructions: Chinese in contemporary South Africa and the region. *African Studies*, 69, 457-479.

Paulme, Denise 1942. Deux statuettes en pierre de la Guinée française. *Bulletins et Mémoires de la Société d'anthropologie de Paris*, 9, 38-43.

Paulme, Denise 1954. *Les gens du riz. Kissi de Haute Guinée Française*, Paris, Librairie Plon.

Paulme, Denise 1960. La société kissi. Son organisation politique. *Cahier d'études africaines*, 1, 73-85.

Pauthier, Céline 2013. L'Héritage controversé de Sékou Touré, "héros" de l'indépendance. *Revue d'histoire*, 2, 31-44.

Person, Yves 1963. Les ancêtres de Samori. *Cahiers d'Études Africaines*, 4, 125-156.

Person, Yves 1968-1975. *Samori: une révolution Dyula*, Dakar, IFAN.

Persson, Mariam 2012. Demobilized or remobilized? Lingering rebel structures in post-war Liberia. *In*: Utas, Mats (ed.) *African conflicts and informal power. Big men and networks* London: Zed Books, 101-118.

Peters, Krijn 2007. From weapons to wheels. Young Sierra Leonean ex-combatants become motorbike taxi-riders. *Journal of Peace, Conflict & Development*, 10, 1-23.

Peters, Krijn 2010. Generating rebels and soldiers. On the socio-economic crisis of rural youth in Sierra Leone before the war. *In*: Knörr, Jacqueline & Trajano Filho, Wilson (eds.) *The powerful presence of the past. Integration and conflict along the Upper Guinea Coast*. Leiden Brill, 323-355.

Peters, Krijn 2011. *War and the crisis of youth in Sierra Leone*, Cambridge University Press.

Peters, Krijn & Richards, Paul 1998. Jeunes combattants parlant de la guerre et de la paix en Sierra Leone. *Cahiers d'Études africaines*, 150-152, 581-617.

Peters, Krijn & Richards, Paul 2007. Understanding recent African wars. *Africa*, 77, 442-454.

Philipps, Joschka 2013. *Ambivalent rage. Youth gangs and urban protest in Conakry, Guinea*, Paris, L'Harmattan.

Pinto, Rogerio F. 2004. Service delivery in francophone West Africa: The challenge of balancing deconcentration and decentralisation. *Public Administration and Development*, 24, 263-275.

Pitcher, M. Anne & Askew, Kelly M. 2006. African socialisms and postsocialisms. *Africa*, 76, 1-14.

Reno, William 2007. African rebels and the citizenship question. *In*: Dorman, Sara, Hammett, Daniel & Nugent, Paul (eds.) *Making nations, creating strangers. States and citizenship in Africa*. Leiden, Boston: Brill, 221-239.

Rey, Pascal. 2007. *Le sage et l'etat. Pouvoir, territoire et developpement en Guinée Maritime*. Doctorat PhD, Université de Bordeaux III.

Richards, Paul 1995. Rebellion in Liberia and Sierra Leone. A crisis of youth? *In*: Furley, Oliver (ed.) *Conflict in Africa*. New York: St Martin's Press, 134-170.

Richards, Paul 1996. *Fighting for the rain forest. War, youth and resources in Sierra Leone*, Oxford, James Currey.

Richards, Paul 1997. War, forests and the future: the environmental understanding of the young in Sierra Leone. *In*: Seeland, Klaus (ed.) *Nature is culture. Indigenous knowledge and socio-cultural aspects of trees and forests in non-European cultures*. London: Intermediate Technology Publications Ltd, 90-100.

Richards, Paul 2005a. To fight or to farm? Agrarian dimensions of the Mano River conflicts (Liberia and Sierra Leone). *African Affairs*, 104, 571-590.

Richards, Paul 2005b. War as smoke and mirrors: Sierra Leone 1991-2, 1994-5, 1995-6. *Anthropological Quarterly*, 78, 377-402.

Richards, Paul & Vlassenroot, Koen 2002. Les guerres africaines du type fleuve Mano. Pour une analyse sociale. *Politique Africaine*, 88, 13-26.

Rivière, Claude 1969. La mobilisation politique de la jeunesse guinéenne. *Revue Française d'Etudes Politiques Africaines*, 42, 67-89.

Rivière, Claude 1971. *Mutations sociales en Guinée*, Paris, Editions Marcel Rivière et Cie.

Rivière, Claude 1977. *Guinea. The mobilization of a people*, Ithaca and London, Cornell University Press.

Roth, Claudia 1997. „Was ist Liebe?" Zum Wandel der Ehe in Bobo-Dioulasso, ein Beispiel. *In:* Sottas, Beat, Hammer, Thomas, Vischer, Lilo Roost & Mayor, Anne (eds.) *Werkschau Afrikastudien. Le forum suisse des africaniste.* Hamburg: Lit Verlag, 198-208.

Sarro, Ramon 2007. Demystified memories: The politics of heritage in post-socialist Guinea. *In:* Jong, Ferdinand De & Rowlands, Michael (eds.) *Reclaiming heritage. Alternative imaginaries of memory in West Africa.* Walnut Creek, California: Left Coast Press, 215-229.

Sarro, Ramon 2009. *The politics of religious change on the Upper Guinea Coast. Iconoclasm done and undone*, Edinburgh, Edinburgh University Press Ltd.

Sawyer, Amos 2004. Violent conflicts and governance challenges in West Africa: the case of the Mano River basin area. *Journal of Modern African Studies*, 42, 437-463.

Schaeffner, André 1951. Les Kissi. Une société noire et ses instruments de musique. *L'homme*, 2, 1-85.

Schlichte, Klaus 2008. Uganda, or the internationalisation of rule. *Civil Wars*, 10, 369-383.

Schlichte, Klaus 2009. *In the shadow of violence. The politics of armed groups*, Frankfurt am Main, Campus Verlag.

Schmidt, Elizabeth 2005. *Mobilizing the masses. Gender, ethnicity, and class in the nationalist movement in Guinea, 1939-1958*, Portsmouth, Heinemann.

Schroven, Anita. 2010a. *Integration through marginality: Local politics and oral tradition in Guinea*. PhD, Martin-Luther-Universität.

Schroven, Anita 2010b. The people, the power and the public service: Political identification during Guinea's general strikes in 2007. *Development and Change*, 41, 659-677.

Schroven, Anita 2019. *Playing the marginality game. Identity politics in West Africa*, New York, Oxford, Berghahn.

Scott, James C. 2006. Cities, people, and language. *In:* Sharma, Aradhana & Gupta, Akhil (eds.) *The anthropology of the state. A reader.* Malden: Blackwell, 247-269.

Seck, Cheikh Yérim 2007. Fin de la récréation? *Jeune Afrique.*

Semadeni, Flurina & Suter, Virginia 2004. „Nous sommes des aventuriers." Ein emisches Mobilitätskonzept in Westafrika. *Tsantsa*, 9, 127-137.

Sharma, Aradhana & Gupta, Akhil 2006. Rethinking theories of the state in an age of globalization. In: Sharma, Aradhana & Gupta, Akhil (eds.) *The anthropology of the state. A reader.* Malden: Blackwell, 1-41.

Shepler, Susan 2010a. Are 'child soldiers' in Sierra Leone a new phenomenon? In: Knörr, Jacqueline & Trajano Filho, Wilson (eds.) *The powerful presence of the past. Integration and conflict along the Upper Guinea Coast.* Leiden: Brill, 297-321.

Shepler, Susan 2010b. Youth music and politics in post-war Sierra Leone. *The Journal of Modern African Studies*, 48, 627-642.

Silverman, David 2007. *A very short, fairly interesting and reasonably cheap book about qualitative research*, London, Sage.

Smid, Karen. 2008. *How tomorrow precedes yesterday: Visions of time and locations of authority for Muslims in the Fouta Djallon, Guinea.* PhD, University of Michigan.

Smid, Karen 2010. Resting at creation and afterlife: Distant times in the ordinary strategies of Muslim women in the rural Fouta Djallon, Guinea. *American Ethnologist*, 37, 36-52.

Smith, Dane F. 2006. US-Guinean relations during the rise and fall of Charles Taylor. *Journal of Modern African Studies*, 44, 415-439.

Sorry, Charles E. 2000. *Sékou Touré l'ange exterminateur. Un passé à dépasser*, Paris, L'Harmattan.

Souaré, Aboubakar 1995. Hinter der Fassade einer Organisation. Handlungsstrategien zwischen divergierenden Legitimitätsdiskursen am Beispiel eines guineischen Unternehmens. In: Von Oppen, Achim & Rottenburg, Richard (eds.) *Organisationswandel in Afrika: Kollektive Praxis und kulturelle Aneignung. Erträge eines Symposiums in Petzow bei Potsdam, 10. Bis 13. Februar 1994.* Berlin: Das Arabische Buch, 107-128.

Spencer, Jonathan 2007. *Anthropology, politics, and the state. Democracy and violence in South Asia*, Cambridge, Cabridge University Press.

Straker, Jay. 2004. *The fate of an African revolutionary curriculum. Forest youth and the cultural production of Guinean nationalism.* PhD, Emory University.

Straker, Jay 2007a. Stories of 'militant theatre' in the Guinean forest. 'Demystifying' the motives and moralities of a revolutionary nation-state. *Journal of African Cultural Studies*, 19, 207-233.

Straker, Jay 2007b. Youth, globalisation, and millennial reflection in a Guinean forest town. *Journal of Modern African Studies*, 45, 299-319.

Straker, Jay 2008. The state of the subject. A Guinean educator's odyssey in the postcolonial forest, 1960-2001. *Journal of African History*, 49, 93-109.

Straker, Jay 2009. *Youth, nationalism, and the Guinean revolution*, Bloomington and Indianapolis, Indiana University Press.

Summers, Anne & Johnson, R. W. 1978. World War I conscription and social change in Guinea. *The Journal of African History*, 19, 25-38.

Svasek, Maruska & Domecka, Markieta 2012. The autobiographical narrative interview. A potential arena of emotional remembering, performance and reflection. *In:* Skinner, Jonathan (ed.) *The interview. An ethnographic approach.* London: Berg, 107-126.

Tait, Gordon 2000. *Youth, sex, and government*, New York, Peter Lang.

Till, Karen E. 2003. Places of memory. *In:* Agnew, John, Mitchell, Katharyne & Toal, Gerard (eds.) *A companion to political geography.* Malden: Blackwell Publishing, 289-301.

Touré, Ahmed Sékou 1963. *La revolution guinéenne.*

Touré, Sékou 1961. *Expérience Guinéenne et unité Africaine*, Paris, Présence Africaine.

Usaid 2008. Property rights and artisanal diamond devleopment (PRADD) pilot program. Policy review: land tenure, natural resources management (NRM), and mining legislation in the Republic of Guinea. USAID Guinea.

Utas, Mats 2005. Building a future? The reintegration & remarginalisation of youth in Liberia. *In:* Richards, Paul (ed.) *No peace, no war. An anthropology of contemorary armed conflicts.* Oxford: Ohio University Press, 137-154.

Utas, Mats 2009. Trapped in the game. Militia and gang members in war and post-war Sierra Leone. *Global Gang Workshop.* Geneva.

Utas, Mats (ed.) 2012a. *African conflict and informal power. Big men and networks*, London: Zed Books.

Utas, Mats 2012b. Introduction. Bigmanity and network governance in African conflicts. *In:* Utas, Mats (ed.) *African conflicts and informal power. Big men and networks* London: Zed Books, 1-31.

Utas, Mats. 2012c. Youth as social age. *wordpress.com* [Online]. 2012].

Utas, Mats & Jörgel, Magnus 2008. The West Side Boys. Military navigation in the Sierra Leone civil war. *Journal of Modern African Studies*, 46, 487-511.

Vieira, Gérard 2005. *L'église catholique en Guinée à l'épreuve de Sékou Touré (1958-1984)*, Paris, Karthala Editions.

Vigh, Henrik. 2003. *Navigating terrains of war: youth and soldiering in Bissau.* PhD, University of Copenhagen.

Vigh, Henrik 2006a. *Navigating terrains of war. Youth and soldering in Guinea-Bissau*, Oxford, New York, Berghahn Books.

Vigh, Henrik 2006b. Social death and violent life chances. *In:* Christiansen, Catrine, Utas, Mats & Vigh, Henrik (eds.) *Navigating youth, generating adulthood. Social becoming in an African context.* Uppsala: Nordiska Afrikainstututet, 31-60.

Vigh, Henrik 2009. Motion squared. A second look at the concept of social navigation. *Anthropological Theory*, 9, 419-438.

Wallerstein, Immanuel 1970. Voluntary associations. *In:* Coleman, James Smoot & Rosberg, Carl (eds.) *Political parties and national integration in tropical Africa.* Berkley: University of California Press, 318-339.

Wastl-Walter, Doris 2011. Introduction. *In:* Wastl-Walter, Doris (ed.) *The Ashgate Research Companion to Border Studies.* Surrey: Ashgate, 1-8.

Weber, Max 2006. Bureaucracy. *In:* Sharma, Aradhana & Gupta, Akhil (eds.) *The anthropology of the state. A reader.* Malden: Blackwell, 49-70.

Werbner, Richard (ed.) 1998. *Memory and the postcolony. African anthropology and the critique of power,* London: Zed Books.

Whyte, Susan Reynolds, Alber, Erdmute & Geest, Sjaak Van Der 2008. Generational connections and conflicts in Africa: an introduction. *In:* Alber, Erdmute, Geest, Sjaak Van Der & Whyte, Susan Reynolds (eds.) *Generations in Africa. Connections and conflicts.* Berlin: Lit Verlag, 1-23.

Wrons-Passmann, Ciaran 2006. Étude sur l'état des lieux des participants du programme DEMO. Unplublished report.

Young, James E. 1992. The counter-monument. Memory against itself in Germany today. *Critical Inquiry,* 18, 267-296.